People and Politics
in the
Middle East

People and Politics
in the
Middle East

Proceedings of the Annual Conference
of the American Academic Association for Peace
in the Middle East.

Edited by
MICHAEL CURTIS

Published by *trans*action Books
New Brunswick, New Jersey
Distributed by E.P. Dutton

Printed in the United States of America
Library of Congress Catalog Number: LC-72440617
ISBN 0-87855-000-3 case
ISBN 0-87855-500-5 paper

Contents

INTRODUCTION 1
    MICHAEL CURTIS
I. ARABS AND JEWS IN THE MIDDLE EAST

ISRAEL AND PALESTINE: THE POLITICAL USE
OF ETHICS 9
    BEN HALPERN

INTERGROUP RELATIONS IN ISRAEL 16
    HUGH H. SMYTHE/SANDRA WEINTRAUB

ETHNIC RELATIONS IN ISRAEL 31
    YOCHANAN PERES

THE PALESTINE ARABS: A NATIONAL ENTITY 69
    DON PERETZ

WHO ARE THE PALESTINIANS? 93
    MARIE SYRKIN

DISCUSSION 111

II. ECONOMIC, HISTORICAL AND GEOGRAPHICAL
PERSPECTIVES

ECONOMIC ASPECTS OF THE ARAB-ISRAELI
CONFLICT 123
    ELIYAHU KANOVSKY

THE BA'ATH IN SYRIA   132
   SYLVIA G. HAIM

ARAB REFUGEES AND THE ARAB-ISRAELI DILEMMA   144
   FRED KHOURI

THE SECOND ARAB AWAKENING   169
   JON KIMCHE

DEMOGRAPHY AND GEOGRAPHY IN PALESTINE   182
   SAMUEL MERLIN

DISCUSSION   205

III. POLITICAL DYNAMICS AND THE ARAB-ISRAELI
CONFLICT

POLITICAL SYSTEMS OF THE MIDDLE EAST:
OPENING REMARKS   216
   IRVING LOUIS HOROWITZ

THE FIASCO OF ANGLO-AMERICAN MIDDLE EAST   220
POLICY
   AMOS PERLMUTTER

THE MIDDLE EAST AND THE GREAT POWERS   250
   F. H. HINSLEY

ENDING THE ARAB-ISRAELI CONFLICT   258
   YEHOSHAFAT HARKABI

CLASHING HORIZONS: ARABS AND REVOLUTION   278
   ABDUL AZIZ SAID

THE NEW LEFT AND ISRAEL   293
   SHLOMO AVINERI

CLOSING HORIZONS: ISRAELIS AND NATIONALISM   303
   GIL CARL ALROY

DISCUSSION   306

INDEX   319

NOTES ON CONTRIBUTORS   327

Introduction

MICHAEL CURTIS

On behalf of the American Academic Association for Peace in the Middle East it was my great pleasure, as chairman of the conference committee, to arrange and open the third national conference sponsored by the Association. With what I trust was not an excess of symbolic overtone we held it in Philadelphia, the Quaker City of brotherly love.

The AAAPME was formed in 1967 as a result of the concern of many members of the academic community in this country about the problems of the Middle East. We felt we should attempt to play some role in the discussion and possible resolution of these problems. The organization does not ally itself with political parties or factions. It does not commit itself to any specific policy or set of policies on Middle Eastern affairs. Those academics associated with it differ among themselves in their political views and outlooks, as members of the academy are wont to do. But they all share in common the belief in the vital need for a just and lasting peace between Israel and the Arab states.

As academics we felt that the particular contribution we could make was to foster an intellectual climate that might help achieve that objective. We have therefore stimulated exchanges of opinion on Middle Eastern affairs in a number of ways. We have sponsored lectures and seminars at many campuses throughout

1

the country, published information material, fact sheets, collections of articles and essays on Middle Eastern topics, held briefing sessions with distinguished officials, Israeli, Arab and neutral, and arranged study missions to Israel, Jordan and the United Arab Republic.

This conference was held in the conviction that greater understanding of the underlying problems that make a pacific settlement in the Middle East so difficult to achieve, could be gained by free and frank exchanges in an academic and non-polemical environment. The individuals who participated in the three panels of the conference did so as fellow members of an Anglo-American academic and intellectual community. They were invited because of their knowledge and expertise in Middle Eastern affairs, not because they represented political organizations, groups or nations.

This is a time when peace in the Middle East seems far off and the sounds of hostilities are heard in an ever insistent beat. The seemingly insoluble dilemma remains that one side calls for ceasefire agreements while the other demands withdrawal of forces from occupied territories before any such agreements can be reached. The threat of another Arab-Israeli confrontation remains acute. The ever-increasing role being played by the Soviet Union adds to the tension. Nations as geographically distant as Morocco, Pakistan and China have become more directly involved in the problem.

The meeting in Cairo of the leaders of the five so-called confrontation or frontline Arab countries concluded on February 9, 1970, that "it becomes imperative for all the Arab states and the Arab people with all their organizations and institutions to mobilize their forces and concentrate their potentials and energies in the face of all the challenges of the battle of destiny." It is our belief that rhetoric of this kind is not helpful for the achievement of the just peace that we all desire so fervently. We have continually urged negotiation not belligerence, rational discussion not militancy. We have encouraged the development of means by which the contending sides can be brought to the bargaining table, not to the battlefield.

My hope was that our conference would be useful in this respect. By clarifying the historical background, by careful analyses of economic, social and demographic aspects of the Middle East, we not only would contribute to understanding of relevant political problems, we also would help lay the foundations for the framing of those proposals on which a peaceful settlement rests.

The papers and proceedings of the Conference are presented here in the belief that they did make some contributions to that objective. As editor of the book, I have taken the liberty of altering the order in which the papers were delivered and of adding some papers that were not delivered at the conference to add some balance to the topics discussed.

I must express appreciation to the staff of the AAAPME, especially to Rivka Simon, Judith Diesendruck and Dorothy Freeman, for the long hours and hard work in making the administrative arrangements for the conference; and to Ann Sinai, who prepared the index. My thanks go also to Mary Curtis, efficient editor for *trans*action Books who ably helped the book through the press, and to Irving Louis Horowitz who made the judicious decision to publish the book.

Rutgers University
New Brunswick, New Jersey

PROGRAM OF THE CONFERENCE HELD AT
PHILADELPHIA, FEBRUARY 14 - 15, 1970

Conference Chairman, Michael Curtis
Department of Political Science
Rutgers University.

PEOPLE AND POLITICS IN THE MIDDLE EAST

I Economic and Social Dimensions

Chairman: Robert Cross, President, Swarthmore College

Ben Halpern, Brandeis University, Dept. of Near Eastern and Judaic Studies
"Israel and Palestine: The Political Use of Ethics"
Eliahu Kanovsky, State University of New York, Stony Brook, Dept. of Economics
"Economic Implications of Conflict in the Middle East"
Yochanan Peres, Harvard University, Dept. of Social Relations
"Ethnic Attitudes Among Jewish and Arab Populations"
Don Peretz, State University of New York, Binghamton, Middle East Dept.
"Palestinians: Are They A Political Entity?"
Hugh Smythe, Brooklyn College, Dept. of Sociology
"Inter-Group Relations in Israel"

II. Historical and Geographical Perspectives

Chairman: David Landes, Harvard University, Dept. of History

Sylvia Haim, London
"The Ba'ath in Syria: Recent Developments"
Fred Khouri, Villanova University, Dept. of Political Science
"The Arab Refugees and the Arab-Israeli Dilemma"
Jon Kimche, London
"The Second Arab Awakening"
Samuel Merlin, Institute for Mediterranean Affairs
"Demography and Geography in Palestine"

III. Political Dynamics

Chairman: Irving Louis Horowitz, Rutgers University, Dept. of Sociology

F.H. Hinsley, St. John's College, Cambridge
  "The Middle East and the Great Powers"
Amos Perlmutter, Harvard University, Center for International Affairs
  "Internal War and External Aggression"
Abdul Aziz Said, American University, Dept. of Political Science
  "Social Differentiation and Political Modernization in the Arab World"

Discussant:

Gil Carl AlRoy, Hunter College, Dept. of Political Science

Arabs and Jews in the Middle East

Israel and Palestine:
The Political Use of Ethics

BEN HALPERN

The so-called Palestine problem confuses political analysts because, even more than other recent disputes (such as the American black revolution, the Nigerian-Biafran war, the Vietnam conflict, or the issues dividing East and West Germany), it introduces distracting moral absolutes into conflicts of specific and normally negotiable interests. When called upon to deal with the established facts, Arabs reply with parables about burglars who break into one's home and then claim its legitimate ownership on grounds of possession. The Israelis, who might be inclined to deal in rational, negotiable terms on the basis of the current status quo, find themselves driven to apocalyptic attitudes by Arab threats that arouse memories of the holocaust. In particular, they are faced with demands to abandon their Zionism: that is to say, they are asked to dismantle a painfully achieved institutional apparatus of statehood and advanced economy, society and culture, manned in all essential functions by Jews, all of whom express a revived national consciousness. Against such a demand Israelis are forced back on their own moral absolutes, for they see themselves defending the right of the Jewish people to survive in sovereign freedom.

Such a confrontation certainly leads to multiple misunderstandings. Those most likely to misunderstand are, of course, third parties closely or remotely concerned with the conflict.

Since they define their interests in the matter rationally, they expect the principals in the quarrel to do likewise. Failure of the principals to do so provokes irritation among outsiders which substantially adds to the confusion.

Between the Jews and Arabs there is at least a common awareness that a clash of fundamental values is involved. Yet this understanding does not lead to mutual appreciation, but rather to mutual rejection of some basic attitudes each side adheres to.

Jews and Arabs have greater reason to study and closely analyze each other's patterns of behavior than do third parties. Not only Israeli Arabists but Arab specialists on Israel familiarize themselves with the enemy with an objective interest and detailed concern greater than is common among third party area special-ists. Moreover, each side has continually learned tactical lessons from the other and adapted its defense doctrine to the procedures of the other.[1] Yet here again close study and even imitation of each other has not led to a deeper essential understanding, but rather the reverse. The more they know each other and the closer their strategic and tactical doctrines converge, the less the combatants seem to share fundamental values.

This is apparent not merely in the Middle East arms race and in the borrowing of tactical and strategic models. It is most strikingly manifested in what one might call the political use of ethics: in the manipulation of symbols and values ranging from sheer propaganda to statements of fundamental attitudes essen-tially determining the political positions of the two foes. In justifying itself to others—and sometimes even to itself—each side has adopted from time to time the language and ideas of the other. Yet this has not contributed to the growth of true mutual understanding. And if there has been such a latent effect, it must wait for peace to be won by other methods before it will make itself felt.

One curious expression of the political use of ethics relates to the Israeli demand for direct peace negotiations with the Arab states involved in the Six Day War. The rational grounds for this position are obvious. In Rhodes, where armistice agreements were concluded, the following conditions applied: the United Nations functioned solely as a channel for initial contacts between the parties; the Security Council resolution under which Ralph Bunche operated — unlike earlier unsuccessful resolutions — made no attempt whatever to predetermine the nature of the ultimate agreements, other than to insist that the parties negotiate an armistice; and Israel dealt separately with each of its antagonists (except Iraq, which evaded any agreement). Subsequently, at Lausanne and Paris, the UN Conciliation Commission tried to mediate and influence agreements between the Jews and Arabs, and held separate meetings with Israel and with the Arab states as a body. The resulting failure was attributed by Israel to the competition in intransigence among the Arabs which necessarily resulted when they negotiated as a body, and to the interposition of third parties between those directly concerned. The experience gave Israel sufficient, rationally grounded reason to insist that next time the negotiations be direct, unprejudiced by third party interposition or attempts to predetermine the outcome, and, if possible, conducted with each of Israel's foes separately. But there are also irrational grounds, perhaps even more basic, for demanding direct talks and formal bilateral agreements.

These grounds, strikingly enough, are formulated by Israelis in terms of Arab, Muslim traditions. In order to have a true peace with Arabs, the Israelis feel, there must be a *sulha*, a ceremony only involving negotiations and formal bilateral agreements, but producing above all an explicit and final reconciliation between Jews and Arabs. Only in this way do Arabs conclude their blood feuds, say the Israelis; and, as they understand the Arabs, without such a procedure the Jewish blood feud will never be considered finished by the Arabs.

A somewhat more technical and refined version of the same point has recently been reported in Israel. What the Jews want, it is said, is the situation known in Islamic law as *sulh*. The best the Arabs are ready to concede to Israel today is an *aman*.

In a sulh, a treaty may be formalized between Muslims and infidels providing for normal peaceful relations upon the cession of territory or payment of tribute following a holy war. Even in early Islamic tradition, when, in theory, peace could never be instituted for more than 10 years between believers and infidels, certain countries were more or less permanently recognized by such treaties as neutralized in the holy wars of Islam. In more recent times Islamic scholars have seen in the sulh and the principle of neutralization a basis on which Muslim tradition could be integrated with the general, secular law of nations and permanent peace between Islamic and infidel states be thus virtually recognized.[2] Israel's current intention is to enter precisely into such relations with the Arabs.

The willingness of some Arabs to talk of a non-negotiated, informal "peace settlement" instead of a treaty is considered by the Israelis as something like an aman: a form of safe-conduct for unbelievers temporarily sojourning in or travelling through Islamic lands, without submitting to the special laws and payments required of other infidels whose religion is tolerated and who enjoy rights of permanent residence. An aman can be claimed or granted in the most informal way, by mere implication; but it is quite specifically and unalterably temporary in character. It has to be replaced within a brief time by full submission of the unbeliever to Islamic authority or by his departure to his own country and the resumption of war.[3]

Thus, the Israelis base their approach to true and lasting peace on their understanding of the Eastern traditions of the Arabs. The Arabs, for their part, draw on the Western and Judaic traditions of the Israelis, as they understand them, in their continuing campaign to eliminate the Jewish state. One does not hear them speak of sulh or aman nor even very much of *jihad*. the holy war, in the forum of Western public opinion. Instead, they seek allies by picturing the Jews, in Western cliches, as a malign international conspiracy or as a bridgehead of Western imperialism. And the solution they offer for the "Palestine problem"—in essence, the same as that which some Israelis refer to as an aman—is to de-Zionize Israel (the state, the economy, the society and culture) and to absorb Jews in a "non-theocratic" state: that is, one in which Jews would live on in sufferance and not by right, after the chief objectionable "theocratic" feature, the constitutional right of Jews to return to their homeland and become citizens there, should have been abolished.

But the Arabs draw not only on general Western values and imagery to explain and justify their position. Like the Israelis who appeal to Islamic values in their search for peace, the Arabs employ the specific values and imagery of the enemy in prosecuting their war against Israel. The most obvious instance is that of the Arab refugees.

There is more involved here than merely the manifest political advantage of being in the position of the victim; an advantage greatly heightened by the fact that the very creation of Israel was decisively advanced by the widely shared humanitarian concern, and even collective guilt, felt by the world for the plight of the Jewish refugees who survived Hitler's holocaust. The Arabs go a significant step further. By a deliberate, concerted effort of indoctrination they have tried to reshape the refugee's situation into an analogue of the Jewish exile, the *Galut*.

Everyone is aware, of course, that Arab children have been learning arithmetic and grammar from textbooks whose examples, paradigms and problems relentlessly hammer home simple xenophobic hatred for the Jewish invader. Equally familiar is the equation between Crusaders and Zionists, leading to the conclusion that the infidels will ultimately be expelled even if it takes 100 years. On the other hand, A. L. Tibawi, in an article published in 1963,[4] noted that "a great and increasing mass of literature and art," expressing what he calls a "new Arab Zionism," had remained "unnoticed not only by independent students of the Palestine problem but surprisingly also by Arabs and Zionists alike." The scope and implications of such Arab use of Jewish symbols is not fully appreciated even today. And in the meantime the doctrine of a Palestinian nation-in-exile has developed from literary indoctrination to a program of a politically organized paramilitary force.

Tibawi's most interesting points relate to the significance of themes of "exile" (*ghurbah*)—alienness, outsideness, of the redemptive "return," and of the shame of being a "wandering people." He stresses that for the Palestinian refugee, Damascus is a city where he is "alien" (*gharib*) and Beirut "a land which is not our land." The insistence on this point extends to the daily recitation in refugee schools of an oath, containing these lines:

Palestine is our country, Our aim is to return. . . .
Palestine is ours. We will never forget her.
Another homeland we will never accept!

The ethico-political significance of this position is clear: it is a direct appropriation by Arabs of the most fundamental moral claim of the Zionists on Palestine. The argument is no longer simply that natives have been dispossessed by invaders, or that the refugees are being inhumanly oppressed and victimized by usurpers who drove them out of their homes. Against these contentions Zionists could argue (and did, to the extent they were still willing to debate abstract issues instead of the concrete, existing dispute) in the following terms: for the Jews, who had no other home, the land of Israel represented their only possible opportunity to preserve their historic national identity, as was their inalienable natural right; but for Arabs, whose national identity is secure and at home over a wide surrounding area, loss of dominion in Palestine represented only a quantitative territorial loss. But if the existence of a specific Palestinian nationality is asserted, for which other Arab lands are not "home" but "exile," and which can survive only in Palestine, then the Arab case is a strict parallel to the Zionist case.

This need not mean that Palestinian Arabs must recognize the legitimacy of Jewish claims to Eretz Israel merely because their own moral claims are now based on arguments appropriated from Zionism. That would only follow if Palestinian Arab nationalism were committed, like Zionism, to peace. Then, like Ahad Ha'am,[5] they might recognize that when two nations have rights in the same territory—and, in this case, allegedly identical rights—the rights of each must be limited by the essential rights of the other. Some territorial compromise or other arrangement for peaceful coexistence of the two would then have to be sought. But if Palestinian Arab nationalism is committed to continuing the war against Israel's existence, it need recognize no such ethically necessary limits to its absolute moral claims.

One has the impression, sometimes, that even this is understating the case. Palestinian Arab nationalism often gives the impression of a tactical expedient rather than an end in itself. One can hardly avoid this conclusion when the national covenant of the Palestinian guerrillas says the following:

Article 1. Palestine is the homeland of the Palestinian Arab people and an integral part of the great Arab Homeland, and the people of Palestine is a part of the Arab nation . . .

Article 12. The Palestinian Arab people believes in Arab unity, and *to fulfill its role in realizing it, must preserve in this phase of its national struggle* its Palestinian personality . . .(my emphasis)

So long as the Palestinian national personality is conceived as a useful weapon in the war to eliminate Israel, then all the protestations that Palestinian Arabs remain alien in Damascus or Beirut and can preserve a deeply-felt national identity only in Palestine seem contrived and quite provisional. One might possibly hope that if the sense of a Palestinian identity irrevocably distinct from other Arab national identities should really take root, it might seek to establish itself and solve its problems in a pact of peaceful coexistence and mutual recognition with Israel. This would be the method most likely to decisively establish a Palestinian Arab nation.

[1] In gross terms of competitive armaments, this point is carefully documented in Nadav Safran, *From War to War*, Pegasus, New York, 1969.

[2] Majid Khadduri, *War and Peace in the Law of Islam*, Johns Hopkins Press, Baltimore, 1955, pp. 144-145 and chs. xxii and xxiii.

[3] *Ibid* pp. 163ff.

[4] "Vision of the Return: The Palestine Arab Refugees in Arabic Poetry and Art," *The Middle East Journal*, Late Autumn, 1963, pp. 507-526.

[5] See *Ten Essays on Zionism and Judaism*, Routledge, London, 1922, p. xviii.

Intergroup Relations in Israel

HUGH H. SMYTHE / SANDRA WEINTRAUB

The young state of Israel, though an officially democratic modern state that has made admirable achievements against very real odds, has found itself in the realm of human relations plagued by behavior grossly out of harmony with the professed values and traditions of democracy and the treasured and hallowed precepts of the great religion of Judaism, which it proclaims as the foundation of the nation.

Some of these difficulties in intergroup relations grew out of the rivalries and tensions in pre-Israeli Palestine, which experienced continual conflict in the years before the British mandated territory was partitioned and the state of Israel was established in 1948. The ethos of the time-history-territorial complex that is Israel encompasses a basically religio-cultural majority group oriented with a pervasive tone that is literate and Western. The period of Diaspora during which Jews were the object of world-wide prejudice as the "eternal scapegoat," helped to make them group centered and patriarchal in social structure as well as largely urban and occupationally commercial. At this stage, Israel is essentially theocratic while professing democracy. The majority Jewish population, at war for years with Arabs in neighboring countries, lives in a small land space whose roughly three million Israeli inhabitants can be generally characterized as educated, individualistic, clannish and enterprising.

The conflict involves problems of religion, language, culture, politics and race. The major human elements are of Conservative, Reform or Orthodox Jewish faith; the latter stress the basic principles of the Torah as fundamental for all in a Judaic state, thus accentuating the religious tinge of the intergroup dynamics. The Ashkenazi or European element, mainly responsible for settling modern Israel and promoting Western ideals, are juxtaposed with the Oriental or Sephardic Jews from North Africa and the Middle East. This precipitates a cultural conflict. Meanwhile, the trend towards secularism arouses the Orthodox and intensifies the difficulty. But there is a large Arab minority (the former majority in Palestine), mainly Moslem, but in part Christian, that chafes under classic patterns of discrimination and segregation, as well as stringent military restrictions. A miscellany of Europeans, Americans, Asians and Africans of various religions, comprise an insignificant population fringe.

Israel, with 7,993 square miles, is about the size of Massachusetts and geographically is made up of four main regions: the coastal plain which extends along the Mediterranean coast, the western mountains, the Negev desert and the Rift valley. The population is unevenly distributed: the Negev desert comprising 70 percent of the total land area, contains only 9 percent of the people; whereas Tel Aviv, 1 percent of the land area, encompasses 35 percent of the population. Obviously the country overall is highly urbanized, being 78 percent urban and 22 percent rural. Population concentration is dense in the center of the territory and becomes uneven and fragmented towards the southern and northern peripheries.

Within this general population configuration, the major ethnic and religious minorities tend to cluster in separate enclaves. Nearly 80 percent of the Israeli Arabs reside in the northern sector; another 15 percent of them are found in the area south of Beersheba. For example, Nazareth now includes both the old, traditional center populated by Arabs and a new adjoining town composed of Jewish immigrants. This pattern is repeated throughout the countryside. Eighty percent of the Israeli Arabs live in rural communities, while among the Jews the proportions are approximately the reverse.

Jewish settlement follows three main lines: secular and religious enclaves, ethnic neighborhoods, and veteran and immigrant sectors. The pre-1948 "veteran" groups are mainly located in the three major cities of Tel Aviv, Haifa and Jerusalem, while post-independence immigrants are concentrated in new towns in the North and South, or in housing estates on the fringes of the major cities. Within the major urban areas veterans predominate in the inner core, while immigrants are scattered along their rims. There is some mixing in the cities. Socially mobile immigrants move into the inner areas, but in general, immigrants and veterans are residentially separate.[1]

There are also distinctions within the immigrant groups. Despite the government's attempt to mix them, in most cases each group forms a relatively distinct cluster. Those who share a common language and tradition have tended to form ethnic neighborhoods, to such an extent that they occasionally make up nearly an entire town. Religious enclaves in Jerusalem and Tel Aviv, for example, include groups who maintain a rigidly orthodox way of life. In these neighborhoods travel is forbidden on the Sabbath, and the modes of dress and speech reflect centuries-old traditions and practices.[2]

ZIONISM, SOCIALISM AND PIONEERING

Against this contemporary framework, intergroup relations are best understood through a quick review of the history of the country. In a certain sense all of Jewish history is a prelude to the formation of Israel. Jerusalem, the dream of the return to Zion, is a recurring theme in Jewish sacred literature. Throughout the centuries there were sporadic small migrations of European and Middle Eastern Jews to the Holy Land. But it was not until the late nineteenth century that a group of 80,000, mainly from Russia, migrated to Palestine and initiated a nationalistic movement.[3] First generations can be critical in a society's development and their traditions may form the core of the nation that is to emerge. In the case of Israel, the ideals of the late nineteenth-century Russian immigrants shaped and continue to mold the institutional basis of Israeli life. Although few in number, these purposeful, dedicated colonists placed their imprint indelibly upon the emerging society.

Zionism, socialism and pioneering were the rallying programs of this founding generation. Zionism called for the creation of a fully autonomous Jewish state. With a socialist creed and true to their radical past, they wished to invest the nation with their highest ideals of social justice, equality, cooperation, the dignity of labor and public-oriented development. As conceived by the founding fathers, pioneering exalts collective over private interests and insists upon constant readiness to undertake national tasks. The *kibbutz* (the collective village) and the *moshav* (the cooperative village) epitomized the pioneer life.[4] Few in number, these early settlers were a homogeneous group, passionate in their dedication to nationalist and socialist ideals.

The period between 1880 and the close of World War I witnessed a slow but continuous Jewish immigration. During those four decades large villages were founded, as well as the city of Tel Aviv. The bulk of immigrants were East Europeans, and the pioneers among them played leading roles in public affairs. Even in this formative stage Jewish immigration was varied. There were religious Jews, along with small bands of Yemenite and Kurdish Jews. Although these groups tended to settle in tiny clusters, their impact was negligible. The European pioneers were dominant; the religious and Middle Easterners were peripheral.

The Zionists conceived of the Jewish state as a haven to which Jews might flee in time of peril. To some extent Palestine did become a place of refuge in the period between the two world wars, when Jews came from Russia, Poland, Rumania and the Baltic countries, and later from the Nazi terror in Germany. Population growth during this period was impressive; between 1925 and 1940 the Jewish community almost quadrupled. This increase was not merely numerical but, more important, encompassed new social elements. Some of those from Poland and Germany did not share the vision of utopian socialism. They represented a middle-class ethic, and in the case of the German immigrants, they also prized their background of "high culture."

Merchants, shopkeepers or professionals, they maintained a certain detachment from the Russians. Separate towns and sections became populated largely by middle-class German immigrants.

With the establishment of the state of Israel in 1948, the government removed all restrictions on Jewish immigration. As a result, from then until the end of 1963, net Jewish immigration was 918,927. This mass immigration produced a socially mixed population. During 1948-1949 the survivors of the concentration camps emigrated to Israel, at first from Czechoslovakia, Bulgaria and Yugoslavia, then from Poland, Rumania and Hungary. Together these groups represented about 300,000 people[5]. There was also mass migration from North Africa and the Middle East, where the Zionist movement hardly existed. Thousands came from Turkey, Iran, Morocco, Tunisia and Algeria. Of Libya's 32,000 Jews, all but 2,000 had come to Israel by the end of 1951 From two countries Jewish communities were brought over almost intact. In May 1949, nearly the entire Yemenite Jewish community of 45,000 were flown to Israel in an extraordinary airlift, while concurrently 125,000 were airlifted from Iraq. Thus mass migration created a truly heterogeneous society.

POST-1948 ASSIMILATION PROBLEMS

It is well to remember that Zionism and utopian socialism did not pull these new immigrants to Israel as with the pre-state immigrants. They fled from their native lands mainly because of insecurity caused by political and economic upheavals. The Russian colonists' ideals of socialism, cooperation and equality had little meaning for these later immigrants. Mass migration therefore introduced a new majority population which had little understanding of or sympathy with these ideals.

Another consequence of this mass migration was the introduction of a non-Western Jewish population drawn from the Oriental Jews. Although small numbers of Yemenite, Kurdish and Moroccan Jews had earlier migrated to Palestine, the massive immigration that commenced in 1948 had not been expected.

Long residence in Muslim lands had made the Oriental Jews life styles resemble those of their Muslim neighbors. Their experience, customs, even their appearance differed fundamentally from those of their European brothers. Israel introduced to the Orientals a different technology, new kinds of social and political relations, and a new system of social values, all of which highlighted differences between the groups.

By the 1950s and 1960s, Israel faced a problem of absorbing and assimilating the great number of Jewish immigrants from the Arab-dominated countries of North Africa and the Near East. In addition to the superficialities of appearance and dress, they differed in family size and in their reactions to goals of industrializing Israeli society. These differences still persist. The Oriental Jews are generally workers or farmers who place little emphasis on education. The European Jews, on the other hand, have skills in administration, a high level of learning, and values derived from Western culture. Virtually all Orientals have in common with their European Jewish brothers are religion and a need for a haven from persecution.[6]

Some European Jews believe themselves superior in cultural equipment, and sometimes they display outright hostility, especially when Orientals want to move next door as neighbors or to marry their daughters.[7] There seems to be a particular resentment to Jews from North Africa, an attitude which suggests elements of racism.[8] Some European Jews exhibit an urgent, almost frantic, desire to assimilate the Orientals swiftly into an Israeli society created and dominated by themselves. Although Orientals make up more than half of the Jewish population, they remain a deprived "minority" in educational and job opportunities, as well as in politics. They have to take what the European elite hands out, so it is understandable that they react with resentment, frustration and apathy, contributing disproportionately to the delinquency problem, and occasionally giving vent to outbursts of violence. Their dissatisfaction with the housing situation has at times exploded into race riots, the most severe being that of North African Jews in Haifa's Wadi Salib slum in 1963. There has also been dissatisfaction with education. Emerging Oriental Jewish leaders are demanding more and more vociferously that schools stop celebrating European customs and values. The Iraqi-born Mayor of Beersheba says, "I'm against assimilation to the European way of living. Every group can contribute something."[9] The Orientals have shown extreme unhappiness with job opportunities available to them. They see themselves becoming the blue collar workers, the bottom layer of the labor force, destined only to be domestic servants, menials and common laborers. And there is also rising dissatisfaction with the official Jewish Agency policy of settling many Oriental Jews in "new development towns," like Kiryat Shemona in the North, Dimona and Arad in the Negev desert. To some this looks like blatant segregation.

It is not surprising that there has been strife even among the victims of prejudice. When Oriental immigration began arriving en masse, the Israeli Government and the Jewish Agency had mixed Jews from different countries in frontier-type villages. The policy failed, as one Jewish leader explained: "There were misunderstandings, racial and otherwise."[10] In the spring of 1965 Moroccans from a community near Ashkelon sat down in protest, demanding to be resettled away from Jews from Tripoli. There have also been tensions between Iraquis and Moroccans, attributed by some to the fact both are low in the pecking order and have nowhere else to direct their hostilities.[11]

Concerned about this unhappy intergroup adjustment, the government has experimented with a program under which each ethnic group lives in its own village, while the children from several villages attend an integrated school and the people from a whole area go to a central, market town. If this program is adopted throughout, it will indicate that the Government has given up hope that the older generation of European Jews will overcome their prejudices towards the Oriental newcomers and hopes that it can save the generation now in school.

EFFECTS OF ORIENTAL IMMIGRATION

The long-range effects of the arrival of large numbers of Oriental Jews are important and significant. They promise to strengthen the hand of the Chief Rabbinate, the head of the Orthodox Judaism, which would like to require everyone to eat only kosher food. On the other hand, the Orientals have little sympathy for the ideology and hopes of the Zionist Jews from Eastern Europe who founded the state, and Israeli leaders fear that Israel will be turned into a nation with values and goals similar to those of its Arab neighbors. If the Orientals, through their numbers and higher birth rate, come to dominate the nation, Israel may become simply another Middle Eastern spot on the map, with the result that nearly six million American Jews will have less incentive to support the country, and (according to Ashkenazi Jewish leaders) Israel's very existence will then be threatened. To prevent this, the Government leadership is trying to assimilate Orientals into the culture of contemporary society and to make the Orientals over into Europeans.

The drive to Europeanize the Orientals, however, is meeting strong resistance. Some Orientals object to the presumption that their culture is worthless. They are not convinced that everything from the ghettoes of Eastern Europe is superior to that of the medinas of their former North African and Middle Eastern homes. They do not want their children to be ashamed of their origins. Although many of them are illiterates, they have real disdain for the "unconscious, unthinking arrogance of European Jews" and believe "it is the very urge to Westernize the Oriental which lies at the root of communal tension in Israel."[12]

Another contributor to tension is the practice of labeling the immigrants with their country of origin. These ethnic tags have become part of the immigrants' sense of identity and have helped to reinforce bonds within the group. But group identification has led to ranking groups in a social hierarchy. Thus whether one is Moroccan or Hungarian has a crucial status meaning. The closer to conformity to veteran European settlers, the higher the status. Europeans or Ashkenazim are ranked higher than Orientals; coming from Britain or Poland makes for more prestige than do origins in the United Arab Republic or Iraq. In addition, there are gradations within each of these categories. Thus, Yemenites now seem to rank higher than Moroccans, perhaps due to their rapid transition from a near-slave status in Yemeni feudalism to a modern citizenship in Israel, with a folk art that has attracted attention, as well as their reputation as good workers and frugal people. On the other hand, Moroccans are considered excitable, dangerous and uncultured. As for the Ashkenazim, they also have sub-ranks. Yugoslav Jews are "good material" who have adapted quickly to the new occupations, while Rumanians, concentrating in small-scale commerce, are stereotyped as grasping, sharp traders.[13]

Oriental Jews, then, are the object of real prejudice. Not only are they lowest on the social and economic scale; they have the lowest level of educational attainment and almost no political power. They seem now to hope that education will make them able to compete with the politically long dominant Ashkenazim.

RELIGIOUS VS. SECULAR JEWS

The ever-present conflict between religious and secular Jews is another sore spot in intergroup relations. The only religious form supported by the state is Orthodox Judaism. As a result more and more Israelis, resenting Orthodoxy's power, which is disproportionate to its numerical and voting strength, are becoming alienated from religious practices. As a consequence the question arises: Will the native-born, or Sabras, come in time to view themselves simply as Israelis rather than Jews? Some feel that this is the way it should be, as in any other nation, while others fear that national identification alone would weaken their ties to Jews elsewhere.[14]

A powerful religious bureaucracy has been superimposed on the political state. There are religious courts; only religious marriages and divorces are recognized as valid.[15] Dietary laws must be observed in all public places. On the Sabbath the Orthodox have imposed their ways to such an extent that there is no public transportation. Some Jews who come to Israel from the United States find it difficult to reconcile this with their American belief in separation of church and state.[16]

There is danger that the religious and the non-religious Jews will become more and more estranged. As it is, they send their children to separate schools, and when children of religious Jews go on to higher education, it is usually to a religious-sponsored college. With the Orthodox youth emphasis is placed on the study of the Torah and the Talmud, with little stress on issues of modern society. The religious Jews are generally in the lower economic groups and live mainly in isolated enclaves in the cities. Thus there is little dialogue between religious and non-religious elements of Israeli society.[17]

In politics, religious parties often represent the important swing vote. The majority parties are forced to compromise, and hand over many important political functions. As a result, religious Jews preoccupy themselves with reconciling modern Israel with ancient Jewish law. The result can be stifling, because that law was not designed to accommodate the problems of modern industrial society. Public officials therefore devote much of their time to seeing how the law can be circumvented without changing it. Still being debated are the issues of autopsy and the proper forms of marriage and divorce.[18]

THE ARAB-ISRAELI MINORITY

Finally, there are the Arab Israelis, now a minority left from the majority of the pre-Israel era. The Arab population of Palestine violently opposed Jewish aspirations. Terrorism and Arab-Jewish clashes were frequent. As a consequence, the Arab and Jewish societies in the League of Nations mandate days were entirely separate entities. When the United Nations effected a partition in November 1947, autonomous Jewish and Arab states were carved out of the Palestine territory (Jordan received part of the territory). Warfare then broke out between Arab and Jew and many Arabs fled from Jewish zones, and it was not long before Jews outnumbered them in what is now Israel.[19] Subsequently the Arab population that remained in the country after 1948 shifted. Some villagers moved from their own communities to others, so that, as with Jews, some Arab villages are divided between veterans and newcomers. There has also been movement to towns and cities, particularly on the part of young people either attracted by the allure of city life or unable to find satisfactory employment in their villages.

Although primary schools in Arab sectors enroll most of the children, Israeli control of the educational process has prevented Arab young people from learning in school anything about their own people, their land their history, or about Arab nationalism. Arabs are also given a one-sided and distorted picture of history.[20] Although a few do go on to receive higher education, they do so knowing that they cannot be sure of employment by Jewish firms after graduation.

The ruling Mapai party, which generally manages to muster the majority of Arab votes, has always regarded Arab villages as a kind of cow, that must be fed in order to keep it alive and to derive milk from it. Mapam, another party, has made some efforts to deal with the problems facing Arab youth. It founded the youth pioneering movement among them and was the first organization to publish progressive Arab literature and to set up producer cooperatives in Arab villages. From time to time Mapam has had to cut back its efforts either for lack of funds or because of administrative intervention from the military government. But what contact has taken place has had an effect. As the Arab youth begins to penetrate the barriers of Jewish society he brings back to his conservative and traditional village new opinions and glimpses of a new way of life. At the same time, even if the young Arabs are able to free themselves economically from their families, traditional ties still bind them. Young Arabs have found the pulls in both directions spiritually exhausting and have sometimes resorted to suicide.[21]

Some Arabs tried to escape the discrimination and segregation in Israel by crossing the border illegally into one of the neighboring states, but they risk getting caught, and imprisonment, injury or death in the process. Some try to escape through assimilation, but they soon realize that Jewish society does not accept them and is far less liberal than Arab society. Young men try to avoid prejudice and discrimination by marrying Jewish girls, although this is not easily done. Others turn to extreme nationalism as an escape. A few Arab villages have tried to initiate some activities for their young people, but until 1962 Israel practiced the same kind of apartheid in athletics decreed by the Republic of South Africa and Arabs were left entirely outside of Israel's sports organizations. Israeli-Arab tensions increased as a result of the June 1967 war, for the number of non-citizen Arabs in Israeli-occupied areas greatly increased.

Palestinian Arabs naturally resent occupation by Israel and are afraid to cooperate with the Jews. They remember that after the 1956 war the returning Egyptians killed the Mayor of Gaza and others because they had "collaborated with the Jews."[22] Israeli efforts to build positive relationships between Arab and Jew have been hampered by the continuing Arab attacks against Israel which feed Israeli feelings that Arabs cannot be trusted.[23] Riots between Jew and Arab can occur again; this potential danger fans prejudices. Since so many Israelis today came to the country to escape oppression in Arab countries, a statement often heard among Israeli Jews is "Don't expect the Arabs to be loyal to us."[24]

One other aspect of intergroup dynamics deserves mention. This is the relationship between the Israeli Jewish and Christian communities. The Israeli Government has not hesitated to interfere in the religious affairs of the various Muslim Arab communities in Israel but intervention in the Christian community of 45,000 has been restricted. The material centers of the Christian community lie outside the frontiers of Israel; and she fears that if Government actions should provoke an unfavorable reaction, aid from the Christian countries might end. However, the situation in the Arab Christian community is by no means the same. This enclave has suffered more than other Christians in Israel, partly because of the widely held Israeli assumption that all Arabs harbor nationalist sentiments. But the Israeli Government's attitude towards the Arab Druze community is more positive. This group has enjoyed differential treatment since 1948, when young Druzes volunteered for the Israeli army. This small sectarian Arab group of some 21,000 seem to have adapted differently and generally to have adjusted to the new socio-political realities.[25]

A concluding word about American Jews in Israel is in order. Like the sprinkling of American Negroes who have gone to live in West Africa in the expectation that they will not feel like outsiders as they did in American society, American Jews have learned through residence that they are outsiders in Israel. The American Jew is called an Anglo-Saxon because he is seen as better off, better educated and highly privileged. He is viewed as someone who has come to Israel because he chose to. Yet many encounter trouble; they find salaries low, taxes high and the standard of living not what they have known. They also discover the schools overcrowded and their educational level lower than they expected. Some young idealistic American Jews, arriving with romantic visions of cooperative living in a kibbutz, quickly find that such group togetherness can place a severe strain on their individual psyches. Under these circumstances it is not surprising that some American immigrants return to the United States within a few years.

Intergroup relations in Israel reveal a skein of conflict in which a variety of dynamic threads can be distinguished. A human relations problem was left unsolved by the former imperial power and the existing conglomeration of disunited people carried over historical jealousies to the contemporary scene. Thus even today dislike is prevalent among the groups. The Western-oriented founders of the modern Israeli state have become the dominant element of the majority Jewish population, look upon their way of life as superior, and want all others to assimilate to it. Some religious, cultural, ethnic and racial minorities resist this design with resultant conflict that can range from name calling to riots to occasional human slaughter. Residential segregation is the rule on a religious, ethnic or cultural basis.

Further, the schism between a powerful minority Orthodox obscurantism and a majority democratic secularism is now approaching the dimensions of crisis. Varying degrees and types of discriminatory treatment exist in all aspects of society, with the Arab Moslem minority aware of the ever-present hostility of the Judaic majority; Moslem distrust is strongly reciprocated by the latter. Oppression of subordinates is justified by the need to unify the nation and protect its security against a surrounding external Arab enemy. "Outsiders" of the faith are at the heart of much internal contemporary conflict, with Westernization in a geographically Middle Eastern environment an exacerbating force. Political compromises during the creation of the state contributed heavily to current intergroup difficulties resulting from political rivalries, a widely varied population and uneven distribution of power.

[1] Alex Weingrod, *Israel: Group Relations in a New Society,* London: Pall Mall Press, 1965, pp. 5-18.

[2] *Ibid.*

[3] "Problems of Integration in Israel," *The American Journal of Economics and Sociology*, vol. 26 (July 1967).

[4] *The New Republic*, September 26, 1965.

[5] M. Louvish, *The Challenge of Israel*, Jerusalem: Israel Universities Press, 1965, pp. 120-122.

[6] Shirley and Sol Kolack, "Can Israel Surmount its Internal Problems," *Trans*action, Vol. 5 (March, 1968), p. 41. See also George E. Gruen, "Problems of Integration and Acculturation Facing Israel Today," New York: The American Jewish Committee, March, 1965.

[7] *Look*, October 15, 1965, p. 69.

[8] Judith Shuval, "Emerging Patterns of Ethnic Strain in Israel," *Minorities in a Changing World*, pp. 97-112. See also, "Israel Admits Negroes Who Contend They're Jews," *The New York Times*, December 23, 1969.

[9] Shuval, *op. cit.* p. 98.

[10] *Look, op. cit.,* p. 69.

[11] *Ibid.*

[12] Walter Zenner, "Ambivalence and Self-Image Among Oriental Jews in Israel," *Jewish Journal of Sociology*, vol. 5 (December, 1963), p. 216; *Look, op. cit.*, p. 70.

[13] Weingrod, *op. cit.* pp. 40-41.

[14] *Newsweek*, November 15, 1965; Dwight L. Baker, "Theocracy vs. Democratic State: The Other Schism in Israeli Life," *Issues*, vol. 20 No. 1, Spring, 1966.

[15] A real controversy on this aspect of Israeli society developed early in 1970. See James Feron, and Irving Spiegel, "Israeli Court Rules a Jew Can be One by Nationality," *The New York Times*, January 24, 1970; James Feron, "Nationality Rule Fought in Israel," *ibid.*; James Feron, "Israel Will Act to Reverse Court," *ibid.*, January 29, 1970; "Israeli Cabinet Votes to Reverse High Court Definition," *ibid.*, January 30, 1970; "Split on Defining 'Jew' Grows in Israel," *ibid.*, February 2, 1970; "Who Is A Jew?," Religion section in *Newsweek*, February 2, 1970, p. 70.

[16] *The New Yorker,* August 22, 1966.

[17] Weingrod, *op. cit.* p. 72.

[18] *The New Yorker, op. cit.*

[19] George E. Gruen, "The Arab Minority in Israel," New York: The American Jewish Committee, March, 1965; Hugh H. Smythe and James A. Moss, "Arabs in Israel-Symposium on Arab-Jewish Relations," *Journal of Human Relations*, vol. 16, No. 1, first quarter, 1968, pp. 89-96.

[20] Weingrod, *op. cit.* p. 69.

[21] Joseph Bentwich, "Arab Education in Israel," *The New Outlook*, vol. 6 (July-August, 1963).

[22] M. Vatad, "Arab Youth in Israel," *The New Outlook*, Vol. 7 (June, 1964).

[23] R. Moskin, "Israel Uptight," *Look*, June 24, 1969, p. 30.

[24] Ernest Stock, *From Conflict to Understanding: Relations Between Jews and Arabs in Israel Since 1948*, New York: Institute of Human Relations Press of the American Jewish Committee, 1968; Martin Lakin, Jack Lomranz, and Morton A. Lieberman, *Arab and Jew in Israel: Case Study in Human Relations Training Approach to Conflict*, New York: American Academic Association for Peace in the Middle East, 1969.

[25] *Newsweek*, September 6, 1965; *Time*, September 13, 1968.

Ethnic Relations in Israel

YOCHANAN PERES

Ethnic relations in Israel must be discussed in relation to the overwhelming problem confronting the nation: the all-involving conflict with the surrounding Arab world. No simple cause-effect relationship between the external struggle and the internal structure can be postulated but clearly Israeli society in general and ethnic group relations in particular are deeply influenced by the Arab-Israeli conflict. On the other hand, social features which developed during two decades of external struggle have by now become actively engaged in this struggle and the characteristics of the opponents and the nature of their conflict have become parts of one inseparable system.

On a more specific level, Israel's ethnic relations can be best described and analyzed in terms of two major relationships: that between European and non-European Jews (the latter will be referred to below as "Orientals."); and that between Jewish and non-Jewish (predominantly Arab) citizens.

This is admittedly an oversimplification. As Table 1 indicates, both the European and the non-European Jewish groups are subdivided into many subgroups which differ in language, level of education, income, life style and many other characteristics. Table 2 indicates that the non-Jewish population is also ethnically subdivided. (One non-Jewish group, the Druzes, are well known for assuming a position favoring the Jews and opposing the Arabs.)

TABLE 1[2]

ETHNIC DISTRIBUTION OF THE JEWISH POPULATION IN ISRAEL

Jewish Citizens of European Descent

Total %	57
U.S.S.R.	13
Poland	17
Rumania	11
Bulgaria, Greece	4
Central Europe (Germany, Austria, Czechoslovakia)	6
Western Europe (Britain, France, Benelux, Spain, Italy)	2
Other European countries	1

Jewish Citizens of American Descent

Total %	1
U.S.A., Canada	0.5
South and Central America	0.5

Jewish Citizens of Asian Descent

Total %	26
Iraq	11
Yemen, Aden	6
Turkey	4
Iran	2.5
Other Asian countries	2.5

Jewish Citizens of African Descent

Total %	16.5
Morocco	9
Algeria, Tunisia	3
Libya	2
Egypt	2
Other African countries	0.5

Total Jewish population: 2,500,000

Although Tables 1 and 2 show that the division of the Israeli population into three groups (European Jews, Oriental Jews and Arabs) does not correspond to demographic reality, I believe that our findings will prove that this simplistic division does organize meaningfully the complex network of ethnic attitudes and relationships.

TABLE 2[3]

NON-JEWISH GROUPS IN ISRAEL IN 1967

Muslims	287,000
Christians	71,000
Druze and others	33,000
Total	391,000*

*Includes the population of East Jerusalem, about 66,000.

Ethnic attitudes cannot be as refined and elaborated as a statistical account. Popular images of ethnic differentiation always embody crude categorization; this is how the three blocs emerged in the minds of most Israelis. In private conversation, newspaper articles, and even in the parliament, "Europeans," "Orientals" and "Arabs" are referred to as the three main components of Israeli society.

Let us now turn to an analysis of the relation between European and Oriental Jews, proceeding later to discuss Jewish-Arab relations (The same order will be followed in presenting the data.)

RELATIONS BETWEEN EUROPEANS AND ORIENTALS

The most remarkable feature of the relations between Europeans and non-European Jews in Israel is their tranquility. Apart from one isolated incident in which shops were looted and a few passers-by attacked, there were no ethnic riots during Israel's two decade history. All attempts to establish ethnic political parties failed. While one to three representatives of such parties occupied seats in the first, second and third Knesset (Israeli parliament), in the last four elections no ethnic party was even in existence. (It should be noted that Israel has a multiparty system, in which about 10 to 15 parties, most of them very small, compete for the 120 seats in the Knesset.)

This tranquility is astonishing if one considers that almost all real leadership positions in the country are occupied by Europeans; that European per capita income is about twice that of Orientals; and that the European tradition and life-style dominate the society. A careful analysis will show that the relationship between these two segments of the Jewish community in Israel is the product of a rather complicated balance of forces. Some of these forces are disintegrative, driving the ethnic groups apart, while other forces are integrative, drawing them together. The outcome of these countervailing forces is not a simple positive relationship but rather a sensitive equilibrium in which a sense of mutual responsibility and common loyalty coexist with covert hostility and underlying tensions.

Factors impeding the integration of Jewish ethnic groups

Dissimilarity: Compared to the differences between ethnic groups elsewhere (such as in the United States), the variations between Jewish ethnic groups in Israel seem to be extremely great. Although all Jews share the same language and religion, they differ in dress, how they relate to each other, and in socialization patterns and family structures. For example, one could compare some mountain tribes that emigrated to Israel from inland Morocco and Tunisia with Jews from America or western Europe. "Primitive society" would not be an exaggerated description of these North African mountain tribes. Even the men were illiterate; they used to live in caves in Morocco, and some of them dug new caves for themselves in Israel, using their houses for storage space; their religious beliefs and practices included many archaic superstitions. By contrast, American and Western European Jews belonged to the most advanced middle class of their Western societies. This is admittedly an extreme example. Most Orientals are much closer to a modern style of living, and many Europeans left environments only in the beginning stages of modernization, such as the rural Ukraine. Nevertheless, it should be emphasized that Israel contains a maximal variety of ethnic behavior patterns and cultures. These differences are most significant wherever close contact and coordination are necessary, such as in schools, factories and the army, but they are also present when political issues have to be decided.

Considerable overlap between ethnic background and economic and demographic characteristics: Issues which would be defined in ethnically homogeneous societies as class differences in Israel have implicit ethnic elements. The majority of Europeans emigrated prior to 1949 (the last large group of European immigrants were survivors of the holocaust who came immediately after the state was established.) The overwhelming majority of Orientals arrived after 1949. Seniority is a vital factor in immigrant societies; very small differences in dates of arrival may influence social status. Those who came first had the opportunity to obtain the most prestigious positions, as well as to occupy the more desirable housing space. Thus, we find that status difference and ecological differentiation overlaps with ethnic background. New-founded towns and villages in the South or far North are predominantly Oriental, while the best neighborhoods in the cities like Tel Aviv and Haifa are predominantly European. The advancement of Orientals to leadership positions is quite selective. In municipal positions (mayors of towns, local labor union leaders) in which leaders are directly accountable to their constituents, Orientals are to be found in increasing proportions. They are less prominent in national politics, where it has become customary to reserve two seats in the government and about 30 seats in the Knesset for Oriental representatives (who are never officially identified as such). There is not one Oriental in the high ranks of the army and very few have influential positions in the academic community. To summarize, the participants in many potential social conflicts are divided along ethnic lines.

Emigration to Israel is perceived as emancipation from minority status: Jews in Europe and America are known to be extremely sensitive to any indication of prejudice or discrimination. This is true also of the Oriental Jews in Israel, although for somewhat different reasons. One of the main incentives for emigration to

Israel is the attempt to rid oneself of an inferior status and to become part of a dominant majority. The fact that in Israel's ethnic stratifications the Orientals did not become part of the dominant group was a frustrating experience. "In Morocco, we were considered Jews, and here we are called Moroccans," is a frequently heard complaint. In other words, many Orientals came to Israel with expectations that made it difficult for them to accept ethnic minority status.

The cultural resemblance of Orientals and Arabs: The majority of non-European Jews in Israel originated from Arabic speaking, predominantly Moslem societies (see Table 1). Naturally, they had incorporated many elements of Arab and Muslim culture into their own social and individual behavior. This has had significant impact upon the interaction of Europeans and Orientals. European Jews exhibit a certain contempt and hostility toward everything which symbolizes the Arab world. Arab music is never broadcast on the radio; Arab art is not displayed[4] and most people would feel uneasy if they spoke Arabic in public places. While no one has ever identified Oriental Jews with the external Arab enemy, it is still important that much of the cultural heritage and life style of Oriental Jews is explicitly rejected by the Europeans as an ethnic group and by the central institutions of Israeli society.

Factors promoting the integration of Jewish ethnic groups

The cultural and ideological factors: In his *An American Dilemma* Gunnar Myrdal points out that the ultimate values ("American creed") held by most Americans imply a full integration of Negroes (and other ethnic groups) into the mainstream of society. One could say that Israel is even more committed ideologically to absolute and egalitarian integration of all Jewish subgroups.

The dominant political ideologies in Israel are socialism and liberalism. There is no conservative party in Israel and no discriminatory ideology has ever been promulgated.[5] The memory of the racist Nazi regime made any reference to the "natural superiority" of any one group over others as well as any public announcement of prejudice distasteful to most Israelis.

The central role that Jewish religious symbols play in Israeli culture and education has also had a unifying effect. Obviously the meaning which Israelis of different backgrounds attach to mythological events like the exodus from Egypt or to rituals like fasting on Yom Kippur is quite different, but whatever the nature of observance, the same symbols are meaningful to everyone.

Zionist ideology adds another dimension. Zionism perceives Jewish faith in different countries and different historical eras as essentially the same. Jews are considered to owe allegiance to each other rather than to the nations in which they live as a minority.[6] Israeli-proclaimed ideology did also address itself directly to the issue of integration, which was announced as one of the most important assignments on the national agenda. Intermarriage between members of different ethnic groups is not only accepted but highly valued. Teachers, physicians and social workers are encouraged to settle among the people they serve and every sign of prejudice is denounced not merely as unethical but more strongly as unpatriotic.

Socioeconomic factors: While the overlap between socioeconomic status and ethnic background is basically an aggravating factor in ethnic relations, the dynamic development of the Israeli economy and the stratification system seems to contribute to ethnic integration. One should keep in mind when reviewing Israel's 20 years of existence that it was a period of rapid expansion. The Jewish population in Palestine increased four times, but other resources like land, capital, expertise and power expanded even more. The process of immigrant absorption has been said to involve sacrifice on the part of the absorbing society, as if the inhabitants shared their homeland with the newcomers. Economic surveys have shown that in fact not only did the oldtimers not lose during the periods of immigrant absorption, but they actually increased their standard of living more than did the immigrants. The gap between average income of oldtimers and newcomers grew during the 1950s while this trend was reversed in the 1960s, when the gap diminished. In any case, established Israelis who were predominantly of European origin did not lose economically in sharing with the immigrants but actually prospered in the process; due to the enormous increase in resources, the economics of ethnic relations in Israel was not a zero sum game.[7]

Jews of European origin not only gained economically from the influx of Oriental Jews, but successive waves of immigration also increased social mobility. As the newcomers took over the lowest positions, more powerful and rewarding roles opened up for the oldtimers. Furthermore, the establishment of the state with all of its branches and agencies (army, foreign office, public health and state-sponsored science) provided new careers for which the better-educated and more experienced Europeans were the natural candidates.

The national security factor: Israel's involvement throughout its entire short history in a fierce conflict in which its very survival was in question obviously had a unifying effect.[8] This unifying effect can be subdivided into three components.

☐ Interdependence of fate. According to K. Lewin, interdependence between members of a group means that their interests are bound together thus a loss for one is detrimental for all. In our case, it is clear that military defeat is perceived to be opposed to the interests of all Israeli Jewish ethnic groups.

☐ A common goal. While interdependence of fate may be passive, like the dependence of all inhabitants of one village upon rain, it can also be expressed by coordinated efforts. This kind of active interdependence is even more unifying since individuals or groups feel that their survival depends upon their cooperation.

☐ An outlet for aggression. If the common goal happens to be defense against a common enemy, there is an additional unifying element. Antagonistic and aggressive impulses then have a legitimate outlet and target.

While we are convinced that the above indicated factors influence the relations between Jewish ethnic groups, we do not know how to estimate convincingly their net effect. Theoretically, it seems that Israel has a good chance to overcome ethnic differences which might have explosive consequences under different conditions. The tendency of ethnic integration is increased if:

☐ A body of cultural symbols exists with which everyone can identify.

☐ If societal resources are in a state of rapid expansion.

☐ If a threat originating from a common enemy is perceived.

While this summary contains an optimistic prediction for the future development of Israeli ethnic relations, as far as Jewish groups are concerned, it also indicates in some measure the price a society in Israel's position is likely to pay.

Appreciation of the unity provided by religious and national symbols might lead to a societal overemphasis of these symbols beyond the level which most members would consider appropriate. This would be likely to strengthen politically those groups which are most closely identified with these unifying symbols beyond their actual proportions, and effectively exclude from equal participation in public life those groups or individuals not associated with these symbols.

The functional necessity of social growth may "addict" the society to the continuous intake of additional resources, whether they be immigration, manpower, land or, most important, capital. A pause in growth may affect this kind of society in a similar way as decline and loss of resources might affect other societies.

Finally, the position of such a society towards its enemies and opponents might tend to harden beyond what would have been expected on the basis of rational self-interest.

These results are not inevitable. Each of them in approaching final realization is likely to arouse resisting forces which are just as deep rooted in Israeli society and culture. Nevertheless, anyone concerned about Israeli society should be aware of these potentials.

Relations Between Jews and Arabs

It is a commonplace that the relationship between Israeli Jews and Arabs as ethnic groups has to be understood in the context of the wider Arab-Israeli conflict. Comparatively speaking, Israeli Arabs belong to the category of enemy-affiliated minorities (most conspicuous examples of which are the Japanese minority in the United States during World War II and the German minority in England during the same period). They have never denied their familial, cultural and religious ties to the belligerent Arab states. In addition, some unique circumstances shape the relations between the two peoples.

☐ Arabs in Israel are a recent minority. Until 1948, there was statistically a clear majority of Arabs in Palestine, although they had no sovereign power.

☐ While a minority within Israel's borders, Arabs constitute the overwhelming majority in the surrounding region.

☐ The Arabs of Israel are a minority without a political and cultural elite. This minority consists of a village population which had been accustomed to following the leadership of towns like Jaffa, Haifa, Nablus and Beirut. The 1948 war emptied some of these towns and severed the connections with the rest. Their lack of trained and accepted leadership increased the vulnerability of the Arabs to Jewish economic and cultural influence.

☐ Palestine was not merely the meeting place of two national movements but also of two different life styles. The modern and sometimes socially innovative Jewish sector confronted a largely rural and traditional community. For many Arabs, contact with Jews was the only avenue to achieving an advanced technology, broadened consumption and modern political ideologies.

While Arabs feel a deep rooted resentment against the Jews they are also attracted to them by a combination of cultural and practical motives. On the one hand, Jews are perceived as responsible for the end of Arab domination over Palestine and for the plight of the refugees. On the other hand, the avenues to both individual and collective progress run close to the advanced and powerful Jewish community. Arab attitudes vary according to the degree of modernization they have achieved. The more traditional, rural Arabs who are still organized in the framework of extended families controlled by "elders" or patriarchs, view Jews mainly as bearers of a foreign way of life, and therefore as a danger to the harmony and integration of their community.

As long as the village community is left alone to pursue its own course, and Jews neither interfere in internal affairs (even in demonstrating different kinds of behavior) nor impede the immediate economic interests of the village, a modus vivendi with a Jewish regime can be found. The traditional village of the Middle East has known and outlived many regimes and developed mechanisms for coping with them, while preserving its own unique structure.

This is not to imply that relations between Jews and the traditional elements are, or ever have been, idyllic. Being a small dense and extremely active society, the Jews did not refrain from interfering in the internal life of the Arab village. Some of this interference was unintentional, such as displaying a modern way of life to the villages, and some was deliberately designed to extend the advantages of modernity to the Arab village. Even though Jewish authorities tried to align with the existing traditional elite, the closeness of the contact brought about a gradual erosion of the authority of the elders.

The younger, modernized Arabs were much less concerned with the stability of traditional rural society, being themselves engaged in conflict with their traditional leadership. These young Arabs agree that the modernization of the Arab village is both desirable and inevitable. They dispute only the speed of the modernization process and the proper means to encourage it. But while the cultural element in the dispute concerning these young and progressive elements is relatively de-emphasized, the political conflict is considerably aggravated. The young educated Hebrew-speaking and European-dressed Arab whose traditional and religious symbols of identity have been eroded, is nevertheless not admitted into Jewish society. As a result, new identity symbols were needed to replace the traditional ones. These new symbols had to be broad enough to embrace the shared experience and interests of Arabs from all over the country and simultaneously sufficiently narrow to differentiate Arabs from Jews. An extreme nationalistic ideology satisfied both these needs.

Thus as modernization proceeded, the cultural and economic conflict between Arabs and Jews weakened while the political conflict was re-emphasized.[9]

The attitude of Jews toward Israeli Arabs is obviously influenced by the struggle against the Arab world. The actual ties of Israeli Arabs to the external enemy are, however, exaggerated by some psychological factors. Israeli Arabs are a weak and obvious scapegoat toward which some of the aggressive impulses engendered by hostility to the powerful Arab world can be channeled. Israeli Arabs are the first non-Jews to live under Jewish domination during the last 2,000 years of Jewish history. Some of the historical fear, mistrust and resentment toward the Gentile ("goy") tended to be transferred to the Arabs, particularly by Jews of Middle Eastern descent who had been dominated by an Arab majority until recently. Sometimes mistrust toward Israeli Arabs was exaggerated by Jewish authorities in response to internal and external criticism of some of the measures taken against the Arab population (such as the military rule and the confiscation of more than 40 percent of Arab land.) Thus while defending the military rule in the Knesset, David Ben-Gurion announced his "understanding" of feelings of animosity on the part of Israeli Arabs, saying that he would feel the same if he were in their position.

Finally, Arabs were regarded by Oriental Jews as a negative reference group—the kind of people, society and culture to be avoided in order to be fully accepted in the European-dominated mainstream of Israeli life.

During the years 1962-1967, the position of Israeli authorities toward the Arab population became considerably liberalized. This can be attributed to a combination of motives: commitment to democratic values (reinforced by increasing pressure by Israeli intellectuals), sensitivity to external public opinion and continuous tranquility of the borders. Thus military rule and other limitations on free movement were abolished. But the level of hostile and prejudiced attitudes among the population at large changed very little, and whatever stability and improvement had been attained during Levi Eshkol's government was all swept away by the June 1967 war.

Jewish hostility toward the Israeli Arab was intensified by the rapid succession of fear during the war and contempt after the Arab defeat. This negative turn in Jewish public opinion was reinforced by the fact that some Israeli Arabs collaborated in Arab belligerent activities.

For Israeli Arabs, the violent 1967 war was a fatal blow to their carefully balanced identity. Their widespread belief that they can maintain a neutral position in the Arab-Israeli conflict was shaken. There was almost no room left for neutrality. When direct communication between Israeli Arabs and their relatives and former friends in the occupied territories was established, the Israeli Arab assumed at first a tutorial role by virtue of his long acquaintance with the Jews and with Israel. But a few months later, the positions were reversed. The traditional authority of the leadership of West Bank towns like East Jerusalem and Nablus was re-established, and many Israeli Arabs felt themselves once again integrated into a wider Arab community. The pressure upon those who wanted to remain impartial became almost unbearable. Loyalty to Israel meant tacit acceptance of Israel's rule over Arab territory, while Palestinian national identification meant acceptance of violent terror raids against their Jewish neighbors. For many young Arabs, it was not only an ideological dilemma, but a practical one as well. Because of their superior knowledge of Israeli geography, language and customs, Israeli Arabs were often pressured to participate in terror raids. And every time such a collaboration is discovered, Jewish mistrust and outrage is aroused. These manifestations of generalized hostility to Arabs in turn discourage Israeli Arabs from remaining loyal. In this way a vicious cycle of suspicion, terror, oppression and retaliation eroded the good will that had been built up during the previous eight years.

THE EVIDENCE

The situations, relationships and processes that were discussed in part 1 were not entirely substantiated by our findings. First of all, these findings relate almost exclusively to perceptions and attitudes; factors like power relations and economic dependencies were not observed directly. Admittedly, the validity of attitude indicators is always somewhat questionable. Even in this study, we have evidence that extraneous factors like the interviewer's nationality or attitude do affect individual responses. Therefore the actual meaning of the exact percentages cited is open to question. Nevertheless, there are some good reasons to believe that the overall trends revealed by the following tables are indicative of the attitudes of various Israeli ethnic groups toward each other

Relations Among Jewish Ethnic Groups

In selecting indicators for inter ethnic attitudes, we attempted to measure these attitudes by conventional means, so that the results might be compared to parallel studies conducted in other countries. Our indicators fall basically into two categories: social distance and stereotypes.

Social distance: Social distance is conventionally defined as the readiness to engage in different kinds of social interaction. The more intimate and binding the social relationship with another person, the less social distance from this person. A typical example of a social distance item, is the readiness to marry or live in close proximity with members of a different ethnic group.

Tables, 3, 4 and 5 reveal considerable social distance between Jews of European and Oriental descent. The majority of both groups seemed to have some reservations about involving themselves "too closely" with the other group and admitted private preferences for intra-ethnic contacts. It is remarkable, however, that only a small minority expressed over antagonism, which seems to indicate that there is a powerful norm against the exclusion of other Jewish groups.

A second conclusion is that social distance between Europeans and Orientals is asymmetrical; Orientals are more likely to accept Europeans. This is particularly evident in comparing Tables 5 and 6. The outstanding difference between Tables 3 and 5 and Tables 4 and 6, respectively, is unanticipated and scarcely explainable. Identical questions about marriage were asked in both, and questions about neighborhoods were similar, yet the distribution was quite different. This difference may be due to the mode of interviewing (the interview vs. the questionnaire), to the location of the subjects (Tel Aviv vs. the entire country), or to their ages (high school students vs. adults). At present, we are unable to isolate these factors. The validity of these distributions, is indicated however, by the fact that the percentage of European high school students who accept intermarriage with Orientals exactly equals the percentage of mixed couples in the entire population of Jewish married couples.[3]

We also found that social distance among Europeans from different countries of origin is considerably smaller than between Europeans and Orientals, while the social distance between Orientals of different countries of origin tends to be even larger than the distance between Orientals and Europeans.

TABLE 4[11]

ATTITUDES TOWARD MARRIAGE AND NEIGHBORHOOD WITH EUROPEAN JEWS.
Respondents: Oriental high school students

	Percentage definitely agreeing	Percentage agreeing	Percentage agreeing but prefer own neighborhood	Percentage disagreeing	Total Workers
Marriage	30	51	16	2	195
Neighborhood	30	55	11	1	195

TABLE 3[10]

ATTITUDES TOWARD MARRIAGE AND NEIGHBORHOOD WITH ORIENTAL JEWS.
Respondents: European high school students

	Percentage definitely agreeing	Percentage agreeing	Percentage agreeing but prefer own neighborhood	Percentage disagreeing	Total Workers
Marriage	15	24	39	21	143
Neighborhood	23	40	35	2	143

TABLE 5[12]

ATTITUDES TOWARD MARRIAGE AND RENTING A ROOM TO AN ORIENTAL JEW.
Respondents: Tel Aviv adults, European.

	Percentage definitely agreeing	Percentage agreeing	Percentage agreeing but prefer own neighborhood	Percentage disagreeing	Total Workers
Marriage	37	20	19	24	204
Renting a room	37	30	7	16	204

In the detailed interviews or in written comments added voluntarily to the self-administered questionnaires, some of the respondents tried to explain their attitudes. Europeans usually justify their refusal to intermarry with Orientals on grounds of cultural gap or different mentality, rather than in explicit claims of racial inferiority. For instance: "I prefer to marry somebody of my own background because of the importance of having the same mentality," or "I wouldn't want to have a cultural gap in my family," or more specifically, "I can't see myself married to a man who wants to have about twelve children."

Sometimes prejudicial overtones are revealed in arguments for a favorable attitude: "I will marry the one whom I love, even if he is Oriental." Most Orientals accept intermarriage; some even prefer it. One outspoken respondent summarized the main arguments for such a position: "I wouldn't only agree, but would even prefer it (to marry a European). First of all, if I marry a girl of my own community, this will not contribute anything to bringing the communities closer. Second, I believe marriage with a European would result in better children."

Stereotypes and Prejudices: There are many specific indications of generally prejudiced attitudes. In order to avoid arbitrary selection of a few, we chose two very broad items, one claiming that unfavorable evaluations of Orientals reflect reality. The second states that although the present backwardness of non-Europeans may be reduced, it can never be totally abolished. We also added a claim that Oriental neighborhoods are dirty, which is well known in the literature on prejudice and stereotypes. In order to minimize possible reluctance on the part of respondents to express prejudiced attitudes, we added the phrase, "Some people say," to each claim. This addition was also intended to disengage the interviewer from these prejudiced statements.

Our pretest indicated that none of the above stereotypes applied to Europeans, so we had to use a special item which stated that Europeans are emotionally cold and unresponsive, the shortcoming most frequently ascribed to them in our preliminary interviews.

Table 6 shows that prejudice against Orientals is, on the average, as frequent among Orientals as among Europeans. This could be interpreted as a certain degree of self-contempt on the part of the Orientals, probably originating from an acceptance of European prejudices.[14] It should be remembered, however, that many may be thinking of other Orientals (not only different individuals but different subgroups), as I will discuss later, in detail. Table 7 shows that even a relatively mild criticism of Europeans as "cold" is rather rare: Only a quarter of Orientals feel that way, and Europeans reject the idea altogether. Orientals perceive Europeans more as a guide or reference group than as an "oppressing majority."

Feelings of Interdependence: In most studies of ethnic relations, the negative aspects of these relations have been carefully explored, but not the positive aspects, such as mutual attraction and feelings of interdependence. According to most studies, the most positive attitude to be expected is that people of different backgrounds are "simply as human beings," that is, to disregard their ethnicity. Our findings indicate that in Israel social distance and prejudice are at least partially balanced by a sense of interdependence and by the desire for a fully integrated society in the future. When asked whether it would be better if there were less members of the other group, a clear majority of both Europeans and Orientals said "no."[17]

Again, the Orientals' attitude toward the Europeans was more favorable; they rejected the notion of less Europeans much more decisively than the Europeans rejected the idea of less Orientals. Some who expressed these attitudes justified them by the need to have more Jews in Israel, whatever their background. Some, however, referred to characteristics of the other group which seemed to them constructive.

"If the Europeans hadn't founded this country, we would have had nowhere to come," one Oriental woman said. Another simply stated, "We need the Europeans; they are the brain." A European respondent said, "The Orientals coming in their great numbers saved the state and its European oldtimers. If they hadn't come, we would now be a negligible enclave in an Arab ocean."

The Desire for Integration: One should analyze ethnic attitudes in the perspective of time: are current characteristics and relation-

TABLE 6[15]

PREJUDICE AGAINST ORIENTALS

Question	Ethnic group	Percentage definitely agree	Percentage agree	Percentage disagree	Percentage strongly disagree	Total Workers
Some people say that for preju-	Orientals	26	17	34	23	246
dices to be abol- ished, Orientals must rid themselves of their short- comings. What's your opinion?	Europeans	23	20	39	18	204
Some people say that even though	Orientals	18	16	30	37	246
Orientals may pro- gress a lot, they will never reach the level of Europeans. What's your opinion?	Europeans	8	17	39	35	204
Some people say that neighborhoods	Orientals	27	38	21	14	246
where Orientals live always seem to be dirty. What's your opinion?	Europeans	20	39	29	12	204

ships perceived as enduring and permanent, or are they flexible, developing towards a more egalitarian (or possibly less egalitarian) solution? Many observers view prejudice as an attitude towards other groups which is not only negative, but also rigid. A prejudiced person is said to believe in his stereotypes as an expression of an eternal truth.

Since in Israel the common historical root with ancient Israel is always emphasized, the notion of inherited inferiority is extremely rare. Ethnic differences are perceived as cultural

TABLE 7[16]

PREJUDICE AGAINST EUROPEANS

Question	Ethnic group	Per centage definitely agree	Per- centage agree	Per centage dis- agree	Per centage strongly dis- agree	Total Workers
Some people say that Europeans are emotionally cold and unresponsive. What's your opinion?	Orientals	13	14	26	47	246
	Europeans	3	8	41	48	204

differences imposed by the various societies of exile. Most Israelis view the differences between ethnic groups as something which can eventually be abolished in the future. In Table 6, we have shown that a majority disagrees with the prediction that Orientals will never be able to close the gap between themselves and the Europeans. Tables 8 and 8A summarize the responses to these questions: "In your opinion, is it desirable that the present differences between ethnic groups in Israel should disappear?" (Table 8A). The main conclusion to be derived from Tables 8 and 8A is that our subjects tend both to expect and endorse the reduction of interethnic differences. These responses do not lend any support to the notion that Orientals in Israel are "forcefully Westernized."[18] As a matter of fact, Orientals are slightly more eager to abolish all differences while Europeans are slightly more concerned about preserving ethnic traditions. Practically no one supports the present level of ethnic differences.

We encouraged some of our interviewees to elaborate the ethnic traditions they would like to preserve. It became apparent that these were almost always limited to the area of home life. An Oriental respondent stated, "Everybody can keep his traditional life style at home. In public places, however, an individual should behave just like everyone else." But even at home, special traditions are made peripheral or aesthetic issues. "We have some old and extremely nice folkways. It would be a pity to lose

TABLE 8[19]

ATTITUDES TOWARDS DIFFERENCES BETWEEN JEWISH ETHNIC GROUPS IN THE FUTURE.

Ethnic group	Percentage saying differences should remain as they are	Percentage saying differences in tradition should remain	Percentage saying all differences should disappear	Total Number
Orientals	2	24	75	195
Europeans	2	34	64	143
Total	3	28	70	338

TABLE 8A[20]

EXPECTATIONS ABOUT DIFFERENCES BETWEEN ETHNIC GROUPS IN THE FUTURE (20 YEARS).

Ethnic group	Percentage saying differences will remain as they are now	Percentage saying no substantial differences will remain	Percentage saying no differences will remain	Total Number
Orientals	13	44	42	246
Europeans	19	58	23	204
Total	16	50	33	450

them." Another typical statement is, "Why shouldn't everybody keep his own tradition, as long as he doesn't interfere with other people's rights?" But even this limited nostalgia is a minority attitude. The majority of Orientals want complete assimilation, and some Orientals explicitly cite the Europeans as a desirable model. "I wish we Persians could overcome all our superstitions and be more like the Europeans—educated, industrious and clean."

Others urge the development of a national and non-ethnic tradition: "I hope a new and unified Israeli tradition will emerge."

Jewish Attitudes Towards Arabs

Hostility and Social Distance: Hostility and social distance increases considerably when Arabs are mentioned. During the pretest, the overwhelming majority of the sample tended to answer each question negatively. We tried to solve that, in part, by adding another extremely negative category, so that degrees of hostility towards Arabs could be differentiated. Tables 9, 10 and 11 reveal the intensity of anti-Arab feelings.

Perhaps the most interesting finding was the tendency of Orientals to be more hostile towards Arabs than Europeans. One might assume that the Orientals, having originated from Arab countries and retaining close ties with Arab culture, customs and language, could serve as mediators between European Israelis and Arabs. However, this is clearly not the case, as the results in Tables 9-11 indicate. Many Oriental respondents explained their feelings towards Arabs by previous unpleasant experiences during their life under Arab domination, but it seems to us that the extreme hostility of Orientals towards Arabs must also be considered in the context of present situations in Israel.

FINDINGS

Orientals naturally aspire to close the gap between themselves and Europeans and to attain a full share of prestige and power. By expressing hostility to Arabs, an Oriental attempts to rid himself of the "inferior" Arabic elements in his own identity, and adopts a position congenial to the European group that he desires to emulate.

TABLE 9[21]

SOCIAL DISTANCE FROM ARABS
A COMPARISON BETWEEN ORIENTAL AND EUROPEAN RESPONDENTS

Item	Ethnic group	Percentage no data	Percentage definitely agreeing	Percentage agreeing	Percentage agreeing but preferring a Jew	Percentage not agreeing	Percentage strongly disagreeing	Total Number
Readiness for marriage	Orientals	1	0	2	6	24	67	192
	Europeans	0	0	11	13	29	56	139
Readiness for friendship	Orientals	2	0	4	23	34	38	192
	Europeans	1	3	10	27	32	27	139
Readiness for neighborhood	Orientals	2	1	7	32	27	32	192
	Europeans	0	4	12	32	27	25	139

TABLE 10
PREJUDICE AGAINST ARABS
A COMPARISON BETWEEN ORIENTAL
AND EUROPEAN RESPONDENTS

A comparison between Oriental and European respondents

Percentage agreeing that:	Europeans	Orientals
It would be better if there were fewer Arabs.	91	93
Every Arab hates Jews.	76	83
Arabs will not reach the level of progress of Jews.	64	85
Disagree to rent a room to an Arab.	80	91
Disagree to have an Arab as a neighbor.	53	78
Total	204	246

[22]Source: (2) in Appendix

If this line of reasoning is correct, then those Orientals most resembling Arabs should be more hostile than others. With this hypothesis in mind, we instructed the interviewers in our second study to record the degree of resemblance of each Oriental respondent to Arabs. Two criteria were chosen: appearance and accent. Table 12 shows that hostility increases slightly when resemblance to Arabs increases. However, they seem to be rather consistent. The slightness of the differences may stem from a ceiling effect: the ratio of anti-Arab prejudice is already high in all the categories of resemblance to Arabs. This seems to indicate that hostility between Arabs and Jews of Middle Eastern origin exists not in spite of but partially because of their many similarities.

Effects of the Six-Day War: As a result of the Six-Day War, social distance and hostility towards the Arabs increased even more. Table 13 shows an increase in 80% of the previous expressions of anti-Arab attitudes between 1967 and 1968. These data were collected before Israeli-Arab participation in terror raids became known. Most Arabs adopted a passive neutrality during the war. Small fringe groups performed ineffective anti-Israeli activities, while other small groups actively helped in the war effort; and the latter received much more publicity than the former. It may thus

TABLE 11[23]

SOCIAL DISTANCE FROM ARABS

A comparison between Oriental and European respondents

Question	Ethnic group	Percentage agreeing	Percentage agreeing but prefer own group	Percentage disagreeing	Total Number
To marry	Orientals	11	5	84	246
	Europeans	9	11	79	204
To rent a room	Orientals	6	4	91	246
	Europeans	13	7	80	204
To have as neighbor	Orientals	12	9	78	246
	Europeans	26	21	53	204

TABLE 12

PREJUDICE AGAINST ARABS AMONG ORIENTALS ACCORDING

TO THEIR RESEMBLANCE TO ARABS

Question—	Arabs understand only force		Arabs will not reach the level of progress of Jews			Total Number
Response— Degree of resemblance	Percentage Agreeing	Percentage Disagreeing	Percentage Agreeing	Percentage Having Reservations	Percentage Disagreeing	
Do not bear resemblance to Arabs						
– by accent	84	15	79	7	13	42
– by appearance	87	13	77	7	17	35
Bear some resemblance to Arabs						
– by accent	86	14	84	6	10	105
– by appearance	83	17	84	5	11	143
Bear resemblance to Arabs						
– by accent	89	11	89	2	9	99
– by appearance	91	9	89	3	8	68

24Source: (2) in Appendix

TABLE 13[25]

NEGATIVE ATTITUDES TOWARD ARABS
BEFORE AND AFTER THE 1967 WAR

	Year	
Percentage agreeing that:	1967	1968
It would be better if there were fewer Arabs.	80	91
The Arabs will never reach the level of progress of Jews.	62	76
Every Arab hates Jews.	73	80
Disagreement to rent a room to an Arab.	80	86
Disagreement to have an Arab as a neighbor.	67	67
Total Number	**200**	**450**

be concluded that the increase of Jewish hostility toward Israeli Arabs resulted from the overall political situation rather than from local interaction. Generally speaking, the position of an enemy-affiliated minority is endangered when an actively violent clash breaks out, whatever their attitudes or actual behavior might be.

The situation of the Israeli Arab is no exception to this rule.

Arab Attitudes Towards Jews

Social distance: Israeli Arabs tend to reject social contact with Jews (Table 14). Friendship is consistently seen as less binding than neighborhood. Some respondents explained that friendship is selective and individual; you can choose your friend, but not your neighbor. Neighborhood also involves the entire family. Many Arab respondents were anxious not to allow the female members of their families to have any contacts with Jews.[26] This attitude is in line with the meaning attached to friendship and neighborhood in an Arab rural life. Most people live in homes which are not purchased but built by or for the family, and rarely change it during the lifetime of one generation. The lack of cars and telephones and the confinement of the women and younger children to the home also intensifies contact with neighbors.

On the other hand, friendship is offered freely. A villager is expected to invite almost every person he meets to eat or at least have coffee with him. If such an invitation is accepted, both men will define themselves as friends, and will exhibit a pleasant

TABLE 14[27]

SOCIAL DISTANCE FROM JEWS

Israeli Arabs	Percentage agreeing to make friends with Jews	Percentage agreeing to live in Jewish quarter	Percentage agreeing to live in house with Jews	Total Number
All respondents	58	42	30	464
Students	53	42	31	181
Parents	69	36	22	98
Young Adults	57	44	36	90
Working Youth	56	44	32	95

although uncommitted attitude towards each other. Thus friendship is less selective and less personal than in western societies.

It would seem, then, that traditional parents would be more inclined than their more modernized sons to make friends with Jews but less inclined to accept Jews as neighbors. Table 14 substantiates this prediction.

While the rejection of social contact with Jews is considerable, it is significantly lower than the rejection of Arabs by Jews. Again, we observe the lack of symmetry in their relations. The Arab minority may feel that they gain by interaction with the Jewish majority, while Jews will tend to exclude outsiders as among other things potential competitors.

An overt show of social distance is usually considered detrimental to the relations between the two groups, but this generalization does not seem to us to hold in all circumstances. For instance, if the dominant group rejects a minority, social equilibrium might be better preserved if the minority similarly rejects the majority.

Thus, attitudes towards social interaction with Jews are not a major problem. Neighborhoods are separate in any case, and Arabs trying to achieve acceptance into the Jewish community are likely to be rejected.

Attitudes toward the State of Israel: Israeli-Arab attitudes toward Israel as a political entity seem to constitute a much more severe problem than do their attitudes towards Jews as individuals. When dissenters question the legitimacy of a society or the validity of its ultimate values, a severe dilemma can be created, particularly if the society is young and not absolutely secure.

As Table 15 shows, Israel's right to exist is not absolutely accepted by our Arab sample. In the category, "Yes, with reservations," the main reservations concern Israel's treatment of the Palestinian Arabs. About half of those giving this response mentioned repatriation of the refugees as a condition for Israel's right to exist. Others emphasized the granting of first-class citizenship to those Arabs now residing in Israel. The most striking difference among the subgroups is between students and their parents.

TABLE 15[28]

HAS THE STATE OF ISRAEL A RIGHT TO EXIST?

Israeli Arabs	Percentage saying yes	Percentage saying yes, with reservations	Percentage refusing to answer	Percentage saying no	Total Number
All respondents	31	49	4	16	470
Students	24	49	3	24	192
Parents	54	41	2	3	96
Young Adults	25	61	4	10	89
Working Youth	29	44	6	20	93

The young Israeli-educated Arab tends to display extreme nationalistic and sometimes hostile attitudes. (Tables 16 and 17). These young people are relatively similar to their Jewish counterparts in most non-political respects. They are also much better equipped (and more positively motivated) to live among Jews. (Table 14).

The traditional village became too limiting for the wider perspectives and higher aspirations of these young Arabs, and those who sought acceptance into the Jewish community were rebuffed. Their experience discouraged others. The alternative open to an Israeli Arab interested in expanding his horizons was identification with the surrounding Arab world. Table 16 indicates that Arab students, and to a degree other young people, feel relatively more "at home" in an Arab country, while their parents prefer Israel.

The Impact of the War: The overwhelming majority of the Arabs in Israel did not predict an Israeli victory (Table 18). The Arab defeat shocked them almost as much as it did the Arabs across the border.

The humiliating defeat of the Arab populations aroused strong sympathy and loyalty on the part of the Israeli Arabs, and tended to increase the Arabs' hatred rather than respect for the state of Israel. Table 20 indicates that more Arabs now feel at home in the Arab world and less feel at home in Israel. Similarly, according to Table 21, fewer Arab respondents see their future as positively bound with Israel.

CONCLUSION

Ethnic relations in Israel are interwoven with other facets of social structure and environment. Some of Israel's ethnic problems seem very close to solution while others may be close to explosion. The distinctive functions which the Oriental Jews and the Arabs perform for Israeli society partly explains the differences.

After European Jewish immigration to Israel began to diminish, mass immigration from the Middle East renewed the young state's development. Orientals occupied the vacant land and houses abandoned by the defeated Arabs, joined Israel's

TABLE 16[29]

DOES THE SUBJECT FEEL MORE "AT HOME" IN ISRAEL OR THE ARAB STATES?

	Percentage in Israel	Percentage in neither	Percentage saying in one of the Arab States	Total Number
All respondents	37	15	48	462
Students	31	12	57	188
Parents	54	18	27	92
Young Adults	35	18	47	88
Working Youth	36	11	53	94

TABLE 17[30]

ARE THE ARABS BOUND TO WAGE ANOTHER WAR?

	Percentage saying yes	Percentage saying yes, if militarily possible	Percentage saying yes, if Israel stays put	Percentage saying no	Total Number
All respondents	35	4	15	46	460
Students	45	4	13	38	189
Parents	21	3	9	66	86
Young Adults	30	2	19	48	89
Working Youth	34	4	22	40	96

TABLE 18[31]

EXPECTED RESULTS OF THE WAR
When the war broke out, who did you think would win?

The Arabs	No One	Israel, but a less decisive victory	Israel	Total Number
67%	18%	5%	9%	457

armed forces and provided a sound justification for mobilizing economic, cultural and political aid from world Jewry. In short, Orientals performed vital functions that contributed to Israel's survival and progress.

The Israeli Arabs were in no position to perform these functions. Even the most moderate and loyal of them could not fully identify with the country's Zionism, with its commitment to Jewish immigration, and most important, with its struggle against the Arab world. These differences in background were further strained when the three main ethnic groups (European Jews, Oriental Jews and Arabs) began to interact.

The Orientals aspired to full integration into Israeli society. This meant a movement away from their Middle Eastern (that is, Arab) background, and toward the dominant European group. Arabs became for the Oriental Jews a "marking-off" group that represented everything resented and dispensable in their own background. The increasing threat of external Arab hostility increased unity among Israeli Jews, while the nonviolent but intense hostility toward the Arab minority was a negative manifestation of this unity.

From the Arab minority's point of view, full participation in the country's social, economic and political life became more urgent, yet the prospects for such participation did not increase. Thus, dynamic and competent individuals who might have been the pioneers of integration under different circumstances became the most outspoken advocates of political hostility. The two groups who could be potential mediators—the Israeli Jews of Middle Eastern background and Arabs with advanced Israeli education—are the least motivated to attain a reconciliation.

TABLE 19[32]

THE PERCEIVED INFLUENCE OF THE WAR ON THE ARABS' ATTITUDE TOWARD ISRAEL
How, in your view, did the war influence the Arabs' evaluation of the State of Israel?

	Percentage rose	Percentage remained the same	Percentage fell	Total Number
Respect	43	17	40	299
Fear	52	34	13	282
Hatred	73	23	4	291

TABLE 20[33]

**FEELING MORE AT HOME IN ISRAEL OR IN AN ARAB COUNTRY
BEFORE AND AFTER THE JUNE WAR**
(High school students only)

Percentage saying	1966	1967
More at home in Israel	62	31
No difference	14	12
More at home in Arab country	23	57
Total Number	117	188

TABLE 21[34]

POLITICAL FUTURE PERSPECTIVES BEFORE AND AFTER THE WAR
What would you like the future of the Israeli Arab to be?
(High school students only)

Percentage saying	1966	1967
They will become part of the Jewish public	6	–
A separate but equal people within the state of Israel	81	53
They will be in a separate state of their own	13	17
An Arab state will arise in the ENTIRE territory of Palestine	*	19
Total Number	116	191

*Not asked.

APPENDIX

The findings presented in the previous pages are based on several studies carried out in Israel before and after the June 1967 war. Our original purpose was to examine the structure of ethnic relations from all perspectives. The unexpected occurence of the war gave us the opportunity to test, by replicating some of our procedures, the impact of the hostilities upon the values and attitudes of Jews and Arabs. The following projects were drawn upon for this essay:

1. A study on ethnic identity and relations among Jewish ethnic groups. The sample included 675 secondary school students of

both sexes and 51 of their parents. A random sample of 117 secondary schools was taken. Written questionnaires were administered to 50 percent of all 11th graders (ages 16-17). Since the questions were too numerous, two different questionnaires had to be used; thus the N in the various tables may vary. Almost all items in both questionnaires were "closed ended." The results of the project are presented more fully in *Ethnic Identity and Ethnic Relations in Israel* a report submitted to the United States office of Health, Education and Welfare in November, 1967 and my doctoral thesis of the same title. (Jerusalem. 1968; in Hebrew)

2. A study of ethnic attitudes among residents of Tel-Aviv. Four hundred and fifty adults were interviewed; 200 of them were interviewed twice (winter 1967 and winter 1968) and 250 only once (winter 1968). An ecological cluster sampling was taken (certain blocks were randomly selected) with an overrepresentation of low status neighborhoods in which Jews of Oriental background are more likely to live. The interviewing was based on a questionnaire which might be described as "open-closed." No preformulated categories were read to the subjects, but once a response was given, it was coded immediately. In cases of doubt, the respondent was asked (*after* giving his spontaneous reply) which of the categories would fit his answer best.

3. A study of ethnic attitudes among Israeli Arabs, carried out in the summer of 1966 and the fall of 1967. The sample of 500 respondents was also clustered. First, eight predominantly Arab settlements were selected according to the following criteria: religious affiliation, degree of urbanization, region and size. Then residents of these settlements were selected according to the following categories:

	Ages	N
High school students	14-18	200
Parents of high school students	35-70	100
Working youth	14-18	100
Young adults	20-35	100
		500 Total

The interviews were performed by the open-closed method mentioned above.

The main problem in all these studies was that objectivity had to be not only maintained but convincingly demonstrated to

coworkers and respondents, so that their confidence and cooperation could be obtained. An investigator studying ethnic relations
in his own society is often identified with his group of origin. In
times of political tension, he may also be suspected of collecting
information for intelligence purposes. We tried to minimize these
fears and suspicions by employing two principles: the groups
studied should be represented in the investigating team throughout all stages of the project; great caution should be taken to
ensure the confidentiality of the data, even at the risk of
weakening the principal investigator's control over field work
procedures.

Among students of the Hebrew University, we were able to
find members of different Jewish groups as well as Moslem and
Christian Arabs willing to cooperate in the project. Arab
interviewers usually interviewed Arab respondents, but some also
took part in the research team from the initial design to the final
report. Confidentiality was ensured by omitting the clearly
identifying information. Interview reports in the Arab section did
not include names or addresses, which made it impossible for the
investigator to follow up the interview or check on the work of
the interviewers. Among Jewish respondents, the level of suspicion was much lower and names and addresses could be recorded.

[1] I am indebted to S. N. Eisenstadt and S. Herman of the Hebrew
University for their guidance and encouragement. The loyal and resourceful assistance of Nira Davis is gratefully acknowledged. Limitations of
space prevent me from mentioning individually my many young Jewish
and Arab colleagues who worked under extremely tense and difficult
conditions to make this study possible.
[2] Source: Statistical Abstract of Israel, 1968. p. 43.
[3] Source: Statistical Abstract of Israel, 1968. p. 45.
[4] Egyptian films are a noteworthy exception.
[5] The one exception is the book *The Ashkenazic Revolution* by K.
Katzenelson, published in 1964, in which the author tried to develop an
ideology of European superiority. This book was, however, violently
denounced by all segments of the public.
[6] The degree to which the imparting of Jewish and Zionist values has
been successful is systematically investigated in S. N. Herman, *The*

Attitude of Israeli Youth To Their Jewishness and to Jews Abroads, (mimeo), Research Report, Jerusalem, 1967. Herman's empirical findings indicate that a definite majority of Israeli youth has a strong and positive Jewish identity, and a sense of responsibility and attachment towards other Jews all over the world. This evidence contradicts the conclusions influenced by the insightful although unsystematic observations of scholars like M. Spiro in his *Children of the Kibbutz* and G. Friedmann in his *The End of the Jewish People?*

[7]These facts were established and interpreted through an interesting exchange between two Israeli economists. In 1961, G. Hanoch reported that the income gap between immigrants and oldtimers was increasing over time, and explained this tendency by the growing income differentiation between manual workers and professionals. He predicted that if no far-reaching measures were taken, social and economic gaps would increase and find political expression. (see: G. Hanoch "Income Differences in Israel" in *The Fifth Annual Report* The Falk Institute, Jerusalem, 1961.) In 1966, another economist, R. Klinov-Malul, cited later findings which indicated that after 1958 income gaps were gradually decreasing. Responding to this challenge, G. Hanoch offered a new explanation: the growing gap in incomes should be understood as a result of the increase in the untrained labor force. (This increase is not exactly synonymous with immigration, as a year or two usually elapses between the arrival of immigrants and their full participation in the labor market.) Unskilled labor and skilled labor are complementary factors of production. Therefore, salaries of unskilled workers decreased relative to incomes of more professional workers. This tendency was less marked in the 1960s when the increase in unskilled labor supply leveled off. In addition to that, more young immigrants achieved better training. While income differentiation between professionals and non-professionals still increased somewhat, this tendency was more than offset by more advanced skills attained by the immigrants so that the overall gap between immigrants and oldtimers tended to decrease. (See original exchange in *The Integration of Immigrants from Different Countries of Origin in Israel.* A symposium held at the Hebrew University. The Magnes Press, Jerusalem, 1969, pp. 97-109 and 123-125 (in Hebrew).)

[8]Whether the threats expressed by several Arab leaders to destroy Israel and kill or expel its citizens were real or propagandistic is irrelevant for our purpose. The unifying function is due to the perceived threat, whether real or not. These considerations were raised previously by J. T. Shuval, "Emerging Patterns of Ethnic Strain in Israel," *Social Forces* Vol. 40, No. 4, 1962, p. 324.

[9]A detailed discussion of these trends can be found in: Y. Peres, "Modernization and Nationalism in the Identity of the Israeli Arab," *Middle East Journal,* August 1970.

[10]Source: (1) in Appendix

[11]Source: (1) in Appendix

[12]Source: (2) in Appendix

[13]See J. Matras, *Social Change in Israel,* Chicago University Press. Chicago. Tables 5, 2.

[14] Actual manifestations of self-rejection are reported by Shuval. See "Self Rejection among North African Immigrants to Israel," in the *Israel Annals of Psychiatry,* Vol. 4, No. 1, 1966.

[15] Source: (2) in Appendix

[16] Source: (2) in Appendix

[17] Europeans were asked if they preferred to have less Orientals in the country, while Orientals were asked the same question about Europeans. This item as an indicator of prejudice has been adapted from R. M. Williams, *Strangers Next Door,* Prentice-Hall, 1964, p. 410.

[18] The argument that Orientals are Westernized against their will and that their specific culture is deliberately destroyed is made by M. Seltzer, *The Arianization of the Jewish State* White Co., 1967. Mr. Seltzer implies that the majority of Orientals want to preserve ethnic differences. However, he fails to present any data to that effect.

[19] Source: (1) in Appendix.

[20] Source: (2) in Appendix.

[21] Source: (1) in Appendix.

[22] Source: (2) in Appendix.

[23] Source: (2) in Appendix.

[24] Source: (2) in Appendix.

[25] Source: (2) in Appendix.

[26] Note that all our Arab respondents were male. Early attempts to interview Arabs of both sexes failed almost completely. A typical reply a female interviewer received when asking to see one of a respondent's four daughters was, "Sorry. But I have no daughters."

[27] Source: (3) in Appendix.

[28] Source: (3) in Appendix.

[29] Source: (3) in Appendix.

[30] Source: (3) in Appendix.

[31] Source: (3) in Appendix.

[32] Source: (3) in Appendix.

[33] Source: (3) in Appendix.

[34] Source: (3) in Appendix.

The Palestine Arabs:
A National Entity

DON PERETZ

My purpose is neither to praise nor to bury Palestinian Arab nationalism but to explain why I think an awareness and understanding of it is essential to peace in the Middle East. Without such attention the movement will certainly continue to be a major source of conflict. Although there are many who would like to dominate, to destroy or to deny it, the Palestinian Arab national movement seems to have become autonomous of any local or outside force. Both its strength and support have been growing. Paradoxically, a principal reason for the strength of the movement is its inherent weakness; that is, its amorphous character, evident in its many fragmentary groups, in a frequently shifting leadership, in the diverse allegiances and alliances that it has formed throughout the Arab world. While the movement has so far failed to receive official recognition in the West, from Israel or in many Arab quarters, all those concerned with peace in the Middle East have become aware of it as a source of disruption and upheaval.

WHAT IS PALESTINIAN ARAB NATIONALISM?

Palestinian Arab nationalism is a national movement that seems to thrive on failure and to grow in proportion to the amount of force opposed to it. Its history since the end of World War I is one of unfulfilled political objectives, of continued fragmentation and diversity, of political divisiveness and internecine bickering among its leadership, but in the final analysis, a history of far-reaching impact and influence on the possibilities of peace in the Middle East.

Since there are many who deny the existence of a Palestinian national entity or of any distinctive group of people called Palestinians,[1] it might be useful to define the group and the entity. The Palestinian Arabs are not unlike many other national groups that have claimed distinctive identity in the twentieth century. There are numerous other groups smaller in numbers, such as those who comprise the nations of Malta, Cyprus, Singapore and several of the Central American Republics. In the Middle East during this century similar groups claiming national identity, but failing to attain it, or obtaining it only recently, include the Armenians, the Kurds and the Jews.

For purposes of practical definition one may say that any group that considers itself a national entity and is so identified by others, although not necessarily by all others, is a national entity. Such groups are frequently recognized by common characteristics including language, history, national ethos, attachment to some identifiable geographic area, and culture expressed in literature, music, art, drama and crafts. These characteristics are sufficient to identify numerous national groups including the Jews of Israel and the Arabs of Palestine. Others may include race, religion or some specific similar creed. However, all of these characteristics are not necessarily integral to establishment of a national entity; a combination of several may suffice.

Prior to World War I there were no distinctive Palestinian people and no political frontiers defining Palestine. Both the land and the people were regarded as part of the Syrian provinces of the Ottoman Turkish empire. Palestinian Arab nationalism emerged after the war in reaction to the rise of two other forces in the territory established as British Mandatory Palestine, the political and security forces of Great Britain and the Yishuv, or organized Palestinian Jewish community. Immediately after World War I, Arab residents of Palestine who were politically organized identified with the Arab nationalism of Syria and were represented in its constituent bodies and parliament in Damascus.

ORIGINS OF THE MOVEMENT

As early as 1918 during the British military administration, Palestinian Arabs attempted to organize anti-Jewish demonstrations.[2] Fearing their potential anti-British character, the demonstrations were outlawed by the military authorities and English troops conducted searches for arms in Jerusalem and in the neighboring villages. Palestinian Arab notables succeeded in convening an all-Arab Palestinian conference during January 1919 which demanded from the Paris Peace Conference: repudiation of the British promise of a national home in Palestine for the Jews; rejection of French claims in Syria; and establishment of a united independent Syrian government as part of the "Arab Nation" in the region of present-day Syria, Lebanon, Israel and parts of Jordan. Muslim-Christian societies were organized to further these demands throughout this area and Palestinian delegates were included among those who attended the general Syrian Congresses in July 1919 and in March 1920 at which Faisal was chosen as king of Syria. However, after the collapse of the Syrian Arab regime, occupation of the country by French armed forces and the institution of civil administration in Palestine, Arab leaders in the latter country began to reformulate a distinctive, separate political position. The result was the Third Palestinian Arab Congress convened in Haifa during December 1920, the first separate Palestinian Arab political convention. (The previous two were the above mentioned Syrian Congresses.) This was the first in a series of five convened by Palestinian Arab political leadership between 1920 and 1928.

The objectives of the Palestinian Congresses were expressed in resolutions which supposedly represented the views of all Palestinian Arabs. They demanded of the British government "in the name of international honour and humanity, and in the name of Moslem and Christian faiths . . . establishment of a National Government in Palestine responsible to a representative Council, to be elected by the Arab-speaking people who were living in Palestine at the outbreak of the Great War, on the same lines and principles which are being applied in Iraq and Transjordan . . ."[3]

The resolutions also expressed dissatisfaction with government support for Zionist policy, including permission for Jewish immigration, official recognition of the Hebrew language and permission for use of the Zionist flag. The Haifa Congress was thus the originating body of Palestinian Arab nationalism and from it emerged the executive committee of the Palestinian Arab Congress, referred to as the Arab Executive.

Leadership of the Palestinian Arab national movement was concentrated in the hands of the landed gentry and the urban middle class. The former represented mostly Muslim landowners and religious leaders living in urban areas but related to rural Arab Palestine through a network of family ties. Although mostly Muslim, the landed gentry cooperated with many of the Christian leaders of the urban middle class. Such tensions as existed between urban Christians and the Muslim Arab gentry were overcome by common opposition to the British mandatory authorities and the Yishuv. Although political leadership lay with a few families of notables, "a certain psychological affinity and some consciousness of a common political purpose existed between leaders and the people at large. The Arab politicians in a sense reflected as well as controlled the attitudes of the people . . . Arab political activity in Palestine was concerned with serious aims and exemplified a definite line of policy.[4] Themes of Arab politics in other countries such as Islam, Arabism and national independence, were also those of Palestinian nationalism. However, "the achievement of national independence under the control of the Arabs . . ." was the end that unified all Arab political groups in opposition to the British Mandate, and this policy rested upon the premise that the Arabs owned Palestine.[5] All Arab political groups refused to accept an equal footing with the "alien Jews."

Political groupings tended to rally around notable families such as the Husainis and the Nashashibis. The former were by far the dominant family in Arab Palestine, and their position was further enhanced after capturing leadership of the Supreme Muslim Council, the authoritative Muslim religio-political body of the country. Their political followers were known as the pro-council party or the *Meglissin* in opposition to the anticouncil party or the *Muaridin* led by the Nashashibis. Both groups were represented in the various Arab Congresses organized during the 1920s.

There was little, if any, social or political content in the programs of the principal Arab political groups. Since they were led by those with vested interest in the social and economic status quo of the Palestinian Arab community, they had little inclination to urge changes in the existing social structure such as were to be advocated in the post-World War II era by various Arab socialist groups.

The policies and objectives of the Palestinian Arab political leadership were transmitted to the urban and rural masses through the complex of ties which the leading families developed throughout Palestine and through the government-organized Arab educational system. Under British mandate, both Arab and Jewish communities were permitted to operate their own educational systems. Although Jewish schooling was supported largely by the local Yishuv, the Arab public schools were organized and supported by the mandatory government. Arabic was the language of instruction, the medium through which Arab consciousness was deeply instilled. In 1937, the British Royal Commission sent to investigate the situation in Palestine was highly critical of nationalist attitudes which it found in both Jewish and Arab educational systems. The Commission pointed out that mandatory government schools, "have become seminaries of Arab nationalism; that the schoolmasters are for the most part ardent nationalists; and that during the disturbances of last year practically no work was done in the Government school."[6] Arab schoolmasters and nationalist leaders felt that they were not given adequate leeway to develop their own nationalist curriculum. The commissioners' recommendation that efforts be made to overcome separatist tendencies by promoting mixed education was ignored.

Characteristic of Arab political organization in Palestine and in the neighboring countries were the deep internal rifts created by personality rather than policy clashes. Factional bitterness was most evident in the rivalry between the Husainis and the Nashashibis. The Palestinian Arab Party developed out of the

Husaini-dominated Supreme Muslim Council. The Nashashibi-dominated anticouncilites formed the rival National Defense party.

Other lesser political groups were also organized during the mandatory period, including several peasant parties during the 1920s. But even they were usually formed by urban notables or middle-class professionals. Continual bickering and infighting among the family factions and competition for leadership vitiated what effectiveness they may have had in rallying mass support in opposition to the mandate and the Yishuv. While their political goals and strategies were nearly identical, the absence of unity led to failure by any group to attain an independent Arab Palestine.

By 1936, resentment of British authority, fear of increased Jewish immigration and the growing strength of Zionist institutions in the country were sufficiently intense to spark a major uprising among the Palestinian Arabs. The chain of incidents began when Arab highwaymen attacked Jewish cars on the road between Tulkarm and Nablus, followed by Jewish retaliation. Mass emotions in both communities were stirred, and Arab and Jewish mobs demonstrated against the respective "enemy." Within days an Arab National Committee was formed in Nablus calling for a general strike in support of Arab nationalist demands, including establishment of a democratic government, prohibition of land sales to Jews and termination of Jewish immigration until "economic absorptive capacity" could be determined. Similar committees sprang up all over the country, and the various Arab factions, now represented by five different political parties, abandoned their mutual hostilities to form a united front in the Arab Higher Committee. In May 1936 the various local committees convened in Jerusalem to organize a passive resistance modeled on Mahatma Gandhi's movement in India. The whole Arab community joined in the effort, and the strike proved to be far more effective than even Arab leaders themselves had thought possible. Passive resistance soon degenerated into full-fledged violent revolution in which trains were derailed, bridges blown up and armed bands, including volunteers from Syria and Iraq, took over parts of the country. Although there were many villagers who did not participate in the revolt, by and large it had the support of most of the peasantry, who joined in attacks on British police and Jewish colonies. Even mass arrests of Arab leaders and members of the Arab Higher Committee during May failed to deter the uprising. At the end of June, 137 senior Arab officials in the Palestinian government presented a memorandum to the mandatory authorities stating that the revolt was caused by the fact that "the Arab population of all classes, creeds and occupations is animated by a profound sense of injustice done to them. They feel that insufficient regard has been paid to . . .their legitimate grievances . . .As a result, the Arabs have been driven to a state verging on despair; and the present unrest is no more than an expression of that despair."[7]

This was followed by other similar memorandums submitted by 1,200 junior officials in the public service and by judges of the Muslim shaira courts responsible to the Supreme Muslim Council.

Unable to suppress the uprising by military force, the British government appointed the 1937 Palestinian Royal Commission to determine the causes of the unrest and to make recommendations. With intervention from neighboring Arab rulers including King Ibn Saud of Arabia, King Ghazi of Iraq and Emir Abdullah of Transjordan, Palestinian leaders were persuaded to call off the revolt to permit the commission to undertake its investigation.

The Royal Commission recognized that the status of Palestine was such that the country could not be regarded "on the same footing as the other Arab countries. [One] cannot ignore all history and tradition in the matter [and] the fact that this is the cradle of two of the great religions in the world. It is a sacred land to the Arabs, but it is also sacred land to the Jew and the Christian."[8] Consequently, the commission recommended that the country be partitioned along lines that would create Arab and Jewish autonomous zones and an area under mandatory control. These recommendations were based upon its conclusions that

> An irrepressible conflict has arisen between two national communities within the narrow bounds of one small country. About 1,000,000 Arabs are in strife, open or latent, with some 400,000 Jews. There is no common ground between them. The Arab community is predominantly Asiatic in character, the Jewish community predominantly European. They differ

in religion and language. Their cultural and social life, their ways of thought and conduct, are as incompatible as their national aspirations. These last are the greatest bar to peace. Arabs and Jews might possibly learn to live and work together in Palestine if they would make a genuine effort to reconcile and combine their national ideals and so build up in time a joint or dual nationality. But this they cannot do. The War and its sequel have inspired all Arabs with the hope of reviving in a free and united Arab world the traditions of the Arab golden age. The Jews similarly are inspired by their historic past. They mean to show what the Jewish nation can achieve when restored to the land of its birth. National assimilation between Arabs and Jews is thus ruled out. In the Arab picture the Jews could only occupy the place they occupied in Arab Egypt or Arab Spain. The Arabs would be as much outside the Jewish picture as the Canaanites in the old land of Israel. The National Home, as we have said before, cannot be half national. In these circumstances to maintain that Palestinian citizenship has any moral meaning is a mischievous pretense. Neither Arab nor Jew has any sense of service to a single state . . .This conflict was inherent in the situation from the outset. The terms of the Mandate tended to confirm it [and] the conflict has grown steadily more bitter . . .In the earlier period hostility to the Jews was not widespread . . .It is now general . . .The intensification of the conflict will continue . . . it seems probable that the situation, bad as it now is, will grow worse. The conflict will go on, the gulf between Arabs and Jews will widen.[9]

Although the Royal Commission recommendations failed to offer any acceptable political solution to the Palestinian Conflict, they helped create political division within both Jewish and Arab communities. In both there were factions that favored accepting the proposals as a basis for compromise, as well as those who ardently opposed them.

The unity that had galvanized the Palestinian Arab national movement during the spring of 1936 was broken. Backed by Emir Abdullah of Transjordan the Nashashibis seemed to have been prepared to accept some version of the commission's proposals. On the eve of publication the leader of the Nashashibis resigned from the Arab Higher Committee. However, the Nashashibi's National Defense party was reluctant to make any overt statement of support for the recommendations. On the contrary, the party felt compelled to keep up with Husainis in opposition to any compromise. The Arab Higher Committee was supported in its opposition to partition by leaders from Saudi Arabia, Yemen, Iraq, Transjordan, Egypt, Syria, Lebanon and Muslim communities in India, Tunisia and Morocco. The threat of partition led to a meeting of 500 representatives from various countries during September 1937 at a Pan-Arab Congress in Bludan, Syria which fully supported the Palestinian Arab Nationalist demands for independence, stating its concern that "Palestine is Arab and its preservation as such is the duty of every Arab."

Soon after the Bludan Conference the Woodhead Commission concluded that implementation of the partition proposal was not feasible. The Arab rebellion was renewed with attacks on British military and governmental outposts and on Jewish settlements. A new aspect of the rebellion was an outbreak of inter-Arab hostilities. The Husaini party now attempted to compel all Palestinian Arabs to follow its policies. Those who did not were to be punished and several hundred Arabs were executed by their fellow countrymen during the later phases of the rebellion.

During 1938 the rebellion took the form of organized guerrilla warfare. Estimates of actual membership in Arab guerrilla bands were not much more than 1,000. As a symbol of national identity the guerrillas wore the native headcloth or Kieffieh, a symbol also adopted by the present-day commandos. Even Arab urban dwellers were required to abandon the traditional red fez as an indication of their support for the national movement. Several of the principal guerrilla leaders, such as Aref Abdul Razzik, became folk heroes whose exploits entered the mythology of Arab nationalism and have become part of the mystique of the present Arab guerrila movement.

Despite the introduction of thousands of British reinforcements, the guerrilla forces were so successful that by October 1938 they had taken over parts of the country including Hebron and Beersheba. According to some observers, the civil administration outside Jewish-populated areas in the larger towns was almost paralyzed. Guerrilla bands even succeeded in occupying Jerusalem's Old City. By the end of the year, with additional major military reinforcements, the British succeeded in recapturing most of the country that had been in guerrilla hands. Dissension within guerrilla ranks was causing the usual political fragmentation. Furthermore, the guerrillas were losing their popularity as a result of measures against those suspected of insufficient nationalist ardor.

By the outbreak of World War II, the movement was in complete disarray, the result of military pressures, disaffection within the Arab community, growing economic unrest caused by the disorders and the political effects of withdrawing the partition proposals. This is ironic, because for all practical purposes, the 1939 British White Paper represented a major victory for the Palestinian Arabs. While the Paper did not immediately concede all objectives of the nationalists, it assured them that these objectives would be realized within the near future. The document sharply restricted Jewish immigration, limiting it to a five-year period when the Jews would constitute a third of the population. Thereafter, additional immigration would depend upon Arab acquiescence. Jewish land purchases would be restricted to small areas of the country. Above all, Palestine would become self-governing within a decade. Although the Mufti of Jerusalem, who led the Husainis and his followers, continued adamantly to insist on immediate independence, a few Arab moderates considered the 1939 White Paper a modest victory.

With the outbreak of World War II, the Palestinian Arab nationalist movement fell into even greater disorganization. The Mufti and his closest followers were in exile abroad. More moderate factions lacked strong leadership and lost much support they had commanded. Even the moderate factions failed to reach any significant political accord with the Jewish community. One such group was the League of Arab Students in Jerusalem. Its members were teachers, officials and students. The group did have specific social objectives including campaigns to improve rural health and literacy. It was also anti-Fascist and sought to break away from the political domination of the notable families. Although the Jewish-Arab conflict was not the major issue for them, its members differed little in their national political objectives and in their opposition to the Jewish national home from other nationalist groups. At a meeting held between a number of Jewish leaders and members of the League of Arab students in Jerusalem during 1941, the latter indicated willingness to cooperate with Jews in economic, social and cultural activity. However, they strongly opposed the principle of 100 percent Jewish labor in Jewish enterprises and boycotts against Arab products and insisted on immediate establishment of an independent Palestine in which Jews, Muslims and Christians had full equality. The student progressives strongly opposed either numerical or constitutional parity between Jewish and Arab communities, expressing fear that once parity was obtained, there was danger that the Jews would become a majority and the position of Arabs would be jeopardized. The talks finally broke down over the question of Jewish immigration when the progressives refused to acknowledge any special prerogatives for Jewish entrance into the country.

Similarly talks between Jewish and Arab moderates about binationalism broke down over questions of parity, Jewish immigration and constitutional structure. The crux of disagreement was over Jewish immigration. Nearly all Jewish leadership, including those who favored binationalism, regarded immigration as an inalienable Jewish right. The major difference among the Zionist leaders was that some felt this right could be compromised by agreement on immigration up to parity. Few, if any, even among the most moderate Arab political leaders were willing to concede Jewish immigration as a right. They regarded it as a concession to be made only with agreement of the Arab majority.

As signs of Allied victory became increasingly evident, even Palestinian Arabs who had advocated collaboration with the Axis powers revised their political stance. By 1943 leaders of the former Istiqlal party sought to revive the national movement and to unify Palestinian Arab leadership. Halfhearted attempts were made to rally the local Arab community at the end of 1943 through the Arab chambers of commerce at their 15th national conference in Jerusalem. Fortunately for the nationalists they were able to unite national sentiment around a new cause, the "defense of Lebanon," for at this moment the French arrested the president and cabinet of Lebanon. Committees on their behalf sprang up throughout Arab Palestine. Through various revived nationalist projects such as the Arab National Fund and the Arab National Bank, Istiqlal leaders now gained access to publicity, funds and contacts throughout the country in a renewed nationalist drive.

Lest they be thought less nationalistic than others and lose leadership of the movement, the Husainis decided in 1944 to reestablish their Palestinian Arab party. They also organized institutions and party organs such as an Arab Bank, local party branches and Arab newspapers. Whereas the Istiqlal leaders were supporting demands for immediate execution of the 1939 White Paper, Husaini followers, not to be outdone, demanded rejection of the White Paper with immediate independence and dissolution of the Jewish national home.

By the end of World War II, the Palestinian Arab party was successfully revived despite the fact that most of its leaders were in exile because of pro-Axis activities. The former Nashashibi faction had been replaced as principal competitor to the Husainis by the ex-Istiqlal leaders now associated with the Arab National Fund. Under their political leadership the Palestinian Arab community gained recognition by the newly formed League of Arab States organized at Alexandria, Egypt in 1944 which gave full backing to their claims for immediate national independence.

It had become evident that within the previous 25 years, there had developed a distinctive Palestine-Arab nationalist movement, and that not only its leadership but the Palestinian Arab community as a whole regarded itself as a national entity and was so regarded by nationalist movements in the neighboring Arab countries. The movement was characterized by all the shortcomings of other Arab nationalist movements in the area including factionalized leadership, lack of any clear economic or social doctrine, and concentration of leadership in the hands of a small elite representing either the landed gentry or the urban middle class. One strength of the Palestinian Arab movement was that religious differences did not play a major role in creating divisiveness. Both Muslim and Christian Arab communities were well represented in the leadership and although Christian Arabs were a small minority of the total Palestinian population, they exercised a strong voice in policy- and decision-making.

Despite its strength and extensive following, the Palestinian Arab nationalist movement did not grow at the rate of its principal antagonist, the Jewish nationalist or Zionist movement, between 1920 and 1945. The Arab movement was in a considerably weaker position at the end of the war than during the 1930s. In contrast, the Jewish national movement had grown both in numbers and strength. Within Palestine the Jewish population had increased from less than 10 percent of the total to nearly a third. Its economic, political and social institutions had been established on strong foundations. As a result of Adolf Hitler's liquidation of their European coreligionists, Jewish nationalists had obtained extensive sympathy in the Western world. During World War II, a large percentage of young men from the Yishuv served in the Allied forces and received excellent military training. Thus, in both absolute and relative strength, Jewish nationalism was established as a major force in competition with the Palestinian Arab nationalist movement.

The Nazi massacres shocked into action both the Yishuv and Jewish communities elsewhere in the world immediately after the war. The intensified demands for immediate and enlarged Jewish immigration to Palestine and for a retraction of the provisions of the White Paper brought the Yishuv into conflict with Great Britain, which sought to stall off any immediate decision about the future of Palestine. Conflict between the Yishuv and the British mandatory government soon sparked uprising on a scale equal to the Arab 1936-39 rebellion. Great Britain, weakened by the war, threw the Palestinian problem into the United Nations which recommended a compromise based on the partition principle established by the 1937 Royal Commission. Both the Palestinian Arab nationalists and their supporters in neighboring

Arab countries as well as other Muslims regarded partition as betrayal of the right of self-determination for the country's Arab majority and decided to oppose it by force.

Conflict between the two national groups erupted within hours after the United Nations General Assembly passed the resolution recommending partition in November 1947. Angry Arab nationalist demonstrations against the resolution occurred at the same time as victory celebrations by the Jews and caused violent clashes. Street demonstrations soon led to organized attacks by armed bands with retaliation and counterretaliations plunging the country into a civil war which the British neither desired nor were able to suppress. Despite the intervention of neighboring Arab states after the departure of the British in May 1948, Arab armies were unable to organize effectively against Jewish nationalist forces. Not only did they fail to defeat the Jewish nationalists, they were themselves so badly defeated that there was complete collapse of the Palestinian Arab communal structure. The breakdown caused a mass flight and, for all practical purposes, the disappearance of an organized Arab community from Jewish-controlled areas of Palestine.

PALESTINIANS BECOME REFUGEES

Defeat in the first Arab-Israeli war of 1947-48 seemed to terminate the history of the Palestinian Arab national movement. Its leadership was discredited and scattered throughout the Arab world. The Palestinian community was dispersed, and its morale was completely shattered, with loss of what self-confidence may have been developed up to this point in history.

During the next 20 years Arabs of Palestine, although identified as Palestinians in their countries of exile, lacked any effective leadership or specific territory in which they exercised political hegemony. The areas of Palestine that were not taken over by Israel were incorporated into the Hashemite Kingdom of Jordan and the small Gaza Strip which was occupied by Egypt. Jordan agreed to grant citizenship to the Palestinians as a way to broaden her narrow population base, for without them the sparse and largely nomadic population of the East Bank barely qualified the kingdom as a full-fledged nation state. Although Palestinians received Jordanian citizenship, were represented in the Jordanian parliament and achieved the highest posts in the Jordanian government, the most nationalistic, especially the youth, regarded the Hashemites as intruders and the kingdom as a political imposition of Great Britain. For all practical purposes the kingdom, especially after it incorporated the West Bank of the Jordan River within its frontiers, became the successor state to Arab Palestine. However, Palestinian rather than Jordanian consciousness was deeply instilled among refugees from Israel and native inhabitants of the West Bank.

In other areas where Palestinian refugees and nonrefugees were concentrated in large numbers—areas such as Syria and Lebanon—they were regarded as a distinctive group of outsiders separate from host country inhabitants.

Since over half the Palestinian Arab community had become refugees from Jewish-controlled areas and since refugee concentrations were the most widespread evidence of their continued existence, "refugee" and "Palestinian" soon became synonymous. This identity was strengthened by attitudes of the refugees themselves, by the host countries and by the international community.

The refugees had a vested interest in maintaining this identity if for no other reason than survival. The vast majority were an unskilled rural peasantry who found themselves living in areas where there was already an oversupply of unskilled agricultural labor. Consequently they were dependent for survival upon the rations and services supplied by the United Nations especially during the decade after the flight. The host countries, except for Jordan, encouraged the identity of "Palestinian" and "refugee" for various reasons. Some were economically unable and others politically reluctant to absorb tens of thousands of outsiders. Egypt, already one of the most overpopulated nations in the world, had little if any space for the Palestinians under its jurisdiction. Since most refugees were Muslims, they were unwelcome as citizens in Lebanon where they threatened to upset the delicate balance between Christian and Muslim populations.

In Syria many natives regarded the Palestinians as a disruptive and unruly element, undesirable as citizens. To grant them citizenship, would mean acceptance of the permanent loss of Arab Palestine.

Annual discussion of the Palestinian Arab refugee question in the United Nations General Assembly further served to strengthen the image of the Palestinian as refugee. Although nearly half were not refugees, having remained in their homes in Gaza, the West Bank or Israel or having departed for other countries where they reestablished themselves successfully, the prevailing image was that of a downtrodden, homeless remnant living in tent encampments. Arab propaganda generally served to strengthen this image by portraying the Palestinians as a homeless entity dependent upon handouts from the international community.

United Nations refugee relief and works projects also helped to maintain the distinctive identity. Although only a little over a third of the refugees, comprising about half the Palestinian Arab population, lived in United Nations camps, they became the most visible manifestation of the Palestinian as refugee. Within the large refugee encampments and in the areas adjoining them, the Palestinians lived for 20 years in closely packed quarters usually separated from host communities, with little social or even economic contact with non-Palestinians.

The camp leaders and employees of the United Nations Services including physicians, social workers, nurses and teachers with whom the refugees came in daily contact were mostly Palestinians. The camps often were given names of areas in Palestine from which the refugees had fled in 1947-48. Refugee children thought of themselves not as Syrians, Lebanese, Egyptians or Jordanians but as Palestinians from Jerusalem, Jaffa, Haifa, Acre, Ramle or other towns and villages where they or their parents had lived.

Perhaps most influential in inculcation of a deeply felt Palestinian national consciousness, especially among the younger generation, was the United Nations Relief and Works Agency for Palestinian Refugees (UNRWA) educational system. Although supervised by the United Nations Educational, Scientific and

Cultural Organization (UNESCO) and financed by the United Nations, all the students, the vast majority of teachers, administrators and supervisors were Palestinians who also had deep feelings about their national identity. This was evident in the names given to schools, the slogans and symbols which adorned school buildings and in the curriculum. A commission of experts appointed by UNESCO in 1967-68, arrived at a number of observations similar to those of the 1937 British Royal Commission after its examination of Arab education in Palestine. The UNESCO commission pointed out that in UNRWA schools, "the choice of historic events selected is almost always centered on Palestine, but an excessive importance is given to the problem of relations between the Prophet Mohammed and the Jews of Arabia, in terms tending to convince young people that the Jewish community as a whole has always been and will always be the irreconcilable enemy of the Muslim community."[10] The commission observed that there were frequent examples taken directly from present-day Palestine and obviously meant to maintain the nostalgia for the " 'usurped homeland' and to strengthen the desire to reconquer it one day." In both history and geography books, there was frequent emphasis on the Arab identity of Palestine. "The term Israel is never used and never features on any map to designate a State entity. The territories constituting the State of Israel are frequently designated as the 'usurped portion of Palestine.' "

The Commission pointed out that in many textbooks: "The Israeli Arab conflict holds a central place . . . Palestine is always in people's thoughts, even if not always mentioned. It influences the choice of poetry or prose for anthologies, the kind of examples and exercises pupils are set, as it conditions the tracing of maps and the wording of their captions." Although in the education they received the Palestinians were identified as Arabs, the identification was that of a distinctive entity which was part of the greater Arab world. Love of the homeland therefore remained deep in Arab consciousness during the post-1948 era even among children who had never seen Palestine.

The close identity of the actual physical land with national consciousness was evident in a survey conducted by sociologists from the Hebrew University among Israeli Arabs during 1967. They noted that:[11]

> Being in the main a rural population, Israeli Arabs have a close, almost mystical relationship with their land. In rural societies possession of land has always symbolized authority and security. A man who acquired wealth, reinvested it in land, and similarly, the sale of land symbolized impoverishment and loss of status.
>
> Even families which stopped working in agriculture did not leave the zone of influence of rural tradition; the more educated among them could give a more sophisticated expression to their love of the soil and countryside.
>
> This individual (or family) bond between Israeli Arabs and their land was frequently transformed into a collective bond. Holding on to the land which is a national Arab possession turns the fact of remaining in Israel from a routine personal attachment into a national aim.
>
> In the literature created by Israeli Arabs during the past 20 years, there is frequent use of agricultural symbols with a national connotation. Love for a girl, for the village and the homeland, are perceived by the Israeli-Arab poet as a single indivisible emotion. The 1948 war is described in this literature as the shattering of a rural idyll (conceived in romantic and nostalgic images) and a severence from a familiar and beloved landscape. Those who remained behind must watch over the inheritance for those who were scattered.
>
> In this way the Israeli Arabs who did not take refuge with the majority of their brethren in Arab countries found a legitimation of their minority status in a Jewish country.
>
> When a nationalist movement was founded among the Israeli Arabs in 1963 (to be banned finally by the authorities), the name "El Ard"—"The Soil"—was found to be the most natural expression of national aspirations.[12]

Nostalgia for the homeland has been evident in the work of Palestinian-Arab writers and artists during the 20-year period after the exodus. The theme of regaining the fatherland, of return and of despair with conditions in exile are widely prevalent in Arab literary and aesthetic themes during this period.

A survey of refugees on the East Bank conducted after the Six Day War by sociologists from the American University of Beirut also emphasized the strong attachment of Palestinians to their homeland. By far the vast majority of both new and old refugees emphasized return to their homes as their chief desire. According to the researchers one of the most evocative responses was:[13] "Your country is like your child ... You cannot be separated from it for a long time. Your country is where you were born and no other country could be dearer to your heart." The survey found that names given to infants born in refugee camps was another indication of the nationalistic state of mind among the Palestinian Arabs. The names included Zeezya (name of a refugee camp), Jihad (struggle), Harb (war) and Aida (the one who is returning).

Despite great pessimism among the refugees about possibilities of immediate return—only 19 percent of the new and a mere 6 percent of the old refugees thought they would return soon—only 3 percent believed that they would never return. Most concluded that still another war with Israel would be necessary to regain their land and homes. The interviewers maintained that few of the Palestinian refugees with whom they spoke thought in terms of a war to destroy Israel. "Only one family spoke of revenge when discussing the probability of war, whereas others talked of a war to win back the rights of Arabs and their honor. As one respondent put it, when asked what he thought Arabs should do in the future: 'peace ... if that is impossible then war.'"[14]

Since the first refugee flight in 1948, the Arabs of Palestine have developed most of the characteristics of a nation in exile. There is a deep nostalgia for a way of life that they believe to have existed before their departure. True, that life style may be very much idealized, much as the "land without a people which was waiting for a people without a land" was idealized among Jews living in the Diaspora. Indeed, the Palestinian Arabs have developed a new Arab Zionism resembling in its emotional content the Zionism of Jews before the establishment of Israel in 1948. Among the Palestinians there is a feeling of rootlessness and of bitterness towards those among whom they have taken refuge. Like Diaspora Jewry, the Palestinians have even become victims of the inverted economic pyramid.

Once a largely rural peasantry whose main occupation was agriculture, they now live in or near large cities and follow economic pursuits of urban rather than rural life. A survey by an Israeli economist of a refugee camp on the West Bank which he believed was not uncharacteristic indicated that [15] "The distribution of workers by occupation reveals an occupational structure similar to that of urban wage-earners. There are very few farmers, and most workers are employed in construction, quarrying, industry, and services. There is even a small number of persons in the liberal professions, and a few white collar workers whose earnings are some 60 percent higher than those of a construction laborer." The employment pattern, the wage and income structure of refugees living in the camp were similar to those prevailing generally among villagers in the West Bank.

Since 1948 many Palestinians have achieved peaks of success in various parts of the Arab world. More than 100,000 Palestinians found employment in the Arabian Peninsula. They can be counted among the leading lawyers, physicians, businessmen and professionals in Arab countries from Libya to Kuwait. Many rose to high government posts in these countries. Nevertheless, rather than attaining or seeking integration into the new environment, most remained Palestinians. Even those who achieved ambassadorial posts retained their own identity rather than become full-fledged citizens of the countries they were representing. In some instances this was because of difficulties in acquiring citizenship, in others because of reluctance to abandon their Palestinian identity.

One of the ironies of this situation is that despite intense feelings of close identity with their Palestinian heritage, they did little to organize in a politically effective manner. Theirs was by and large a grass roots sentiment rather than one artificially stimulated or imposed by an elite leadership. While they failed to organize themselves, the host countries in which they lived often took political advantage of their Palestinian consciousness, exploiting the feeling as a weapon against Israel.

Prior to the June 1967 war, Egypt, Jordan, Syria and Iraq organized groups of Palestinians into so-called commando organizations to conduct guerrilla warfare against Israel. These activities were often undertaken by mercenaries recruited from the most depressed elements of society. There was no widespread mass movement with broad popular support among the Palestinians. Various attempts prior to 1967 to organize Palestinian political organizations were usually initiated by host governments for their own political advantage. The Egyptians at one time organized a Palestinian government in exile, and the Jordanians established a quasi-political Palestinian entity. But none of these groups successfully galvanized public opinion. An attempt was made to legitimize the Palestinian national movement by the Arab states when they gave formal recognition at the 1964 Cairo summit conference to the Palestine Liberation Organization (PLO). However, the verbal pyrotechnics of the organization's leader, Ahmed Shukairy, brought little credit to the PLO nor did it succeed in attracting international support to the cause of Palestinian Arab nationalism. Before 1967 it can be said that the Palestinian Arab nationalist movement was largely a political tool of various Arab governments. While the emotions and feelings of Palestinian national consciousness were genuine, they remained unorganized in any successful mass movement.

FROM REFUGEES TO NATIONALISTS

The defeat of Syria, Jordan and Egypt in the June 1967 war had a traumatic effect on Palestinians living in the Arab world, especially upon the younger generation. The disaster left them disillusioned, not only with their own divided and disreputable leadership but also with leaders of all Arab countries. There was also a wide disillusionment with the strategy and tactics of Arab governments in dealing with the problem of Palestine. The younger generation was determined to speak for itself rather than permit non-Palestinians to be their spokesman.

During the previous 20 years a new generation of young Palestinians had grown up, highly educated, many in Western universities and estimated at between 50,000 and 100,000. Among Palestinians 80 to 90 percent of the eligible age-group received basic education, comparing favorably with the Arab world as a whole where the comparable enrollment rate was 53 percent. The younger generation was almost adamant in its determination to assert itself. This was evident in the spate of new underground organizations organized after June 1967. Estimated at several dozen, they differed from the pre-1967 organizations in their asserted independence from any Arab government, in the intensity of their motivation and in their insistence on total political objectives expressed in determination not only to defeat Israel but to eliminate the Jewish state and its Zionist character. Most of the new organizations were military or paramilitary, differing from the prewar guerrilla bands by their recruitment of young professionals who had succeeded in fields such as engineering, medicine or teaching. Whereas among parents of the younger generation there could be found many who had fled Palestine in 1948 who spoke in terms of fond rememberance of their association and friendship with Jews, there was little if any such feeling among the new generation of zealots.

The new nationalism and its organized movements of the post-1967 era have changed the prevailing image of Palestinians throughout the Arab world and among the Palestinians themselves. They no longer are thought of as downtrodden refugees, but as a national entity, almost an elite entity, which has stimulated the imagination of Arab youth from Casablanca to Kuwait. This image contrasts with that of the older generation of Arab political leaders including the now aging military charismatics. The new Palestinians are regarded like the Algerian rebels during the 1950s. While the commander of Fatah and leader of the PLO, Yasir Arafat, is the most notable and conspicuous of the various commando leaders, his individual charisma still has not reached that acquired by Egypt's President Gamel Abdel Nasser. prior to the 1967 disaster.

The commando group charisma is transmitted throughout the Arab world through posters and recruiting drives on university campuses, through writings of Arab political theorists and in literature or poetry extolling the Palestinians. There is hardly a single Arab university campus that does not display posters and slogans calling attention to the deeds of the new Palestinians. While a high percentage of commando communiques are either exaggerated or completely false, they are widely believed because Arab youth is hungry for victories such as these. If they cannot be accomplished in reality, their mythology is accepted as equally valid. As in nearly all other nationalist movements, mythology plays a significant role, perhaps more important than historical chronology. More significant than their military victories or defeats is the image that the commandos have created of the new Palestinian national entity replacing the refugees as its most visible evidence.

It would be a disservice to the quest for peace in the Middle East to dismiss the new Palestinian nationalism as a transitory phenomenon that will disappear after a few retaliatory raids. The number of recruits in the Palestinian commando organizations has not diminished but increased several fold during the past two years. Most startling was the rise of support received by the commandos after the Karameh retaliation in 1967. After Karameh the number of volunteers in the various Palestinian organizations grew appreciably, and the intensity of commando activities was not diminished but increased to a higher level than before.

Manifestations of Palestinian Arab nationalism in the post-1967 era resemble trends in the period between World War I and World War II. Both periods are characterized by deep emotional intensity, by insistence on total political objectives, by refusal to recognize the national rights of the principal antagonist and by divisiveness within the ranks and among leaders. These short-comings should not obscure the significance of the Palestinian nationalist movement. Failure to recognize the realities of Palestinian nationalism can only lead to indefinite continuation of the conflict and make peace in the area even more remote.

As long as Israeli or Zionist nationalism and Arab nationalism continue to pursue total objectives, failing to recognize that Palestine is integral in the national aspirations and identity of the antagonist, the conflict will continue. As long as Arab nationalists deny the existence of Hebrew or Jewish national identity and as long as Israelis continue to deny the existence of a Palestinian national entity there can be no hope for peace in the Middle East.

[1]In an interview with Frank Giles published in the *Sunday Times*, London June 15, 1969 Prime Minister Golda Meir stated: "There was no such thing as Palestinians . . . They did not exist."

[2]This section reviews the origins of Palestinian Arab Nationalism for the benefit of those who are unfamiliar with the movement and to recall past history for those who are knowledgeable of it. Among the excellent sources for this background are: The 1937 *Palestine Royal Commission Reports*; The ESCO Foundation's *Palestine a Study of Jewish, Arab and British Policies*; Yaacov Shimoni's *The Arabs of Palestine* (Hebrew); and Aaron Cohen's studies of Arab-Jewish relations.

[3]ESCO Foundation for Palestine, Inc., *Palestine: A Study of Jewish, Arab and British Policies* (ESCO) Yale University Press, New Haven, 1947, Vol. I, p. 475.

[4] *Ibid* p. 471.

[5] *Ibid.*

[6]Great Britain, *Cmd.* 5479 *Palestine Royal Commission Reports,* London, 1937, p. 340.

[7] *Cmd.* 5479, pp. 401-403.

[8] *Ibid.* p. 41.

[9] *Ibid.* pp. 370-372.

[10] UNESCO, Executive Board, 82 Session, 82 EX/8, Paris, 4 April 1969, *Annex I* p. 3; *Final Reports* 24 February 1969, *Annex II* pp. 3, 5, 9.

[11] Yochanan Peres and Nira Yuval-Davis, *Some Observations on the National Identity of the Israeli Arabs,* Department of Sociology, Hebrew University, Jerusalem, Israel.

[12] See: Rashed Hussein, " The Beauty and the Village, She is My Land" in: *Ma al Fajar* (At Dawn), Nazareth, 1957 (Arabic); Jamal Ka'war, "A Dream Which Burst" in: *"Ajina't min al Jalil"* (Songs from Galilee), Nazareth, 1958 (Arabic); The authoress Naj'ah Ka'war-Farah tells of the struggle of an old Arab who refuses to leave his land, and who clings to it as the olive trees hold on to the soil in which they grew, in spite of his wife's pleasure to emigrate to one of the Arab countries where her children are living, in Naj'ah Ka'war-Farah "The Bitterness of the Two Alternatives" in: *Leman a-Rabiva* (To whom the Spring), Nazareth 1963 (Arabic), all cited in Ibid. See also "Visions of the Return: The Palestinian Arab Refugee in Arabic Poetry and Art," A. L. Tibawi, *Middle East Journal* Vol. 17, No. 5. 1963.

[13]Peter Dodd and Halim Barakat, *River Without Bridges: A Study of the Exodus of the 1967 Palestinian Arab Refugees*, The Institute for Palestine Studies, Beirut, 1968, p. 59.

[14]Ibid; p. 60.

[15]Yoran Ben-Porath, *Some Economic Characteristics of a Refugee Camp: Preliminary Results*, reprinted from *Middle East Developments*, Truman Center Publications, No. 3, Jerusalem (October 1968), pp. 43-44.

Who Are the Palestinians?

MARIE SYRKIN

On November 2, 1969, the fifty-second anniversary of the Balfour Declaration, the *New York Times* published a full page advertisement calling for a "Nixon Declaration" which would view with favor the establishment of a Palestinian state in which Jews, Christians and Moslems would live on the principle of "one man, one vote." The Arab sponsors of this advertisement urged President Nixon to assume the role of "peacemaker" and "reverse the process begun by the Balfour Declaration" by undoing the "dismemberment and mutilation of Palestine, its mutilation from a land sacred to and inhabited by Moslem, Christian and Jew, to a land which is the exclusive domain of a few." Simultaneously, the Arab signatories called for the implementation of the United Nations resolutions regarding Palestine without specifying whether this demand included the 1947 Partition Resolution which set up a Jewish state in a part of Palestine for the very reason that Arabs and Jews were not living in peace with each other.

I am certain that many a good citizen, wearied by bloodshed and rumors of a widening war in the Middle East, must have been favorably impressed by this apparent evidence of Arab moderation. Instead of the customary threats of extermination, offers of amity and coexistence were being publicly extended. That this offer was contingent on the dissolution of the Jewish state may not have immediately struck the casual reader, though the only difference between this proposal and the familiar Arab cries for the destruction of Israel lay in the failure to specify that Jews would be driven into the sea. After Israel ceased to exist, its citizens, or some of them, would be permitted to dwell as a minority in a hypothetical Palestinian state in which they would presumably be as safe and happy as the Jews of Egypt, Iraq or Syria.

Obviously, Israel is unlikely to accede to a formula for its extinction no matter how graciously phrased. A return to the status before 1947 will hardly commend itself to those for whom Jewish independence was both dream and necessity. From the Israeli point of view the only novelty in the latest Arab propaganda tactic is its resort to euphemisms. Taking a cue from public relations advisers who have deplored the sanguinary rhetoric which preceded the 1967 war, Arabs are determined to mute some of their pronouncements. The Nixon Declaration, bristling with goodwill, is a case in point. An ecumenical Palestine will obviously sit better with church groups and liberals than the prospect of another holocaust.

The more strident counterpart to the peaceloving Palestinians who simply invite Israel to disappear is the guerrilla whose bombs inspire the revolutionaries of the Left. In the current Middle East scenario the pathetic Arab refugee has been replaced by the husky Palestinian commando; during the recent United Nations debate on refugees, Arab spokemen made no secret of the change of emphasis. Instead of refugees maintained in constantly swelling numbers in United Nations Relief and Works Agency (UNRWA) camps, the scene is dominated by organized guerrillas, well-stocked with the ubiquitous Russian arms, and supported by oil royalties from Saudi Arabia and Kuwait as well as UNRWA rations. The rallying cry has changed from "repatriation" to "liberation." Not bound by tenuous considerations of cease-fire lines, the terrorist groups can maintain tension along the northern and eastern borders, while Eygpt wages its war of attrition across the Suez Canal. In addition to whatever military advantage may be gained from such harrassment of Israel in anticipation of the promised fourth round, the guerrillas play a significant part in the continuing political struggle against Israel. As a movement of national liberation they have captured the imagination of much of the Left, who hail them as the Vietcong of the Middle East; their slogans and acts of terror arouse instant sympathy among disciples of Frantz Fanon and devotees of the Third World. Even those not automatically turned on by revolutionary jargon are troubled by the vision the commandos raise of a lost Palestinian homeland temporarily obscured by Zionist chicanery but now emerging into the light of day. The focus of the ideological debate has shifted. For the Palestinian refugee whose problems could eventually be solved by compensation, resettlement and partial repatriation, has been substitued a dispossessed Palestinian people whose aim is restoration.

ARAB PROPAGANDA AND ARAB AIMS

Arab strategy may prove inimical to the best interests of the Middle East and the welfare of its own peoples, but it has shown itself unfailingly resourceful in keeping the pot boiling. The Arab states' political exploitation of the refugees by preventing their resettlement and absorption is too familiar to require comment. As the claims to refugee status of a second and third generation born in the UNRWA camps grow thin, a new tactic has been devised. The substitution of the burly Palestinian exile for the frail refugee has changed the terms of the argument and disposed of any solution save the elimination of Israel. Even Israel's withdrawal to the 1967 borders would not quiet the Palestinian's demand for his homeland. While the Arab states re-occupied the territories they lost in 1967, the guerrillas would remain free to undo the evils of the Partition Resolution of 1947. Gamal Abdel Nasser has made no secret of this strategy.

Though the immediate military success of this scheme may be limited, the emergence of the commandos has undoubtedly borne fruit on the propaganda front. A reappraisal of the Zionist idea appears to be taking place post-facto. Judging from articles and letters to the editor whose composers increasingy bolster their positions by references to the history of the mandate, confidence in the moral validity of Israel's case has been shaken among people who formerly accepted the rise of Israel as the rectification of a historic wrong. Some are now disturbed not only by the endless warfare and its grim aftermath of human suffering but by the very existence of Israel itself. Despite all its wonders and achievements should it be there? In this context the wrongs done the Arab refugees of 1948 merge with the fresh problems generated by the Six Day War of 1967, particularly that of Palestinian nationalism.

The suffering of the Arabs who abandoned their homes and villages in 1948, and in lesser measure in 1967, is incontestable, and I do not propose to argue again whether they were the victims of Israel or of the failure of the Arab design to liquidate Israel. Whether they fled or were driven, whether the Israelis were savage or generous victors, is no longer the essence of the debate. A refugee problem can be settled in the Middle East as elsewhere in the world; an irredenta with all the profound passions it arouses is another matter. Hence the continuing debate on the Arab/Israeli conflict, particularly insofar as it presumes to question the continued existence of the Jewish state, must frankly face the new problem posed by the Palestinians.

Are we witnessing the synthetic creation of a Palestinian identity as a weapon in the anti-Israeli arsenal? In the total evaluation of Arab and Jewish rights this question looms large. The Palestinian nationalist, whether in costume or true guise, is a new factor in the Arab-Jewish conflict; and one treated respect-fully by Israeli commentators many of whom argue that the origin of Palestinian nationalism is irrelevant to the issue. Supposing it did spring belatedly out of the head of Arab nationalism merely as a hostile response to Israel? The lad is alive and kicking and calling him bastard will not exorcise him. But by the same token Israel is also there; if its ouster is demanded on the grounds of illegitimacy then the counterclaims must be examined. Can the newcomer be fed only at the expense of the Jewish state or is there room elsewhere in the family domain for his natural development?

The question of origins is not merely academic. The Fatah terrorist who attacks an El Al plane in Zurich justifies his act on the grounds that the first Zionist Congress took place in

Switzerland in 1897 so ushering in the "horror" of Zionism to the world scene. Commentators of all shades of the political spectrum seek to determine future policy according to their view of what actually took place in the last 50 years. Obviously, if the British sponsorship of the Zionist endeavor was a bad business to begin with, at best an error of judgment as Dean Acheson discreetly indicates in his recent memoirs, or at worst, a gross injustice as Arnold Toynbee would have it, then the possible accommodations of the present must be made with such history in mind. Even those who believe that truth is best served by granting the clash of two wrongs or two rights will fit their prescription to their diagnosis of the cause of the trouble. Any view of what should be done now to achieve a peaceful settlement between Arab and Jew is bound to be practically affected by a determination of the extent of the injury. A dispossessed Palestinian people, able to flourish only within the area of the Jewish state, would require compromises from Israel other than those to be made for the same number of dislocated refugees. For this reason a discussion of Palestinian nationalism is not a futile semantic exercise. There is little hope of devising a satisfactory territorial solution if the existence of Israel is really predicated on the ruthless dispossession of a people from its homeland—something radically different from the dislocation or resettlement of individuals as an aftermath of war, a familiar process in Europe and Asia during the twentieth century.

PALESTINIAN SELF-DETERMINATION

The first point to be made is that the characterization of Palestinian nationalism as "artificial" does not come from Zionist adversaries but from classic Arab sources. In the period before and after the issuance of the Balfour Declaration, Arab nationalists consistently protested the use of the name "Palestine" or the adjective "Palestinian" to demark them from other Arabs in the region. All the declarations of the nascent Arab nationalist movement from 1880 on concentrated on "the unity of Syria" with no references to Palestine as other than "south Syria." Nothing could be more explicit than the statement of the General

Syrian Congress in 1919: "We ask that there should be no separation of the southern part of Syria, known as Palestine, nor of the littoral western zone which includes Lebanon, from the Syrian country. We desire that the unity of the country should be guaranteed against partition under whatever circumstances."

The Arab Congress meeting in Jerusalem in 1919 formulated an Arab covenant whose first clause read: "The Arab lands are a complete and indivisible whole, and the divisions of whatever nature to which they have been subjected are not approved nor recognized by the Arab nation." George Antonius, the Arab historian, makes sure that there will be no misunderstanding on this score. In *The Arab Awakening* (1939) he writes: "Except where otherwise specified the term Syria will be used to denote the whole of the country of that name which is now split up into mandated territories of (French) Syria and the Lebanon, and (British) Palestine and Transjordan."

The extremist Mufti of Jerusalem originally opposed the Palestine Mandate on the grounds that it separated Palestine from Syria; he emphasized that there was no difference between Palestinian and Syrian Arabs in national characteristics or group life. As late as May 1947, Arab representatives reminded the United Nations in a formal statement that "Palestine was . . . part of the Province of Syria . . . Politically, the Arabs of Palestine were not independent in the sense of forming a separate political entity."

Before the creation of the Jewish state the whole thrust of Arab nationalism was directed against what its proponents viewed as the dismemberment of an ideal unitary Arab state. Even the setting up of several independent Arab states was viewed as a subtle thwarting of Arab nationalism, not its fulfillment. Nor was there a change after the establishment of Israel. In 1952, Charles Malik, the well-known Arab scholar and statesman described the process dourly: "greater Syria was dismembered, the southern and northern parts being put under different administrations." And his demonstrative comment on the settlement "of countless Jews on Syrian soil" not Palestinian, should be noted.

With an eye to the future, the Arab Ba'ath party, which describes itself as a "national, popular revolutionary movement fighting for Arab Unity, Freedom and Socialism," declared in its constitution (1951): "The Arabs form one nation. This nation has the natural right to live in a single state and to be free to direct its own destiny," and equated the battle against colonialism with the "struggle to gather all the Arabs in a single, independent Arab state." No mention of Palestine, except as usurped Syrian territory, tainted any of these formulations. So rabid a figure as Ahmed Shukairy had no hesitation, while head of the Palestine Liberation Organization, in announcing to the United Nations Security Council that "it is common knowledge that Palestine is nothing but southern Syria." (May 31, 1956.)

ARABS AND JEWS IN NINETEENTH CENTURY PALESTINE

From the foregoing it is obvious that for Arabs "Palestine" was merely an inaccurate name for a sector of the Middle East whose separate designation was the result of imperialist plotting against Arab independence. Unlike its role in Jewish history and tradition, in Arab eyes Palestine was neither the cradle of a nation nor a holy land. It aroused none of the memories or special attachments given a homeland. Arab national passion was engaged by the concept of a greater Syria or an even larger united Arab state, not by this tiny segment which had become detached through the *force majeure* of foreign colonialism. In the lexicon of Arab nationalism the independent existence of a Palestine state, like the existence of an independent Lebanon, represented a violation of the Arab national will.

Historians have repeatedly pointed out that Palestine as a political unit ceased after the Roman conquest of the Jewish commonwealth, and that it was restored centuries later as a distinct political entity by the British Mandate for the specific purpose of establishing a Jewish national home. Admittedly this fact of ancient history would have little relevance to the present if up to the Balfour Declaration there had ever developed an Arab diaspora, which like the Jewish diaspora, had an emotional fixation on Palestine. Nothing of the kind took place. Even when the desert Arabs revolted against Turkish rule during World War I, the Arabs in Palestine were so little concerned with independence that they continued to fight alongside the Turks till liberated by the Allies.

The concept of Palestine as a separate national entity arose among Arabs as a purely negative reaction to Zionism after the Balfour Declaration. Those Arab spokesmen who originally welcomed the setting up of a Jewish homeland in a small portion of the territories freed from Ottoman rule made no pretense that they viewed the abstraction of Palestine from the total area assigned to the Arabs as other than the loss of a number of square miles. Emir Faisal signed his celebrated agreement with Chaim Weizmann (January 1919) on behalf of the "Arab Kingdom of Hedjaz," and in his letter to Felix Frankfurter, then a member of the Zionist Delegation to the Peace Conference, the Emir wrote a few months later (March 1, 1919) "We are working together for a revived Near East, and our two movements complete one another. The Jewish movement is national and not imperialist. Our movement is national and not imperialist, and there is room in Syria for us both."

The Arab guerrillas who justify their demand for bases in Lebanon as in Jordan and Syria with the argument that the Arabs are one nation and therefore have the right to use each others' territories interchangeably, are operating completely within the tradition of orthodox Arab nationalism. Some sophisticated Arab spokesmen have become aware of the pitfalls presented by Arab avowals that they are all one people with no difference between Jordanian, Palestinian or Syrian. The editor of the Amman weekly, *Amman al Masa* has warned that such reasoning might make the notion of the resettlement of Arab refugees "respectable," since its advocates could justly claim that the refugees were merely being moved to another part of their Arab fatherland, whatever its name. Such considerations, however, trouble neither the guerrillas who move freely across the borders of the Arab states as citizens of the Arab nation, nor their sponsors. The same Syrian Ba'ath leaders whose program calls for one Arab state are the most zealous supporters of the terrorists whose purpose is to recover the Palestinian homeland.

The youth born in Lebanon or Jordan who is taught on the one hand that the Arabs are one people whose land was cut up by the imperialists, and on the other that his family was thrust out of a Palestinian Eden whose allurements increase with each decade of Israeli achievement is not likely to be worried by logical niceties. Whatever the contradictions, current Arab strategy is not likely to renounce a successful technique. Nevertheless, in the face of the evidence no proponent of Arab nationalism would deny that the Palestinian variant is a very recent mutation.

Equally to the purpose is the fact that the absence of such a distinct Palestinian nationalism provided a rationale for the Balfour Declaration. In their various negotiations with the Arabs in regard to the territory liberated from the Turks the British were faced with demands for a greater Syria, a kingdom of Hedjaz, an Arab state, never for an independent Arab Palestine, for the reasons already indicated. The Arabs who opposed the Balfour Declaration and the mandate objected to a foreign intruder in their midst and to the diminution in any measure of their vast holdings. All this is human and understandable. Just as understandable on another level is the not ignoble calculation that allotted 1 percent of the huge area freed by the Allies for the establishment of a Jewish national home. Lord Balfour expressed the hope that the Arabs would recall that the great powers had liberated them from the "tyranny of a bestial conqueror" and had given them independent states. He trusted that "remembering all that, they will not grudge that small notch—for it is no more geographically whatever it may be historically—that small notch in what are now Arab territories being given to the people who for all these hundreds of years have been separated from it."

It is necessary to repeat this statement because contemporary anti-Israel polemics—from the high-minded exhortations of Noam Chomsky to more primitive rantings—maintain the fiction that the British and the Jews proceeded with a total disregard of an Arab presence in Palestine. In support of this accusation all kinds of stray bits from Theodor Herzl and lesser luminaries have been exhumed, though their bearing on the actual political deliberations which culminated in the Balfour Declaration was nil. The many pages devoted to analyzing the Sykes-Picot Agreement, the McMahon Letter or the recommendations of the King-Crane Commission—all pre-Mandate documents—indicate that however proponents varied in the solutions or interpretations they offered, every aspect of the Arab case was weighed and considered; it did not go by default as rewriters of history like to pretend. The King-Crane Commission, appointed by President Woodrow Wilson to study the question of the Palestine Mandate, brought in an outspokenly hostile report; it urged the abandonment of a Jewish national home and proposed instead that Palestine be included "in a united Syria state" for which the United States should hold the Mandate. The very nature of the anti-Zionist opposition—American, British and Arab—its indifference to Palestine except as part of an Arab whole, made the reasoning of pro-Zionists like Lord Balfour plausible. Their psychology may have been faulty; the Arabs did and do grudge the "little notch," but nothing could be more irresponsible than to foster the myth that Arab national feelings were ignored by the promulgators of the Balfour Declaration.

ZIONIST CONTRIBUTIONS TO PALESTINE

The same holds true for the Zionists. Those who lived to graduate from Utopian visions to the hard bargaining tables of diplomacy were foolhardy innocents only in the extent of their hopes for Jewish-Arab cooperation in the Middle East. They were thoroughly aware that Palestine, though denuded and sparsely inhabited, had a native population. They came prepared with agricultural studies and demographic charts demonstrating that soil reclamation in Palestine would make room for more Arabs as well as Jews and would provide a better life for both. They were certain that the Arabs would prosper materially as the result of Jewish settlement, and they took account of the more delicate matter of Arab national feelings. Weizmann, a more reliable authority on this subject than romantic predecessors like Herzl whose idyllic vision of coexistence of Arab and Jew in *Altneuland* bore no relation to the facts of life, declared unequivocally that the Zionists assumed that the "national sentiments of the Palestinian Arabs would center in Baghdad, Mecca and Damascus, and find their natural and complete satisfaction in the Arab kingdoms which resulted from the Peace Treaty settlement in the Near East."

The Zionists proved poor prophets with one vital exception. Paradoxically, their coming did make more habitable room in Palestine. I refer of course to the period of Jewish settlement until the establishment of the state—the period in which the Jews strove unsuccessfully to live in peace with their Arab fellow-citizens. If peaceful Jewish colonization beginning at the turn of the century had resulted in the dispossession of the local population this would have been a more serious indictment of Zionist policy than the subsequent flight of refugees in later wars. No such dispossession took place. Since the current indictments of Israel include not only the urgent troubles of the present, but the "historic wrong" done the Arabs through their dispossession by Jewish settlers, this must be clearly established. Instead of diminishing, the Arab population increased spectacularly in the three decades after the Balfour Declaration. It grew from 565,000 in 1922 to 1,200,000 in 1947—an increase of 100 percent and striking evidence of the stimulus provided by the agricultural development. During the same Egypt showed an increase of 25 percent, while Transjordan, lopped off from Palestine in 1922, and also under a British Mandate but closed to Jewish immigration, remained static.

Not only the local Arabs prospered because of the better sanitary and economic conditions created by Jewish labor. After the Balfour Declaration Palestine changed from a country of Arab emigration to one of Arab immigration. Arabs from the Hauran in Syria as well as other neighboring lands poured into Palestine to profit from the higher standard of living and fresh opportunities provided by the Zionist development.

All reports agree that prior to the Jewish return Palestine was a dying land. Throughout the nineteenth century the favorite adjectives of travellers describing the Holy Land, beginning with the French Count de Volney who visited the country in 1785, are "ruined" and "desolate." Each successive writer mourns the further decline of the country. A. Keith (*The Land of Israel*) writing some decades after Volney, comments: "In his (Volney's) day the land had not fully reached its last degree of desolation and depopulation" and he estimates that the population had shrunk by half. By 1883, Colonel Condor (*Heath and Moab*) calls Palestine bluntly "a ruined land." And, of course, Americans are familiar with Mark Twain's shocked account of the Holy Land's total "desolation" which introduces a somber note into his *Innocents Abroad*.

THE REFUGEE PROBLEM

Up to World War I the picture of Palestine is one of waste land inhabited by impoverished, disease-ridden peasants in debt to absentee landlords residing in Beirut, Damascus, Cairo or Kuwait. The transformation of the country comes when the sand dunes and marshes purchased by the Jewish National Fund from absentee landowners at fancy prices are reclaimed at an even greater expenditure of Jewish lives and labor. The Valley of Esdraelon, today one of the most fertile regions of Israel, the location of flourishing kibbutzim, was described by the High Commissioner of Palestine for 1920-1925 in the following words: "When I first saw it in 1920, it was a desolation. Four or five small, squalid villages, long distances apart from one another, could be seen on the summits of the low hills here and there. For the rest the country was uninhabitable. There was not a house or tree."

Not to exculpate the Jews but to defend British policy, the not overfriendly British Secretary of State for the Colonies declared in the House of Commons (November 24, 1938): "The Arabs cannot say that the Jews are driving them out of the country. If not a single Jew had come to Palestine after 1918, I believe the Arab population of Palestine would still have been around 600,000 at which it had been stable under Turkish rule . . . It is not only the Jews who have benefitted from the Balfour Declaration. They can deny it as much as they like, but materially the Arabs have benefitted very greatly from the Balfour Declaration."

In the light of the grim present, a recital of former benefits rings hollow if not downright offensive. But this much emerges from the record. In 1948, the Jewish state created through partition in one-sixth of the territory originally envisaged by the Balfour Declaration emerged without dispossessing a single Arab. Pre-state Zionist settlement had brought Arabs into the country instead of driving them out, uninhabited land had been made habitable, and the abstraction from Arab sovereignty of the territory on which the Jewish state aroused represented no blow to the goals of Arab nationalism as till then expressed. Had the account between Arabs and Jews been closed in 1948 with the acceptance by the Arabs of the compromise represented by the Partition Resolution, it would have been difficult to place the Arabs in the loser's column. The Jews had their miniscule, much amputated state. The original area envisaged by the Balfour Declaration in 1917 had been approximately 3 percent of the former Turkish Provinces but by the time of the Mandate in 1922, the promised land had been whittled down to less than 1 percent (.8 percent) through the truncation of the territory east of the Jordan for the purpose of establishing Transjordan. The Jewish state that emerged after the partition resolution shrank further to one-half of 1 percent. In other words, where six independent Arab states had emerged to enjoy sovereignty over a million and a quarter square miles, the Jewish state was ready to dwell in peace with its neighbors within its 8,000 square miles. But this balance could not be struck. Arab calculations were different and the attack of the Arab states on newly declared Israel, with all that followed in its wake, changed the book-keeping.

Now there were to be dispossessed Arabs who would continue to multiply but without flourishing, while the Jewish state would expend on war and defense the energy and tenacity that had formerly been expended on the desert. From this point on, the drama unfolds with the fatality of a self-fulfilling prophecy. The Arabs, who in the thirties had raised the false spectre of dispossessed Arabs, created the reality of the Arab refugees. I have written elsewhere about the refugees (See "The Arab Refugees," *Commentary*, January 1966) and will not rehearse the familiar arguments as to Arab and Jewish responsibility. However one element of relevance to the present discussion should be noted, particularly as it has escaped the attention it merits.

All kinds of reasons have been offered for the wild flight of the Arabs from Israel in 1948 when hostilities started: they were driven, they were terrified, they acted in obedience to the orders of the Arab high command, etc. Whichever of these explanations is believed or dismissed, none makes adequate allowance for the swiftness and readiness with which the flight took place. People picked themselves up as though they were going from the Bronx to Brooklyn, not as though they were abandoning a homeland. Part of the speed was due to irrational panic, part to the assurance of return after the victory, but it was undoubtedly abetted by the subconscious or conscious feeling that flight to a village on the West Bank or across the Jordan was no exile. The Arab who moved a few miles was in the land he had always known though not in the same house. He arrived as no stranger and any differences between himself and his neighbors were due to local antagonisms not national alienation. The West Bank which had been Palestine till its seizure by Abdullah in 1948, Jordan which had been Palestine till 1922, offered the familiar landscape, language and kin of the abandoned village. No tragic uprooting such as befell the Jews in Europe lucky enough to survive, or the countless millions shuffled around in World War II by the victors, particularly by the Soviet Union, took place.

Television interviews have familiarized us with the Arab refugee pointing from his hillside barrack toward his native village in Israel. Sometimes a well-dressed young Arab student indignantly claims to behold the house his family left behind. His anger is understandable. Nobody enjoys seeing his property used by others even if compensation is available. But the very proximity of the abandoned neighborhood, while tantalizing, is the true measure of how little national loss the Arab from Palestine suffered. Even for so slight a cause as a new subway or urban relocation people are shifted larger distances and to stranger surroundings than the changes endured by the majority of the Arab refugees. Nasser had no qualms about dislodging whole villages for his Aswan Dam despite the objections of the inhabitants, and the impressive ease with which the Soviet Union repeatedly shifted huge numbers of its people to further some social or political purpose is a matter of record. Only in the case of the Arabs has village patriotism been raised to a sacred cause.

Arab refugees left so readily not because of cowardice, but because departure represented no fundamental wrench; they had a choice. I refer to the aftermath of the 1948 fighting. Even in June 1967 the comparatively small number who crossed into Jordan did so in the inner assurance that both banks of the Jordan were home regardless of the physical privations endured as a result of the war. The mobility of the Arabs as refugees or guerrillas within Jordan, Lebanon and Syria indicates strikingly the strength of Arab nationalism and the tenuous character of the Palestinian attachment except as a political tactic against Israel.

What bearing has all this on the present? Guerrillas will not be disarmed by documents irrefutably demonstrating that they are really southern Syrians, nor by British census figures which prove just as convincingly that Jewish settlers did not displace their Arab neighbors. The refugee camps, with their potential for violence, continue to exist and the furies fed by a humiliating defeat show no sign of abating. Under these circumstances is any accommodation short of the destruction of Israel possible? A fourth round, whatever its outcome, will provide no solution. Should the Arab states with the active aid of Russia succeed in destroying Israel, a harvest of horror will be reaped for generations, as after the "final solution" of the Germans. Should Israel win again—the probable result unless the Soviet Union openly intervenes in behalf of its clients—Arab rage will not be lessened. The prospect of fortress Israel, besieged by hostile millions, will become a bitter parody of the vision of the Jewish state which animated its founders.

ARGUMENTS AGAINST A PALESTINIAN STATE

The answer to the apparent impasse is not a Palestine state in which Jews—if we take at face value the assurances given—will be relegated to the status of a steadily dwindling minority. And any one who has read the fine print of such Arab proposals knows how even the promise that the Jews will be allowed to live is amplified by references to "Zionists," "foreigners" and "imperialist criminals" to whom the amnesty would not extend. A small number of Arabic-speaking Oriental Jews might qualify for citizenship under these generous provisions. (It should be clear that no bi-national state is intended. The latter, though advocated by some Israeli groups before the declaration of the state, never found a response among Arabs.) That the Jews of Israel remain sceptical of Fatah soothing syrup may be taken for granted. In any case, even if they believed that they would be neither exterminated nor deported, it would be hard to persuade Israelis that some moral imperative demands the snuffing out of their country. They cannot understand the tenderness toward every variant of Arab nationalism allied to a brutal disregard of the sole national hope of the Jews.

As they see it, no development in the contemporary world has weakened the ideological argument for a Jewish state. On the contrary, the wave of romantic internationalism which threatened to swamp Zionism as a form of parochial nationalism has long receded. Emergent nationalisms are burgeoning all over the globe with the full blessing of the anti-colonial Left whose latest discovery is Palestinian nationalism. In the midst of this ardor for movements of national liberation it is difficult to convince survivors of the Hitler era that Jewish nationalism is the only heretical specimen. Remembering not only active persecution but the barred doors and closed immigration quotas of every land during the holocaust, Israelis are unlikely to agree that the only people with no national need are the Jews. Surveying the globe from European Poland to Asian Iraq, they would reverse the order: no people is still in such desperate need of national independence if only to ensure physical, let alone cultural, survival. "They killed us because we had no country," Jewish refugees in Israel repeated over and over again. And they view indifference to the fate of Israel as simply another manifestation of an ineradicable anti-Semitism which interchangeably exploits the slogans bequeathed by Hitler and Stalin, be it the Elders of Zion of medieval legend or the "Zionist imperialist" of communist doxology.

Ideology aside, no Israeli of the pioneer generation will take seriously charges that his coming displaced the Arabs. His personal experience in the process of rebuilding the country testifies otherwise. That is why more concern on this score is to be found among some sabras—not because the young are perverse or more ethically aware than their ruggedly idealistic parents but because they have no memory of the country to which their elders came. Golda Meir knows that her toil in malaria-ridden Merhavia made an uninhabited spot livable, just as she knows that her grandchildren in Revivim, a Negev kibbutz, are creating another oasis in the desert. In human terms is this good or bad? Every farmer and kibbutznik will indignantly echo the question. A scientist at the Weizmann Institute may less rhetorically point out that only a dozen Arabs lived on the waste on which Rehovoth was founded in 1891. Even a city dweller in Tel Aviv will remind you that Jews built this bustling city on a sand dune; the only ones displaced were the camels who used to parade slowly along the beach. All are united in the conviction that their coming enlarged the habitable area for both Arab and Jew.

The post-1948 inhabitant of a former Arab house in Jaffa or Jerusalem must resort to a more modest rationale. He cannot speak grandly of his creative role as a remaker of land and bringer of light. If he is an Oriental Jew he may call to witness the house and possessions of which the Arab despoiled him when he fled from Iraq, Yemen or another of the Arab countries from which half a million destitute Oriental Jews escaped to Israel in an informal population exchange. A Western Jew will use the mundane terminology of *realpolitik*: what morality demands that foiled aggressors escape scot-free? Besides Israel is prepared to discuss compensation for abandoned Arab property anytime the Arabs want to negotiate a peace settlement.

The Israeli government has repeatedly announced its readiness to negotiate "secure and agreed" borders whenever the Arabs are ready to discuss peace. Though there are differences of opinion in regard to what should be retained or returned, for the overwhelming majority of Israelis the conquered territories, with the exception of Jerusalem, have no value in themselves; barring peace, their occupation makes defense against attack easier. The Sinai desert which three times served as the staging ground for Nasser's armies, the fortified ridge of the Golan Heights from which Syrians shelled the Israeli settlements at will, the enclave of fedayeen in Gaza, are cases in point. Neither the empty Sinai nor the Golan Heights present a human problem. Gaza and the West Bank are another matter. There live the bulk of the Arabs displaced by the fighting of 1948.

The most reasonable solution among the many informally-discussed, the one which does least violence to the vital interest of the parties concerned, is the proposal to set up a Palestine entity on the West Bank and the East Bank of the Jordan. To begin with, the actual territory was part of historic Palestine, till 1948 and 1922 respectively. The area represents five-sixths of the territory originally set aside for the Jewish home by the Balfour Declaration. It is the place where most Arab refugees already live for the reasons of consanguinity and proximity already indicated. The dominant role of the Palestinians in Jordan is an open secret. Such a Palestinian state could serve to satisfy newborn Palestinian nationalism and in conditions of peace prosper economically in partnership with Israel. The emergence of such a state would mean compromises for both parties to the conflict. Israel, regardless of victory, would have to accept the narrow confines of its much amputated state, and the Arabs would have to come to terms with the reality of Israel.

Since the likelihood of the immediate acceptance of what could be a rational solution is for the time being remote, such questions as the role of King Hussein's shaky throne in such arrangement or whether the state should be known as Jordanian Palestine, need not be argued. The proposal, however, serves as a reminder that the Palestine homeland is already basically in Arab hands and that it does not have to be recovered—unless such is the real objective of the agitation—on the corpse of Israel. Given an honest will to peace, the exact delineation of borders and such problems as the compensation for abandoned property lend themselves to negotiation. But such negotiation, to be meaningful, must be preceded by the recognition that the new national need of the Palestinian and the ancient one of the Jew can be satisfied within the confines of historic Palestine without the destruction of either Israel or Arab Palestine.

DISCUSSION AT THE FIRST PANEL
February 14, 1970

Kanovsky: My first question is to my distinguished colleague Professor Peretz. It refers to the matter of Arab-Palestinian nationalism. I'm not a political scientist or a sociologist and therefore I can claim no expertise whatsoever in this particular area. Nonetheless, Peretz makes the point in his paper, and I think very correctly, that for all practical purposes, the kingdom of Jordan, especially after it incorporated the West Bank of the Jordan in 1948, became the successor state to Arab Palestine. He qualifies this by stating that Palestinian rather than Jordanian consciousness was instilled deeply in the refugees from Israel and the native inhabitants from the West Bank. I think both of these statements are true. But, one has to look at the developments which have taken place since 1948. In fact, Jordan was the only one of the Arab states which gave citizenship en bloc to the refugees and the Palestinians within its borders. This is something that one has to emphasize very strongly. Now, I don't know the social relationship between the Palestinian population and the original population of the East Bank. What I do know is that according to the statistics compiled by various authorities, over half of the refugees in Jordan had been absorbed economically into the country. In fact, we do know that there was a very large exodus from 1948 until the Six Day War, from the West Bank to the East Bank, due to the fact that there were greater economic opportunities in the East Bank. The exodus was in the range of 200,000 300,000. Bear in mind that the West Bank population in 1966 was roughly 800,000; so when one speaks of such a large migration to the East Bank, this indicates that there was a considerable absorption. The other countries did not accord citizenship for various internal political reasons. The Lebanese because they didn't want to disturb the delicate balance between the Christian and the Muslim populations. The Syrians because of confessional problems in their country. The Eygptians for their own reasons. Now I'm not going to discuss the true border of Palestine, or whether the original border encompassed the East Bank or not, but I think it is basically true that the successor state to Arab Palestine is the kingdom of Jordan. One can speculate about the political consequences, but I think these are facts one has to take into account.

Peretz: You are saying that there has been economic absorption of Arab refugees in Jordan and other Arab countries. Palestinians did rise to the highest positions in many of the surrounding countries. But the fact remains that despite this economic success the Palestinian identity that they carried with them not only remained but became even more intensified. The 100,000 Palestinians who are in Saudi Arabia and in Kuwait and other places, do not consider themselves citizens of those countries but Palestinians. Those who acquired Jordanian citizenship, acquired it by and large not out of any great confidence or love for King Hussein, but for a very practical reason: in order to get a passport. They wanted to be able to go to the Arabian peninsula and make a living, to be able to emigrate and get jobs abroad, to be able to get an education in the United States. During this period, something like 50,000 Palestinians graduated from universities, and became a very strong nationalist element. One of the points you made was that white collar and professional groups were among those who were most affected by the war. It's these white collar and professional groups that are at the backbone of the nationalist movements. In essence it's really not objective factors, such as language, race, religion, historical chronology that make nationalism. Subjective factors such as historical mythology are much more important. The identity of a group is created when its members feel they are a group. The Palestinians in Syria, in Lebanon, in Jordan, in the Gaza Strip, in the Arabian Peninsula, in the universities in the United States, still consider themselves Palestinians.

Kanovsky: I think we're taking everything as a sort of conglomerate. What I'm trying to do is to dissect it. I think there is a very basic difference between the Palestinians in Jordan, and the Palestinians in other Arab countries. And one of the very important reasons for that difference is the fact that the Palestinians in other countries have not been granted citizenship. They work in Kuwait, they work in Saudi Arabia and in other countries, but they are not granted citizenship. Now I understand the reasons for it, and the political problems involved in these things. I think your original statement, that the kingdom of Jordan has become the successor state to Arab Palestine, has a large element of truth in it. But I don't think it is proper analysis to take the whole picture without dissecting the elements in it. In Lebanon, the Palestinians have to receive special permits to be able to work. And of course, unskilled workers, which is what most of them are, find it very difficult to receive these permits. In the Persian Gulf states, they receive permits only if they are needed. There are many examples of this. At the time of the creation of the so-called Arab Common Market, there was a proposal to grant unlimited transit or travel rights to all countries involved in this particular market. Iraq and Kuwait objected because they found it was politically difficult. Therefore, one has to distinguish between the Arabs, both refugees and non-refugees of Palestine in Jordan, and those in the other Arab states. In Jordan, there has been an attempt made to absorb them. In the other countries, there has been a very conscious attempt to minimize their influence. Their labor skills have been utilized only to the extent they are needed for the economy.

Peretz: I agree with you that it is important to make the distinction. But the distinction is irrelevant to my central point, which was that a concept of Palestinian nationalism exists. Many Israelis deny this. The Prime Minister of Israel denies this. But their denial is a factor that works against peace in the Middle East. Some people believe that Palestinian nationalism is an artificial concept; in the words of one of the panel members a deliberate and calculated tactical expedient, rather than a natural development that grew from the roots of the people. I feel that this attitude is one that works against peace. And as long as this attempt to make invisible men of two million people who feel that they have a vital concern prevails, it's going to perpetuate rather than end the conflict. I agree that the Palestinians, as long as they refuse to see that there is such a thing as a concept of Israeli nationalism, or Jewish nationalism or Jewish national identity, will also contribute to this conflict. But the conflict will not end as long as either side regards the other as an invisible man.

Smythe: I want to suggest to Professor Halpern that it is unreal to insist upon or even ask for a *sulh* at this phase. Settlements in international relations today really can only result in or achieve what we call "tolerable adjustments." So why ask for that which is unreasonable?

Halpern: I think perhaps I ought to make some remarks on other matters than the question put to me. First, a brief one, about the usage of terms like "Oriental." It seems to me that the term "Western" is equally objectionable. The dominant culture in

Israel today really is not properly described as a Western civilization. The language that is spoken there, is spoken not with the accent of Eastern European Jews, but with some kind of a watered-down adaptation of the accent of non-European Jews. The influence of Arabs on the entire external behavior of Israeli sabras is very extensive. The political structure of Israel resembles in many respects as much Eastern European democratic central-ism, in the pure meaning of the term, as it does anything in the nature of Western tradition. I would also like to point out that initially, in the late eighteenth century and at the beginning of the nineteenth century, when Ashkenazim began to come as newcomers to Israel, they found themselves thrown upon the mercies of the Sephardic community. They were totally domi-nated. This went on throughout the nineteenth century, in spite of the fact that parallel to the authority structure established by the Sephardim over the centuries, a new authority structure was being established by the newcomers. This new structure was established not by a single Western group, but by each group contributing a part of the structure. It is a very complex thing.

Now, I should like to deal with the questions that were put to me about a sulh and the problem of the Palestine entity. In reverse order. I think it should be made clear first of all, that all the facts cited by Professor Peretz have never been denied by anyone. The question is, what is their pertinence with reference to peace? And I can't see that they have any particular pertinence in the manner in which it was presented.

We are discussing the concept of the Palestinian entity. An entity refers to a political grouping that is able to exercise claims and enter into engagements with other political groupings. Again, we have to distinguish between various uses to which this conception may be put. If the purpose is to establish that the issues as between the Palestinians and the Israelis will not be resolved simply by the humanitarian solution of the problem of the individual Arab refugees by repatriation of some and resettlement of others, that is one thing. But if the purpose is to support the claim of the Palestinians to a homeland coupling the entire area of Israel with other areas then, of course Israel cannot accept this. What's more no one else does: neither Nasser, nor Hussein, nor the Russians nor the Americans nor for that matter even the Palestinians themselves. It has been argued that the Palestinian Arab people believe in Arab unity and that to fulfill its role in realizing this unity it must preserve at this stage of its national struggle the Palestinian personality. But, the question of a Palestinian entity would not be resolved by that fact alone. Suppose Israel disappeared from the map? Then the problem would arise whether this entity wished to assert itself again after it has achieved the purpose of eliminating Israel. To ask Israel to recognize the Palestinians as a national entity is not the same thing as to ask Israel to recognize the facts of the attachment of the people to its land, and the memories which they have built up around it, and to understand the feeling of separateness of the Palestinians caused by the way they've been treated by everyone including their Arab brethren.

Certainly Golda Meir understands this. What Golda Meir is being asked to tell Israel to accept is something quite different. I think it is incumbent on academicians to make these distinctions even though they may not appear in the literature that they consult. I would like to say too, that it is not historical myths, not sentimental attachments, but primarily the demarcation of political boundaries and the establishment of a continuous history of sovereignty that determine the lines within which nations exist. I'm not talking about nationalities, I'm talking about nations. The Belgian nation differs from the Dutch nation because in the Netherlands' battle with the Spanish, the battle stopped at a certain point which became a perfect boundary. On one side of the boundary was Belgium and the other side Holland.

Switzerland exists as a nation solely owing to the fact that a federation was established which had certain accepted boundaries. The Palestinian people, which unquestionably over the past 20, 30 or 40 years have built up a sense of identity and a tradition which everybody understands, is a candidate for such national status if they really desire it.

They can achieve it realistically today if they sign a peace treaty with Israel to which both agree. That would definitely establish a Palestinian entity. Now, Golda Meir says she doesn't recognize a Palestinian entity as existing today. But I would say, that if there had been a group capable of negotiating and carrying out an understanding with the Israeli government on behalf of the Palestinian people, and which was able to maintain that position in the face of all opponents, there would today have been an agreement with that entity.

Now as to sulh. In my paper I discussed the ethical basis for positions. Ethics is certainly far from being a realistic foundation on which to conduct political discussion. Now, with regards to ethics, the only question you can ask is whether a demand is justified. The demand that there should be a real peace, a real reconciliation on the part of Israel, and that this should be the condition upon which Israel is ready to endanger the security that she now has is a totally justifiable demand. It is as realistic as any other demands being voiced today. I think it is probably the most likely outcome for the immediate future and that once people thoroughly have understood this, then it may be realistic to talk in terms of real peace.

Peres: I would like to raise one point in connection with Professor Peretz' presentation. I think he presented the situation as a parallel situation where no complete parallelism exists. It is true that Golda Meir said that she does not recognize the Palestinians. But it is also true that there exists an important minority in Israel, consisting of perhaps the majority of Israeli intellectuals and some important political figures like the Secretary General of the Israeli Labor Party (which is the largest party in Israel), that does recognize the Palestinian entity. By saying that both nations look at each other as if the other party was invisible, we are implying a parallelism where there is none. The fact is that no sizeable, no salient Palestinian minority came up with a statement that it recognized the national rights of Jews to establish their state in Palestine, or whatever boundaries it would grant Israel. If we had a parallel situation, if there were such minorities, they could work together towards a solution. But we, the minority of Israelis who do recognize the Palestinians, don't see a comparable minority on the Arab side. I think Professor Peretz systematically ignores Israeli opposition to the formal party line. He always cites the Israeli view as if it were only the official position of Golda Meir, which is, I think, a great oversimplification.

Now, I would like to answer Professor Smythe very briefly on the question of discrimination in Israel. I think he over-emphasized the powerlessness of the Orientals or Middle Easterners. Orientals are very powerful in local politics. I estimate that there are 30 or 40 Middle Eastern members of the Knesset. Finally, there is a myth of forced Westernization of the Middle Easterners. I found, in both my samples, that Middle Easterners want to adjust themselves to what I call European culture and to what Professor Halpern rightly spoke of as a special mixture of East European and unique Palestinian or Israeli culture. They want to adjust to this even more than the Europeans want to adjust them. They want to have their differences extinguished more than do the Europeans. So there is no forced Westernization; there is social change which is to a large extent voluntary.

The panel was opened to questions from the floor:

Question: I would like to address myself very briefly to Professor Peretz. It seems to me that he unduly romanticized the Palestinian national movement in the true spirit of the Levantines. As a matter of fact, Golda Meir, you have stated, does not recognize a Palestinian entity. Neither did the Arabs. Nor did the Palestinians themselves recognize or consider themselves an entity. If this was the case, why didn't they form a state when they were on the West Bank which is now the occupied zone. This was the economically most viable part of Palestine. Professor Peretz has himself stated that in the first stages, they were recruited from the so-called underworld. And it was later on in the interest of the Arabs that the Arab nations and their politicians, aided by the national pride of the Palestinians, blew up the movement. Professor Peretz, I'd like to know whether you could establish that there was at any time a Palestinian language, a Palestinian nationality or when, if ever, was Palestine an Arab national state. And is the word "Palestine" associated with the word "Arab"?

Peretz: I think I pointed out that prior to World War II there was no such thing as a Palestine entity, or a group of people that considered themselves Palestinians. But the concept of Palestinians, the idea of a Palestine people as an entity is one that developed after World War I, in the period between World War I and World War II. But this feeling is one that developed with much more intensity in the period between 1948 and 1967. And it was created as a result of a grassroots feeling among the people who considered themselves Palestinians. A national entity, any national identity, is not something that is primarily determined by objective factors such as language, race or religion, but is something that is determined by what a people feels itself to be. Just as the Kurdish people consider themselves a nation, just as the Armenians considered themselves as a nation, the Palestinians consider themselves as nation. And until you and other people who deny the existence of this concept, recognize that there is such an entity, the conflict will continue.

Question: I wonder if the members of the panel would address themselves to the controversial proposal that has been discussed in Israel and elsewhere, concerning the establishment of a

Palestinian state in the West Bank. This proposal assumes that Israel could establish a state unilaterally without the cooperation of any other country in the Middle East, and that this state could presumably solve some of the problems with respect to Arab refugees. I would appreciate it if any members would address themselves to the pros and cons of this proposal.

Peres: This suggestion was made very shortly after the war. I myself wrote an article in an Israeli daily immediately after the war proposing exactly this, and we believed that it would be possible. What happened was that no authoritative body could be formed in the West Bank or in the Gaza Strip that could stand up against the criticism from the entire Arab world and establish a government under Israeli supervision because its members would be seen as Quislings. Also, officially Israel didn't provide enough support to make a really independent Palestinian state possible. I still believe that if these two conditions could be met a state could be formed. If there could be found a considerable body of Israelis or Palestinians who would be willing to establish and to lead such a state, and if official Israel would give them a free hand and allow real independence, this would be an excellent foundation for resolution of the conflict.

Peretz: I would agree that a first step towards a solution of this problem would be the recognition of the identity of the Palestinians but I cannot see that a valid legal state can be established under the protection of Israel, any more than the people of Armenia or Kazakhstan or Uzbekistan, can be considered independent under the protection of the Union of Soviet Socialist Republics, or Bohemian Moravia under Nazi Germany. As far as the acceptance of this in Israel, I would refer you to the *Jerusalem Post Weekly* of January 26, 1970, in which appeared an interview with Arveh Eliav, the new Secretary General of the Israel Labor Party. Among the things mentioned in this interview was the extent to which many of his colleagues had labelled him a defeatist for even raising such a possibility. I wish it were true that this concept has been increasingly accepted, but I haven't seen that everybody recognizes it. I wish many more people in Israel had the wisdom to recognize the validity of this concept.

Halpern: You're quite right that a Palestinian entity established on the West Bank under the sponsorship of the Israeli government would have been regarded by everybody as a puppet state. And that is precisely the reason why, apart from exploring the possibility, the Israeli government did not follow it much further. Secondly, a condition to the ability of such an idea to achieve peace would be that this should not preclude the possibilities of making peace with the neighboring Arab states. And it would have done precisely that. To recognize the Palestinians, unless they had first eliminated the state of Jordan, would have meant to undercut the position of the Jordanian government and to make impossible any agreement with Jordan. And the other Arab states have similar interests. Now, we have had facts presented regarding the attachment of the Palestinians to their homeland and the culture—rudimentary culture, polemical culture, but a culture nevertheless—that has been built up over the past 20 or 40 years. I do not believe that everybody here recognizes these facts academically, but I would say that everybody, specifically Israeli official policy, recognizes Arabs residing in Israel as a distinct nationality.

Israeli Arabs are treated and have been treated by the state of Israel as a distinct Arab nationality. If it turns out to be impossible to arrive at a solution that would make possible the peaceful restoration of areas densely populated by Arabs today to Arab sovereignty, and Israel sustains her position, the remaining Arabs in the territories controlled by Israel will constitute an Arab nationality, recognized as such and treated as such.

Kanovsky: I am going beyond the confines of my particular discipline and venturing into areas in which I have no special expertise. Nonetheless, I know that when I study economics, I try not only to find out what the situation is, but also to find in which direction the economy is moving. It seems to me that sociologists and political scientists should do the same thing. Some of us have stated that in Israel there is discrimination against Middle Eastern Jews. There is no denying this. The question that is more relevant is, what is the trend? Is the trend towards greater discrimination, or towards lesser discrimination? The fact is that the percentage, not just the number, the percentage of Middle Eastern Jews, who are graduating from high school and who are graduating from universities is continually rising. The rate of intermarriage between Sephardic and Ashkenazic groups is continually rising. This is especially true of those who were born in Israel. Regarding the Arabs in Israel, there is no doubt that there is discrimination. But again, the question should be asked, what was the trend before the Six Day War? The fact is that the trend was towards giving them greater civil and political rights—the abolition of the special military passes and so on. Let me make a last statement, as an Orthodox Jew; and I'm making this very pointedly. One gets the impression, and I'm speaking specifically to Professor Smythe, that the Orthodox Jews that he knows are those with the long black Kaftans, and the curls and the long beards and so on, who are stoning buses in Jerusalem. Let me just apprise him of a few facts. Orthodox Jews in Israel do not constitute a small minority. They are, at a minimum, 25 percent, and if I use Ben Gurion's estimate, it is probably closer to a third. The fact is that in terms of education, there are various public schools, for those who select religious and those who select general education. Not only is the percentage in religious education roughly 35 percent, but more importantly, the trend is upward. Every year, there is an increase in the percentage of those voluntarily choosing to send their children to Orthodox schools. It would be foolish for any society to ignore even a 10 percent minority, as we know from experience in the United States. Certainly to ignore a minority ranging from 25 to 33 percent would be absurd. One must recognize that Israel, like any state, has its distinctive problems. Religion and nationalism are uniquely intertwined; there is no doubt about their interconnection. And it has existed all through the ages.

Economic, Historical and Geographical Perspectives

Economic Aspects
of the Arab-Israeli Conflict

ELIYAHU KANOVSKY

The economic aspects of the Middle East conflict do not make
the headlines. Indeed, most of what passes for serious discussion
or analysis of the economic questions involved is superficial and
often fallacious. During a recent study of some of these
questions, I became very much aware that in the responsible press
and even in professional journals. the economic aspects of the
conflict are either ignored or dealt with in an offhand or
erroneous manner. What is even more disturbing is that at least
some policy makers are uninformed or misinformed about
economic matters; and while economic matters are not necessarily of overriding importance, they are certainly one important
variable, as I shall attempt to demonstrate with the three
countries that are most directly and most actively involved in the
Arab-Israeli conflict: Jordan, Egypt and Israel.

IMPACT OF THE WAR ON JORDAN

Jordan is emphasized not because of its primary military
involvement—Israel and Egypt are the main antagonists—but
because of the fact that misinformation regarding its economy
and the impact of the June 1967 Six Day War on its development
is very prevalent. Shortly after the war, Middle East specialists
and the news media quoting them were predicting the economic

collapse of the country. The almost unanimous opinion was that without the West Bank, Jordan was no longer a viable economic entity. Jordan was making rapid strides before the war in terms of production, incomes, rising living standards and so on. But if by a viable economic entity one means a high ratio of investment to resources, a diminishing balance of payments deficits, reduced foreign aid or an increasing share of self-financed investment, the record fails to show such achievements. The predictions of economic collapse were based on the following facts: the loss of the West Bank, which meant that tourism would be sharply curtailed; the severance of the base of agricultural prosperity and exports; and the loss of the remittances received from the many Jordanians working mainly in the oil-rich Persian Gulf area. When Jordan did not collapse, it was argued that the country had been salvaged by the $110 million annual subsidy received from Saudi Arabia, Kuwait and Libya.

What has really happened is briefly the following: After a short-lived decline the economy began to revive quickly in early 1968. Investment by the government was increased substantially, followed by rising private investment. Industrial production and exports as a whole have risen sharply. Foreign aid was of crucial importance, but the fact that *domestic* revenues rose to levels exceeding those of the prewar period indicates that the economy was advancing very rapidly. Without raising tax rates, domestic revenues from the East Bank alone in 1968 were equal to those received in fiscal year 1965-66 in prewar Jordan. All the economic indicators for the first half of 1969 point to a continuation of the sharp upward trend.

Anyone who had the necessary training and bothered to study and analyze the official statistics could perceive these developments. And yet we find a recent "economic survey" in the *New York Times* stating: "Jordan, while she has no large-scale long-term prospects, enjoys a hollow prosperity based on the 40 million pound annual subsidy from Saudi Arabia, Libya and Kuwait. This enables Jordan to endure the gradual destruction of her economy by warfare with Israel." This was a dispatch from Beirut, and was the sum total of the correspondent's report on the economy of Jordan. One can only assume that his Beirut informants were the same ones who had predicted economic collapse two and a half years earlier. When the data showed rapid development, rising exports and increasing production and incomes, they had to conclude that this was a "hollow" prosperity. How could the report speak of the gradual destruction of the economy when the economic indicators were pointing upward? All of these so-called experts had ignored the fact that during the 20 years preceding the Six Day War the greatest emphasis on economic development had been in the *East* Bank. The East Bank had the major irrigation projects and industrial development and had become the economic center of the country. The United States Embassy in Amman, which had earlier been among the pessimists, began to backtrack in its subsequent reports and to speak of Jordan's "remarkable" resiliency. What is more remarkable is how poorly informed they had been.

Let me emphasize that all this does not mean that the war has had no impact on the economy. Certainly in the absence of hostilities progress could have been even greater. Certain sectors of the economy and border areas have suffered as a result of the war. But the United States Embassy in its mid-1969 report stated that there was relatively little current unemployment in the country. The official economic data show a 14 percent rise in over all GNP in 1967, a slight rise in 1968 in spite of the drought, and a significant increase in 1969. Foreign aid in 1968 (official transfer payments to the central government) was JD 22 million higher than in 1966, in addition to loans. Essentially this enabled the country to increase its foreign exchange reserves to unprecedented levels. At the end of 1968 they were JD 40 million higher than at the end of 1966.

EGYPT'S ECONOMIC DECLINE

Myths are as numerous and as persistent about the economy of Egypt as about Jordan's. We are told that the Egyptian economy was growing at a respectable rate before the Six Day War (between 6 percent and 7 percent annually) and following a temporary postwar downturn has begun to resume its prewar expansion and that Egypt has through various measures switched from a position of chronic prewar balance of payments deficits to smaller deficits or even surpluses. It is said that the Aswan Dam and other reclamation projects have brought about significant increases in agricultural production, and that the massive industrialization program is bearing fruit in large (12 percent) increases in industrial production, following the temporary postwar slowdown. Whatever problems the Egyptian economy has are mainly attributed to the growth of population and the ratio of other resources to population growth. These official Egyptian data are partial in every sense of the word. A well-known authority on the economy of Egypt told me that when the government's department of statistics officially changed its name (before the Six Day War) to the Central Agency for Public Mobilization and Statistics, there was a good reason for it.

What are the facts? The Aswan Dam (and the other reclamation projects) increased the potential for agricultural production significantly. Between 1960 and 1967 over 800,000 acres were reclaimed, but the cropped area increased by only 100,000 acres. Agricultural production declined steadily between 1965 and 1968 and on a per capita basis there has been a steady drop since 1962. The massive industrialization program during the first half of the 1960s increased the potential for production. In fact, the rate of growth of industrial production during this period was only approximately equal to that of the previous 15 years, and there was a sharp slowdown during the two or three years preceding the war, at the very same time that the completion of many industrial projects should have accelerated the rate of growth. Egypt was the recipient of large-scale foreign aid before the Six Day War, both from East and West. Commodity exports increased very slowly, and between 1965 and 1968 were almost stagnant.

The large prewar trade deficits have been curtailed, according to the official reports. The problem is that those who quote these reports, and that includes many so-called experts, fail to read the footnotes that show how misleading the reports can be. The reports exclude imports received within the category of foreign economic aid; they exclude the imports of various government departments, as well as the massive military shipments; and they exclude the imports of oil products. In fact an examination of the Soviet statistics on exports to Egypt—excluding military shipments—as compared with the official data on Egyptian imports from Russia, show discrepancies of 100-150 percent.

There can be no doubt that the Six Day War affected the Egyptian economy. The loss of the Suez Canal revenues, the sharp decline in tourism, the reduction in oil revenues as a result of Israel's occupation of the Sinai Peninsula; the destruction of the major Suez oil refineries and the evacuation of over one half million residents from the Canal area are all well-known. However, it is difficult to determine what part of these losses is being paid for by foreign aid from the Arab oil states and from the Soviet bloc countries. The large increase in military expenditures is certainly a burden to the economy. However, the economic stagnancy is not only due to the war. The problems of the economy antedate the war, and are as much a result of gross economic mismanagement as anything else. There does not appear to be any danger of a serious economic downturn, but stagnation can be a crucial problem for any society, especially one that has promised so much and delivered so little.

DEFENSE AND DEVELOPMENT IN ISRAEL

The impact of the Six Day War on the economy of Israel was rather complex. By Middle East standards Israel's economy is highly developed and, in many respects, approaches that of the advanced Western European countries. Its military budget absorbs about the same share of gross national product as Egypt's, but the cost of the war to Israel greatly exceeded her military budget, since with full mobilization in 1967 almost 25 percent of her labor force was diverted from civilian production. The Six Day War began when Israel was in the throes of a serious recession with unemployment levels of about 12 percent. But the full-scale mobilization hardly reduced unemployment. The majority of the unemployed were unskilled and could not replace the skilled personnel that had been mobilized, either in civilian or military capacities. The brevity of the war and contributions from Jewish communities abroad reduced the economic costs of the war to tolerable levels. However, the postwar situation became increasingly serious. Defense budgets, as well as indirect military expenditures, rose steadily in 1968 and 1969, and further increase is indicated in 1970. A large part, if not most, of this increase is due to the arms race. The massive postwar Soviet arms shipments to Egypt, estimated at over two billion dollars, spurred Israel's leadership to purchase military equipment from any dealer, and the postwar French arms embargo accelerated the pace of investment in domestic military production.

Within a few months after the war the economy began to turn sharply upwards. I shall not go into detail, but it should be emphasized that this was partly due to the military victory and the subsequent rise in local military expenditures. During the latter half of 1967 and in 1968 and 1969, the GNP grew at an annual rate of 12-13 percent in real terms. By the latter half of 1968 and especially in 1969 serious labor shortages developed. These were due both to the rapid growth of production and the higher level of mobilization, as compared with the prewar period. To some extent these shortages were ameliorated by the use of Arab labor from the territories occupied by Israel, and by the subcontracting of work to industrial firms and workshops in the West Bank and the Gaza Strip. Investment, which had been declining between 1965 and 1967, rose very sharply, especially in the industrial sector. Industrial production rose by 29 percent in 1968 and 18 percent in 1969, and industrial exports by 26 and 17 percent, respectively. By international standards, the expansion was extremely rapid. In effect the rapid growth of the economy helped to hold down the relative burden of the defense effort. However, the result of these developments was a deterioration in the balance of payments in 1968 and an even more serious problem in 1969. In spite of the sharp rise in exports, including income from tourism, the trade deficit in goods and services increased very sharply. The foreign exchange reserves which had risen in 1967 as a result of contributions from abroad during the war, dropped by $100 million in 1968 and over $250 million in 1969. The reserves at the end of 1969 reached a critical level.

What accounted for the deficits and the consequent decline in reserves? The answer one commonly reads is that this was due to the defense burdens, both direct and indirect. This is largely true, but does not reveal the whole truth. Per capita personal consumption in 1968 and 1969 rose at an unusually rapid pace. One might explain this phenomenon as a sort of "catching up" with the two previous years when per capita private consumption declined slightly. The internal social-political structure of the country imposes serious obstacles to official efforts to curb these increases. In large measure these deficits represent an unusually large increase in investment in many sectors of the economy, both those directly and indirectly related to defense as well as in housing, transport and communications, and export-related industries. These investments are considered important in terms of future expansion of production and in particular in stimulating exports. The growing volume of immigration, especially from the West, adds to the importance of large-scale investment to provide housing and other services, as well as to increase employment opportunities. However, the short-run impact of investment is to add to the volume of imports and to increase the balance of payments problems.

I suppose that in a more normal period—whatever that means—the Israeli leadership might be satisfied with a slowdown in the pace of economic growth to a rate more in keeping with that of other countries. However, the feeling of many Israeli economists and of the political-economic leadership seems to be that the rising defense budget necessitates rapid economic growth lest the relative burden of military expenditures becomes increasingly onerous. In other words, the goal is apparently to stimulate economic growth to keep pace with the rising defense budget, so that it does not greatly exceed the current level of 20 percent or more of the gross national product. Some steps were taken in 1969 and early in 1970, to curb the rise in private consumption, and I anticipate that additional measures will be taken.

Finally, a few words regarding economic developments in the various areas taken by Israel in June 1967. The press and the other news media confine themselves to reports of the various incidents of fighting, curfews, and so forth. This is regrettable, though one can well understand why these events make the headlines. What is less understandable is that the professional journals dealing with Middle East problems seem to completely ignore the economic developments in these areas, or at best to deal with them superficially.

In each of the areas taken by Israel there has been a basic restructuring of the economy, which has had a favorable impact on certain sectors and an unfavorable impact on others. In the West Bank and the Gaza Strip there has been a strong uptrend in the development of light industry as a result of the opening up of the Israeli market and the increasing trend towards subcontracting to various firms in these areas. Overall industrial production exceeded the prewar level by the middle or end of 1969, and the trend was sharply upward. For various reasons the development of industry was neglected in these areas before the war. In the West Bank there has been a restructuring of the agricultural sector towards the production of those products which are needed in Israel. In spite of the opposition of many Israelis—including some powerful political leaders—the trend towards integration of these economies with that of Israel is continuing, and the use of Arab labor from these territories is rising. On an overall basis the rate of unemployment in the West Bank has been reduced below the prewar level but this has left serious pockets of unemployment especially among the professional and white collar groups. In the Gaza Strip the rate of unemployment is very high but is steadily falling. The annexation or unification of East Jerusalem has had far-reaching economic effects. The sharp reduction in tourism and the competition with Israeli establishments has created serious problems for certain groups of Arabs, particularly those that were previously in the upper-income levels. On the other hand the 4,000 or more who commute daily to work in West Jerusalem—about one third of the labor force—are far better off in terms of real incomes than before the war. This is also true of some who have businesses or work in East Jerusalem. But there are many Arabs who are at least relatively and often absolutely worse off than before the war. In part this is due to the imposition of a relatively highly egalitarian socioeconomic structure upon an area that had been accustomed to the high degree of inequality common to many underdeveloped countries. Presumably the thousands who came to vote in the municipal elections in the fall of 1969 were those groups which had benefited.

I have no simple, pat solution to the economic problems involved in the Middle East conflict. All I am suggesting is that in our endeavors to bring about a just and durable peace we must take account of all aspects of the problem, and keep abreast of all developments—political, military and economic. The failure to do so, especially on the part of policymakers, can only add to the difficulties involved in achieving a just and lasting peace.

The Ba'ath in Syria

SYLVIA G. HAIM

Journalists talk with great assurance of the Ba'ath, its alignments with one or other of the great powers, its socialism or lack of it, and more recently of the Ba'ath and the Neo-Ba'ath. Leaving day-to-day political activities aside, I shall attempt to describe the climate that favored the growth of a movement such as the Ba'ath, and will try, in some small measure, to focus a rather diffuse picture. In order to do this I shall deal with a very obscure personality, Zaki al-Arsuzi.

It is commonly accepted that the Ba'ath (Resurrection), as a party was founded in 1940 by Michel Aflaq and Salah al-Din al-Bitar. At its origin, the party had no special connection with the military; as a movement, its activities consisted for a long time of talks and discussions at various social gatherings and coffee shops. Both founders had been born in Damascus in 1911, had the usual local schooling and then went on government scholarships to study at the Sorbonne. Aflaq read history, and Bitar mathematics. They returned in 1934 to teach in secondary state schools in Damascus; they soon founded a magazine called *al-Tali'a* (Avant-Garde). In 1940 they founded the Ba'ath party; in 1941 they tried to organize demonstrations in support of Rashid Ali's coup in Iraq, but without great success. They resigned from school teaching in 1942 on the grounds that the schools were under the influence of the mandatory power, and concentrated their activities on the party. In 1943 the party declared its solidarity with Lebanon which was fighting for independence. Not until 1947, however, did the first congress of the Ba'ath take place.

It is possible to supplement this skeleton with some information recently come to hand. I refer particularly to two publications; *al-tajriba al-murra (The Bitter Experience)* by Munif al-Razzaz who was for a time Secretary-General of the National Command of the Ba'ath (1965-66). The second book, *al-ba'ath (The Ba'ath)*,[2] Beirut 1969, is by Sami al-Jundi, a dentist by training, and Syrian Ambassador in Paris until he was recalled and imprisoned by the regime, as a result of his having published a book in German called *Juden und Araber*, Munich 1968.[3] It would seem that he mentioned in the preface to the German edition (which I have not seen) that the then Syrian Minister, Makhos, had asked him to get in touch with the Israeli Foreign Minister and that he had asked for an order in writing; he has also denied absolutely that he ever agreed to be present at such a meeting.[4] There was obviously a lot of recrimination which is irrelevant for the present discussion, and this may well have been a pretext to recall and imprison him in the Mezze prison in Damascus. It is also probable that his fate was connected with the falling into disfavor of the rest of his Ismaili relatives. He is now a refugee in Beirut, and like so many other refugees, busy writing his memoirs and some fictional transposition of autobiographical experiences.

In *al-ba'ath* Jundi describes the beginnings of the movement, the present organization of which did not take place until 1957, as haphazard, its success depending upon the impulsiveness of its members, mainly writers and men of letters, and on their emotional responses. Contrary to the usual belief that the Ba'ath was the creation of Aflaq and Bitar, Jundi claims that the two people who played a principal role in its foundation were Aflaq and Zaki al-Arsuzi about whom very little, if anything, has been mentioned in the various histories of the party in English. These two men were in constant disagreement with each other, but their vision and their temper were reflected in the pattern of the members' behavior.[5] He goes back to the thirties in order to trace the origins of the movement to its parent *'usbat al-'amal al-qaumi* (The National Action League), which lasted from 1932 till 1940 and which rallied Syrian youth around itself. Up to 1938 when Alexandretta was ceded to the Turks, the National Bloc which consisted of political leaders found it a convenient organization. A clash soon arose between the League and the government; but the League's efforts to organize the National Youth and the Iron Shirts on Nazi and Fascist models did not make great headway, and are irrelevant to the present discussion.

It is, however, interesting to dwell a little on the League's policy of non-cooperation with the mandatory power even if this meant the refusal of government jobs. The League was badly hit by the death of its first secretary, Abd al-Razzaq al-Dandashi, and by the fact that its second secretary, Sabri al-Asali, accepted an opportunity to become a deputy and had therefore to be expelled, and finally when Arsuzi himself withdrew his membership in 1939. This spelled a natural death for the National Action League. A new effort to create the National Arab Party *(al-hizb al-qaumi al-arabi)* by Arsuzi in 1939, with a defined creed, does not seem to have taken off either, and yet it is worthwhile to dwell a little on it. The leopard was taken as its symbol because of its nature as an easily aroused and aggressive animal rather than the grave and ponderous lion.

The creed was:

☐ The Arabs are one nation.

☐ The Arabs have one leader who will make manifest in his person the possibilities of the Arab nation which he represents and to which he gives the truest expression. This mystic quality that Arsuzi attributes to his leader, a sort of politico-religious ruler, is very much the result of his own religious background. Arsuzi is an Alawi, the Alawis being a Muslim sect who believe in a hidden imam, and like the Druse and Ismailis, the other minority groups active in the Ba'ath party, they have many esoteric practices.

☐ Arabism is the national consciousness.

☐ The Arab is master of fate (i.e. of his own fate). This last statement is very significant because the Arab National Party believed that it had to start at the beginning, that is before Islam.

If it were to free others, it had first of all to free itself from the beliefs and traditions it had inherited. The master believed therefore in going back to the noble values of the Jahiliyya (Age of Ignorance: pre-Islamic period).

This party did not survive for long, and Arsuzi went to Iraq as a teacher in 1939. Various efforts to organize other local Arab parties, mostly with a socialist coloring, were stillborn.

It is necessary to give here some information about Aki al-Arsuzi. An Alawi from Alexandretta, he was the leader of Arab resistance to the mandate's policy in Alexandretta. His father too was known for anti-Ottoman activities and had been exiled to Konya.[6] Arsuzi, a school-teacher who had read philosophy at the Sorbonne, soon came into trouble with the mandatory government and was released from his teaching post in 1934. With the Franco-Turkish treaty of 1936 and the subsequent ceding of the province to Turkey, he emigrated to Damascus. He spent 1939 to 1940 as a schoolteacher in Iraq hoping to awaken the nationalist consciousness there. In less than a year however, he returned to Syria highly disappointed with the Iraqi rulers, whom he described as tools of imperialism and murderers of King Ghazi whom many Arab youth had admired. It is interesting to note that there is a mention that until 1940 Arsuzi preferred to speak in French and that only in 1940 did he come to study Arabic seriously. His writings, which I have read extensively, disclose the following picture:

I arrived to Damascus as a university student, and met Zaki al-Arsuzi the second day after my arrival. He was beautifully spoken, a poet bright with images, fecund in his metaphors and irony, biting in his satire, able immediately to transform social and political concepts and visions. I remember that he used then to talk to us about Neitzsche and the three stages of the mind. He was good looking and neat, gentle in appearance. When he spoke however, he appeared vehement and savage as though he were revolution personified. His large green eyes would blaze with angry passion as though he was a bird of prey bent on destruction.

It is difficult for those who got to know him later as an ironical stoic philosopher, then as a ruined body which shone until his death with a limpid poetic flame to believe and accept this picture of him.

He used to insist on the need to form a party; we therefore met on November 29, 1940 (anniversary of the ceding of the province to Turkey). We were only six and we met in a small room where one of us (Abd al-Halim Qaddur then a student in the Law College) used to live. He gave us a lecture on democracy, communism and Nazism which went on for four hours nonstop and in which he plumbed the depths and was so removed from surface superficialities that these seemd to have no existence on earth. He was heated and emotional. He started with Descartes and ended with Houston Stewart Chamberlain . . .

They decided then and there to found a party and to call it the Arab Ba'ath (Arab resurrection). The six members present took the oath "with simplicity and without formalities."

I have dwelt at such length on this description because it illustrates first of all the kind of modest and haphazard way in which the movement started and secondly it shows clearly the kind of master-disciple relationship which has helped to foster illusion at the cost of realism and to encourage the sort of passive contemplation of past glories that can somehow, it is hoped, be revived. The narrator adds that with the 24 liras dues that he collected, he bought a high chair for the master and low chairs for the others to sit on. They used to meet in a small and poor house where Arsuzi and a group of refugee students from Alexandretta used to live and dream of the glories of Arab history. Describing the mood prevalent then among this group, Jundi writes:

We used to live by this hope [of resurrecting past Arab glories], strangers in the midst of our society which was making us more and more lonely. We were rebels against all ancient values, enemies to all that humanity had accepted. We rejected all ritual, all relations, all religions; we sought battle in every spot. We were a savage axe. Society persecuted us so we defied it, we went on destroying with a lot of cunning as well as stupidity all institutions. We were infants who were growing older but became, with the passage of time, even more infantile.

Jundi adds that the attacks which were made on them were all correct: they were against all existing leaders without distinction; they were atheists in spite of what later Ba'athists have said in defense of themselves. They believed in the mysticism of religions and their humanistic tendencies but not in other people's religious tendencies. They were greatly influenced by Nazism and its emphasis on race, and read particularly Nietzsche, Fichte, and Houston Stewart Chamberlain.

I will point out here that references to the purity of race when used by the Master are in order to explain the present day weakness of the Arabs. The Arabs were pure in the Jahiliyyah, Islam was born in Arabia and brought by the Prophet in order to reinforce the noble and pure qualities of the Arabs. But alien elements adopted Islam, and here it is not a question of Jewish and Christian converts to Islam, but mainly a question of other nations, the Persians and Turkish for instance, who adulterated the pure and noble qualities of the Arabs. I will also emphasize that there is no question of racialism as typified by the Nazi final solution. The attraction of Nazism was a practical one. Jundi writes: "Whoever has lived in Damascus at that period will appreciate the inclination of the Arab people towards Nazism, for it was the force which was taking up their cause. The defeated, by nature, loves the victor."

However, in spite of his ideology, Arsuzi did not join forces with the Axis; on the contrary he declined Italy's advances towards a union.

The membership of the party remained a handful, and the members seem to have been mainly busy reading, writing and translating. In June 1941, Arsuzi was exiled from Damascus and three of the members were imprisoned; the rest fled. In 1942 there was another attempt at activity, but poverty and suspicion were destroying the Master. He started to feel persecuted and to suspect all those around him as spies. Even his disciples were not free from his biting criticism. "His tension and suspicion transferred itself to us," Jundi says, "The party became a collection of anarchists with the same way of thinking and the same logic; their interpretation of events was almost identical, but they did not trust anyone; they loved the people and hated the individual; they held the whole sacred, but they despised the parts." The group scattered in 1944; the Master moved to Lattakia and from there to Tarsus where his mother died in poverty and where he declined in misery and poverty, withdrawn and bitter, engaged only in authorship and in teaching.

There is now rather sharp disagreement among the Ba'athists about who was the real founder of the Ba'ath: Aflaq or Arsuzi Strong feeling is aroused by this and not all writers treat the subject as cooly as Jundi. At least one author denounces Aflaq as a thief who together with his disciples and students found in Arsuzi's thought the nationalist ideology they were seeking; he accuses Aflaq not only of having stolen this ideology but also of having exiled Arsuzi from the intellectual field and relegated him to obscurity.[8] This seems very sharp language considering that there is hardly any originality of thought in either men; both of them seem to have had a similar education and the only difference is one of selection and adaptation of ready-made European theories.

This selection and adaptation is as much the result of differing personalities as of the changing political scene and power patters of the last four decades.[9] It is however a little curious that in all the writings of Arsuzi and of Aflaq that I have read neither mentions the other. It seems that the two men were in constant disagreement, in spite of their perhaps equal influence on the movement. Judging from the writing of both, it does not seem unlikely that Arsuzi had the greater influence in creating a Ba'athist climate of thought. He writes in a reasonably precise and clear language that he has a wide knowledge of Arabic literary sources at his command. Aflaq's writings, on the contrary, strike me as rather obscure and confused or, as the same unsympathetic writer puts it, "foggy".[10] In fact, Aflaq is often described as a silent and enigmatic personality as well as rather slow of speech; this, according to the generosity of lack of it of the commentator, is taken either as an indication of the depth of his personality or of his dimness.

It is however quite clear that since the events of February 1966 and Aflaq's flight from Syria, Arsuzi's role and influence is being discussed and emphasized. I shall again draw on Sami al-Jundi in connection with this. He claims that he took to Arsuzi in 1941 a lithographed manifesto written in his own style and signed "the Arab Ba'ath", which was passed on to him by a friend, Arsuzi immediately saw in it an imperialist plot to block his way to the people by creating a movement bearing the same name as his own.

At that time Professors Michel Aflaq and Salah al-Din al-Bitar founded a party which, at the start, they sometimes called the Ba'ath (Resurrection) and at other times *al-Ihya'* (Revification). We must remember that these two words mean the same thing. The two movements were similar, even identical. Almost all our companions (Maitre Muhsin Shishakli and myself being perhaps the only exceptions) were the students of Aflaq and Bitar at College. The members of their Ba'ath used to call sometimes on Maitre Arsuzi and suffer his biting criticism and scorn.

Our intellectual formation was the same: we were two Ba'aths which had diverged.

When Rashid 'Ali al-Gailani came to power, *al-Ihya'* suddenly appeared and talked about aiding Iraq to victory. It led the wave of enthusiasm and stove to send volunteers to Iraq. The two Ba'aths exchanged attacks, and faith in Arsuzi weakened. (Arsuzi it seems was critical of Rashid 'Ali's coup because he considered it untimely and sure to fail). The members, even those who trusted his opinion, started to question his practical ability. He clashed with them as he clashed with public opinion by foretelling the failure of Gailani. He was a person who would not forgive anyone who did not trust his judgment.[11]

It seems, however, quite clear that because of his rather tempestuous personality and his falling out with the French authorities—in June 1941, he was exiled out of Damascus—he should lose some of his disciples who rallied around Aflaq. "Arsuzi did not belong to the Party but was forever present in it . . . It was Aflaq who gave the party a lot of its romanticism which is essential for every beginning, and stamped it with his own intellectual character and involved thought."[12] This seems a fair summary of the state of the movement at the time.

However, the point I want to make now is not concerned with the problem, which is rather academic and of no political significance, about the real founder of the Ba'ath. Most of these arguments have taken place since 1963 when the Ba'ath came to power and the process of its disintegration as a coherent political party had started. The question to be asked is: Why this need to persevere with an ideology and a party which had, at no time, a large membership, and which would not have become known were it not for its successful wooing of the army officers from the mid-1950's, a wooing which has caused discomfiture on the part of the civilian founders of the party.[13] The membership of the party in 1952 is given by Jundi as 500 consisting mainly of college and secondary school students of country origins and not city dwellers; it increased to 2,500 in 1954, after it had merged with Haurani's socialist party and become *al-Ba'ath al-Arabi al-ishtiraki*. The need to have a semblance of a party and an ideology can be best guaged perhaps by the fact that General Salan Jedid, himself an Alawi, and perhaps the most important personality in Syria today operates from the modest position of Assistant Secretary of the Regional Command of the Party. His civilian front man and Prime Minister is Secretary General of the Party. A wry Dascene joke current at the end of 1965, "Three soldiers govern Syria with two shoes" is quoted by Jundi, the two shoes being the Prime Minister, Nur Al-Din al-Atasi, and Yusuf Zulayyin.[14]

The other book mentioned above, by Munif al-Razzaz, *al-tajriba al-murra*, is unique as a document of recent political history in Syria and of internal conflicts, Munif al-Razzaz, a Jordanian (of Syrian origin?) fled from Jordan because of his Ba'athist activities. In 1965 he took over from Aflaq as Secretary General of the Ba'ath. With the bloody victory of the military within the Ba'ath in February 1966, Razzaz fled to Beirut where he wrote his book. Although a socialist, he is highly critical of Stalin to whom he compares Salah Jedid and his methods; the techniques of both of them he likens to the rules of a game of chess where only the king is victorious. Ideals are useful as a means of attacking rivals and are liable to be changed at every stage of the struggle.[15] Like Aflaq he is extremely bitter at the way the military subverted the foundations of the party and gained control over it. There are now loud denunciations about the way the military infiltrated the party meetings and thereby started controlling it to the extent that the original founders such as Bitar and Aflaq had to flee the country.

Looking back to the union with Egypt in 1958 it seems quite clear that it was the Ba'ath party itself which actually pursued Nasser, who was undoubtedly quite willing to be pursued, in order, to put it very simply, that he should come and save them. And although Haurani, originally of *al-hizb al-arabi al-ishtiraki* (the Arab socialist party) before it merged with the Ba'ath, was the first to agitate for secession from the union and has maintained this position throughout, Aflaq and Bitar seem to have seesawed in their attitude and to have managed for a while at least, to delay the commitment to a clear decision.[16] After the secession from Egypt in 1961, the party was so divided within itself, that it is difficult to keep track of the various factions. There were the Nasserites, the Hauranites and above all the anti-Nasser Syrian Nasserites as Razzaz so calls them. These latter were the group of officers[17] (among them Salah Jedid, Hafid Asad, and Muhammad Umran) whom Nasser had kept under surveillance in Cairo. They came to adopt his political tactics although they hated him.[18] They are sometimes called *al-musta' jilun* (the impatient ones); this description has stuck to them because a lot of commentators, including Razzaz, claim that these men came to believe in revolutionary methods because they could not wait for the slow process of converting the masses. It is these men who have come on top since February 1966. It is not my intention to sort out the ensuing battles of recrimination, invective and murder, but to give some idea of the atmosphere prevailing in the party, and to raise a few questions. Is it not possible that the military did not in fact subvert the party but that the Ba'ath itself, with its origins in a master-disciple relationship, a mystic ideology, admiration of activism and visions of resurrection, has within itself the germs of glorifying military power? Ever since the early fifties, Aflaq and the civilian Ba'ath in general have been infiltrating the army and wooing the officers. Jundi points out that Aflaq even tried to become the respectful mentor of Zaim, the first military dictator of Syria as early as 1949.[19] Another question worth pursuing is the reason why it is necessary for the ruling group to cling tenaciously to the myth of the existence of a party which they seem to have destroyed; note that Jedid is only Assistant Secretary of the Regional Command of the Ba'ath operating behind the screen of his civilian front man, Atassi, Secretary General of the Party and President of the Republic.[20] Even if we are to accept the undoubted fact that it is useful to operate within an already existing framework, is it possible to explain away such a tenacious desire to adopt an all-embracing ideology merely on the grounds of its utility? A worthwhile line of further investigation would have to study developments not only within the general framework of Arab nationalism and socialism but also in reference to minority and sectarian groupings and perhaps to family relationships.

[1] Munif al-Razzaz, *The Bitter Experience*, Beirut 1967.

[2] Sami al-Jundi, *The Ba'ath*, Beirut 1969.

[3] This book has since appeared in an Arabic edition, *Arab wa yahid*, Beirut 1968, and in a French translation, *La drome palestinien: Pour sortir de l'impasse*, Paris 1969.

[4] See his book *Kisrat khubz (A Crust of Bread)*, Beirut 1969, p. 13.

[5] al-Jundi, *op. cit.* p. 33.

[6] Foreign Office Documents, F.O. 882/15, p. 31.

[7] al-Jundi, *op. cit.* p. 25.

[8] Muta' al-Safadi, *Rizb al-Ba'ath*, Beirut 1964, p. 66.

[9] See Gordon H. Torrey, "The Ba'ath—Ideology and Practices" in *Middle East Journal*, Autumn 1969, for a description of Aflaq's socialism and his views on racialism and other similar questions generally discussed by Arsuzi.

[10] Safadi, *op. cit.*, p. 74.

[11] Jundi, *op. cit.*, p. 29.

[12] *Ibid.*, p. 33.

[13] Footnote in text, p. 11.

[14] Jundi, *op. cit.*, p. 146.

[15] Razzas, *op. cit.*, p. 138.

[16] See Malcolm Kerr, *The Arab Cold War* 1958-1964, London 1965, and Ben-Tzur, *loc. cit.*

[17] *Ibid.*, p. 84.

[18] *Ibid.*, p. 56.
[19] Jundi, *op. cit.*, pp. 51-52, 54-55.
[20] Martin Seymour, "The Dynamics of Power in Syria Since the Break in Egypt," in *Middle Eastern Studies*, January 1970, p. 39.

Arab Refugees
and the Arab-Israeli Dilemma

FRED J. KHOURI

The Palestine War of 1948 uprooted hundreds of thousands of Palestinian Arabs and created an embittered, restless refugee population living in crowded, wretched camps in the four Arab states bordering Israel. Over the years, as the number of refugees steadily mounted, their discontent intensified, and their militancy and political influence grew and spread throughout the Arab world. The Six Day War of June 1967, by causing tens of thousands of Palestinian refugees to leave their homes once again and by forcing more than 200,000 Egyptians, Jordanians and Syrians to become refugees for the first time, added major new dimensions and complications to the already perplexing refugee problem. My purpose here is to discuss the principal facts surrounding the critical role of the Palestinian refugees, before analyzing the views of both Arabs and Israelis and presenting recommendations for the resolution of the refugee issue.

THE ARAB EXODUS

Serious clashes broke out between the Arab and Jewish communities in Palestine immediately after the United Nations General Assembly passed its partition resolution on November 29, 1947,

The material contained in this paper is largely based on my book, *THE ARAB-ISRAELI DILEMMA*, published by Syracuse University Press in 1968.

and by the early part of 1948 some 30,000 upper- and middle-class Arabs had left Palestine. As the fighting intensified, many more frightened Arabs fled their homes. After April 1, the Arab exodus accelerated as a result of several successful Jewish military offensives into Arab areas and terroristic attacks by Irgun and the Stern Gang (such as the massacre of 250 civilians in the village of Deir Yassin) which were launched to encourage Arabs to flee whenever Jewish forces approached. Even before the armies from the neighboring Arab countries formally intervened when the Palestine Mandate came to an end on May 15, 1948, about 200,000 Palestinians had already become refugees, although, on several occasions before May 15 and in certain limited areas only, some Jewish officials had encouraged Arabs not to leave.[1]

During the Palestine War itself, many tens of thousands of Arabs fled because according to Count Bernadotte's report to the UN, (A/648, Part II), there was "panic created by the fighting in their communities, by rumors concerning real or alleged acts of terrorism, or explusion" on the part of the Israeli forces. Israel expelled large numbers of Arabs in order to: provide land and buildings badly needed for the Jewish immigrants pouring in; reduce to the minimum the Arab population in the Jewish state; give Israel a "trump card" in future political bargaining; and interfere with Arab military operations.[2] Illegal Israeli military offensives in the Negev and Galilee during the second truce in 1948 and 1949 caused many more thousands of Arabs to quit their homes; and additional thousands were expelled from the Negev and the Syrian-Israeli Demilitarized Zone after the armistice of 1949.[3]

Early UN Efforts to Resolve the Refugee Problem

During the spring and summer of 1948, the neighboring Arab states tried to help the Palestinian refugees; but they soon found themselves unable to cope adequately with the needs of the hapless refugees, most of whom lacked shelter, food, and had lost their possessions in Israel. In response to Arab appeals, Count Bernadotte initiated an emergency relief program with the help of the World Health Organization and other UN specialized agencies. He asked Israel to allow the return of some of the refugees after careful screening to eliminate security risks. But Israel refused on the grounds of security and the continuance of a state of war. The UN mediator disappointed with Israel's response, reported (A/648, Part III) to the UN that "no settlement can be just and complete if recognition is not accorded to the rights of the Arab refugee to return . . . home."

In the hope of dealing with the increasingly serious refugee situation, which threatened to cause more strife in the area, the UN General Assembly passed two important resolutions in the fall of 1948. The first [212(III)] set up a Director of UN Relief for Palestine Refugees and provided money for relief purposes. The second [194(III)], passed on December 11, established a Conciliation Commission for Palestine and instructed it to "take steps to assist the Governments and authorities concerned to achieve a final peace settlement of all questions outstanding between them" and "to facilitate the repatriation, resettlement and economic and social rehabilitation of the refugees and the payment of compensation" to them. A key section was contained in paragraph 11, which resolved

that the refugees wishing to return to their homes and live in peace with their neighbors should be permitted to do so at the earliest practicable date, and that compensation should be paid for the property of those choosing not to return . . .

The Conciliation Commission, composed of representatives from the United States, France and Turkey, began its activities with high hopes of bringing about an early peace settlement as well as an early return of the refugees. However, it soon discovered that the views of the Arabs and Israelis were difficult to reconcile. Convinced of the urgency of the refugee problem, the commission decided to concentrate on trying to implement paragraph 11 of Resolution 194(III) in the hope that this would not only help to relieve human misery but also lead to a peaceful settlement of the other major points in dispute.

The Arabs insisted that the refugee question had to be dealt with according to the terms of UN resolutions before they would seriously discuss the other issues. Jordan and Syria indicated to the commission that they would receive those refugees not opting for repatriation. Egypt and Lebanon held that they were already too overpopulated to be able to absorb any significant number of refugees. Israel, for her part, initially insisted that the return of the refugees was contingent on the establishment of formal peace on the grounds of security. Soon, however, Israel began to reject the principle of repatriation and to hold that, even if a peace agreement were reached, a final solution of the refugee problem would have to be based on the resettlement of all or nearly all of the refugees in the Arab world.[4]

By the spring of 1949, UN and American officials (including President Harry S. Truman), came to believe that the Arabs would be ready to make peace if a substantial number of the refugees were repatriated, and expressed growing impatience with Israel's adamant position on repatriation. They began to exert increasing pressures on Israel to accept the return of at least 200,000 to 300,000 refugees.[5]

In response to these pressures, Israel reluctantly indicated that if she could annex the Gaza Strip she would take over responsibility for the refugees there. Since this was not acceptable to the Arabs, the Conciliation Commission or the United States, Israel then offered to repatriate 100,000 refugees, on the condition that she could resettle them to suit her own interests. Not only did this proposal prove unacceptable to the Arabs, the commission and the United States, but, as a result of mounting internal opposition to any repatriation, Israeli officials quickly withdrew their new offer and reassured their people that they would stand fast against the principle of repatriation. From then on, the greatest concession that Israel would make, besides contributing to a fund to compensate resettled refugees, was to agree to a "reunion of family" plan which allowed for the return of a limited number of refugees separated from their families still in Israel.[6]

In May 1949, in Lausanne, Switzerland, the Conciliation Commission succeeded in bringing together Egypt, Lebanon, Syria, Jordan and Israel and all parties signed two identical but separate protocols stating that the signatories were willing to use the 1947 partition resolution boundaries as a "starting point and framework for the discussion of territorial questions." The Arab signatories revealed that they had significantly altered their position from outright opposition to the partition resolution to partial support of it, because continued opposition to it in their weak military position would be self-defeating and because UN enforcement of its provisions would force the Israelis to give up at least part of their territory. However, Israel disregarded the protocols she had previously signed and made it clear that she would not abide by the territorial and refugee provisions of the November 29, 1947 and December 11, 1948 resolutions, even though these had been clearly reiterated in UN Resolution 273(III) admitting Israel to the UN. In the meantime, some Arabs also revealed their great reluctance to accept Israel.[7]

Having failed to solve the refugee question by political means, the Conciliation Commission decided, in August 1949, to try a different approach. An Economic Survey Mission was instructed to recommend large-scale development projects which would ultimately bring about the reintegration of most of the refugees into the economic life of the area. However, it quickly discovered that there were many political and emotional obstacles to economic development and that neither the Arabs nor the Israelis were ready to provide the cooperation necessary for large-scale and area-wide projects. It therefore recommended small-scale "pilot demonstration projects" and the continuation of UN relief for the refugees.[8]

In the light of these recommendations, on December 8, 1949, the UN General Assembly unanimously—with Israel's consent—established the United Nations Relief and Works Agency for Palestine Refugees (UNRWA), with a budget of $54,900,000, and reaffirmed, as it did annually thereafter, the right of the refugees to repatriation or resettlement with compensation, as stated in paragraph 11 or Resolution 194(III).

In the summer of 1951 the United States persuaded the Conciliation Commission to make one more effort to find a solution of the refugee and other issues. The commission proposed (A/1985) that Israel repatriate "specified numbers of Arab refugees in categories which can be integrated into the economy" of Israel and that the remainder be settled in the Arab world with Israel paying them a "global sum" based, in part, on "Israel's ability to pay." Both the Arabs and the Israelis opposed this new proposal. The Arabs charged that it disregarded valid UN resolutions. Israel not only continued to object to any significant repatriation, but she now argued in addition that the recent major exodus of Jews from Iraq and other Arab countries had produced a virtual exchange of populations. Israel's position on compensation also hardened on the ground that Iraq had not paid for properties left behind by Iraqi Jews. Moreover, disputes between Israel and Syria over Lake Huleh and between Egypt and Israel over restrictions on Israeli shipping through the Suez Canal had intensified Arab-Israeli hatred and made them less willing than before to compromise their differences. Failing again to make any real progress, the commission suspended its efforts at conciliation and concentrated on trying to deal with limited technical fields, such as refugee bank accounts blocked in Israel, areas in which it was able to make some significant progress.

Responding to mounting pressures from an impatient Congress, in October 1953, President Dwight D. Eisenhower sent Eric Johnston to the Middle East to obtain Arab and Israeli acceptance of a plan for the regional development of the Jordan River system. It was hoped that such a scheme would not only solve the refugee problem but also open the way to a peaceful settlement of the other issues as well. Agreement was reached over certain technical aspects of the project, but a combination of political factors, border incidents, an Arab-Israeli arms race, and anti-Western feeling in the Arab world prevented any final agreement.

In August 1961 the Conciliation Commission appointed Dr. Joseph E. Johnson as a special representative, again due to American pressure, to explore practical means for dealing with the refugee situation. He suggested that each refugee be given an opportunity to express freely his preference for repatriation or resettlement, with Israel being allowed, subject to a UN review, to reject certain refugees as security risks. Repatriation and resettlement would take place gradually, and Israel would contribute to a special fund for compensating those refugees opting for resettlement. While the more moderate Arabs supported Johnson's proposal, other Arabs, led by the Palestinian refugees, objected to some parts. Israel, in turn, rejected the proposal, again opposing any significant repatriation.

In the years that followed, Israel persisted in holding that the refugee question could not be resolved separately from a final peace settlement, which had to come about through direct negotiations and which would provide for only a limited "family reunion" scheme and no other repatriation. The Arabs again called upon the UN to implement paragraph 11 of Resolution 194(III). They also pressed the UN to set up a custodian to administer and protect Arab refugee property in Israel, but also to no avail. While the UN in annual resolutions reaffirmed the validity of paragraph 11, it never seriously tried to implement it.

UNRWA AND THE REFUGEE PROBLEM

Having failed to resolve the refugee question, the UN continued to provide relief services and works projects through UNRWA, partly for humanitarian reasons and partly to prevent the plight of the refugees from causing further unrest in the Middle East. At first the Arabs were hesitant about cooperating with efforts to establish a large-scale development program because they feared that this would undermine the right of the refugees to repatriation or compensation. After reassurances on this matter from UN officials the Arab League Council agreed in June 1950 to accept major projects as long as refugee rights were not endangered. By the end of the summer of 1950, the Conciliation Commission was even able to report that it had

> received the impression that these [Arab] governments are inclining more and more to the view that the problem cannot be fully solved by the return of the refugees to their homes; and that consequently the settlement ... of a considerable number of refugees in the Arab countries must also be contemplated in order to achieve a complete and final solution of the problem.[9]

By 1954 UNRWA was able to report some progress. Iraq had accepted about 5,000 refugees, and Libya was willing to absorb 6,000. Israel had assumed full responsibility for some 19,000 refugees then living within her borders. Jordan had offered full citizenship to all Palestinians in her territory, and Syria allowed all refugees residing there to seek employment on the same basis as her own citizens. UNRWA had begun a small vocational training program and its graduates were readily able to find jobs. A limited number of refugees had been supplied loans for setting up small business enterprises. Several agreements had been concluded with Syria, Jordan, and Egypt for development projects.[10]

At the same time UNRWA indicated that, because of a high birth rate, the total number of refugees had been rapidly increasing. While many thousands of names were illegally on the refugee rolls, at least as many thousands were denied relief because of lack of funds. Besides, there were about 300,000 hardship cases among the Palestinians—among them 165,000 "economic refugees" (Palestinians unable to earn a living because their farms were in Israel while their homes remained in Jordan); 60,000 unemployed natives of the Gaza Strip; and 7,000 Azazme Bedouins forcibly expelled by Israel in 1950—who were in desperate need of help which UNRWA was not able to provide. For a number of reasons, the organization had not been able to resettle or repatriate any significant number of the refugees. The most important of these were: 1) the lack of physical resources in the area and of skills and training among the refugees; 2) the lack of adequate UNRWA funds; 3) the intensification of Palestine Arab nationalism, as well as the attitude of the Palestinian refugees and its influence on Arab governments; and 4) the unfavorable political conditions in the Middle East [11]

Of the four host states where nearly all of the refugees lived, Jordan, Eygpt and Lebanon were poor in natural resources and already overpopulated. Only Syria was relatively well endowed with land and water resources. Consequently, only a part of the total number (which reached one million by 1957) could have been resettled in the host countries even if all potential development projects had been completed and most of the Palestinian refugees would have had to cross national boundaries or demarcation lines before they could have found sufficient jobs and land. In any case, even the Arab states with the greatest resources, such as Syria and Iraq, had rapidly growing populations and their governments were reluctant to give priority to the Palestinian Arabs over their own poverty-stricken citizens in any schemes of economic development. Their own basic needs and those of the Palestinian refugees could not simultaneously be satisfied. Besides, most of these refugees lacked special skills and the Arab Middle East was an area already generally saturated with farmers and unskilled workers. UNRWA had been able to provide vocational training or university education to a small number of the refugees who had no difficulty in finding jobs and becoming self-supporting. These same officials noted that it was not enough to supply aid for the economic development of the Arab world for the "same technological process that brings higher total employment also brings a decrease in the relative need" for unskilled workers. Thus, even if the refugees had been willing to cross international boundaries and were allowed to do so and even if massive development projects had been begun in the area, most of the refugees would still have remained "virtually unemployable" without some kind of special training. In short, any major resettlement of the refugees, even under relatively favorable circumstances, would have created difficulties and problems for the Arab states directly involved.[12]

UNRWA's work was also curtailed by a serious lack of money. Only $37,000,000 of the $200,000,000 reintegration fund established by UN General Assembly Resolution 513(VI) was received by UNRWA. Approximately $18,700,000 of this amount had been spent while the rest was kept as essential working capital. After 1955, major financial difficulties were primarily responsible for forcing UNRWA to give up further plans for promoting large-scale development schemes and to concentrate on smaller and cheaper self-help projects and business grants to a limited number of individuals—and these had to be cut still further after 1956. Thanks to special aid from governments and private groups in the 1960s, UNRWA was able to increase modestly its vocational training program and its number of grants for university education.

The growth of Palestine Arab nationalism and the embittered attitude of the refugees created other obstacles. UNRWA and Conciliation Commission reports (A/1255, A/1288, A/1367, A/1451) emphasized that the Palestinian refugees still passionately desired to return to their homes—a desire encouraged by the annual UN General Assembly resolutions reiterating the right of refugees to repatriation. Having won the sympathetic support of the Arab masses, the refugees were able to apply effective pressures on most of the host governments. Their influence was especially strong in Jordan (where the refugees constituted one-third of the population and other Palestinians another third), Syria and Lebanon. Because the refugees in the Gaza Strip were generally unable to move freely out of this area, they were unable to exert any significant influence on the Egyptian government and people prior to the June 1967 war. Gradually, as Palestinian nationalism grew and as large numbers of the refugees began to move to other parts of the Arab world, the Palestinians began to spread throughout the Arab world their intense feelings of hate and frustration and their strong conviction that a grave injustice had been done to them.

A number of unfavorable political developments in the Middle East during the 1950s added to the complications. Serious border clashes, raids and counterraids and a growing arms race brought about a major deterioration in Arab-Israeli relations. Moreover, Israel's attitude hardened over the years as a result of the activist parties' success in the 1955 Knesset elections, and the return of Ben Gurion to the government first as Defense Minister and then as Prime Minister, the replacement of the moderate Moshe Sharett by the militant Golda Meir as Foreign Minister, the closer ties with France, and the support from Jewish groups throughout the West. Simultaneously, increasing instability and rivalry between a number of Arab governments made it more difficult for even moderate leaders to appear ready to compromise their differences with Israel. In fact, the weaker the internal position of an Arab leader, the stronger the anti-Israeli stand he felt himself obliged to take, at least in public.

The intrusion of the cold war into the Middle East added further to the complications. Soviet aid and political support encouraged strong anti-Western feelings throughout the Arab world, and this made it more difficult for the West to exert influence on Arab views and actions. Western political, economic and military aid to Israel, which was largely responsible for the growth of anti-Western feelings in the Arab world, only encouraged Israeli self-confidence and intransigence.

THE JUNE 1967 WAR AND THE REFUGEE PROBLEM

The unresolved refugee problem also played a major role in producing those developments that led to war in June 1967. Since neither Israel nor the UN were willing to carry out the UN repatriation provisions, embittered refugees convinced increasing numbers of Arabs that they had no alternative to the use of force to obtain what they considered to be "justice." Thus, Fatah and other activist Palestinian organizations were formed, and in January 1965 Fatah launched a series of guerrilla raids on Israel—the first such operations since 1956. Except for Syria most of the Arab states were reluctant to aid the commandos before the June War. It remained basically an organization of Palestinians seeking to restore Palestine Arabs to their homes and their "homeland." The revival of these commando activities—as well as Arab response to provocative Israeli encroachments on Arab-owned or disputed lands in the Israeli-Syrian Demilitarized Zone—precipitated Israeli retaliatory attacks on Jordan, Syria and Lebanon.[14] In turn these attacks triggered more commando attacks and border incidents. There followed more destructive Israeli retaliations, such as at as-Samu in Jordan in November 1966 and on Syria on April 7, 1967, and strong threats made by top Israeli officials in early May of an assault on Syria. These events, plus internal developments in Egypt and other Arab states, caused Gamal Abdel Nasser to send large military forces into the Sinai, to request the removal of the United Nations Emergency Force (UNEF) from the demarcation lines and Sharm el-Sheikh overlooking the Strait of Tiran, and then to close the strait to Israeli shipping and to contraband goods on neutral ships heading for Israel. These and other provocative Arab actions and bellicose statements then led Israel to make a "preemptive" air strike and land offensive against Eygpt, and the June War was on.[15] A strong case can therefore be built from the historical facts to support the conclusion that without the refugee problem there probably would have been no commando attacks and retaliatory raids, and no May 1967 crisis and no June War.

Israel's military victory and her seizure of the Gaza Strip, the West Bank of the Jordan, Sinai, and Golan Heights, created a new refugee problem as well as complicating the old one. By December 1967 UNRWA reported (A/SPC.121) that more than 140,000 refugees from the Palestine War and over 280,000 Syrians, Egyptians and Jordanians who had been living in the conquered territories had already fled to Arab-controlled areas and that "perhaps as many as 300,000" Egyptians had been forced to move as a result of the renewed fighting in the Suez Canal sector. Israel now found herself with nearly 550,000 of the 1,300,000 UNRWA-registered refugees under her control.

As had happened during the fighting in 1948, during and after the June War large numbers of Arabs fled in panic at the prospect of fighting around their homes. In some areas, as reported by a number of neutral observers,[16] there were Israeli efforts to encourage them to leave. In addition, many Arabs—such as pensioners, civil servants, those dependent on remittances from family members working in various Arab countries, and those living in areas hit by serious postwar unemployment and food shortages—left for financial and economic reasons.

On June 14, 1967, the UN Security Council unanimously adopted Resolution 237 calling upon Israel "to facilitate the return of those inhabitants who have fled the areas [of military operations] since the outbreak of hostilities." Despite UN and American pressures, Israel allowed only about 14,000 refugees of some 170,000 applicants from the West Bank to return, plus several thousand from the Gaza Strip and Golan Heights. In the meantime, and at least until early 1968, several thousand Arabs each month left the Gaza Strip for East Jordan—often, again, with Israeli encouragement.[17]. Some Israeli officials (including Defense Minister Moshe Dayan) frankly admitted that they were happy to see the Arabs leave and were reluctant to permit many of them to return since their absence would make it easier to administer and to annex some if not all of the conquered territories. There would be, too, less danger that the occupied lands would radically alter the Jewish composition of a "Greater Israel", and a stronger political bargaining weapon for Israel in any future negotiations with the Arabs.[18]

The new Arab exodus created in the Arab world another large group of restless, frustrated and angry refugees who blamed the international community, as well as Israel and the Arab states, for their plight, who refused to allow their fellow Arabs and governments to forget their unhappy situation, who provided the greatest support for commando activities against Israel and who demanded forceful actions from their leaders to enable them to regain their homes and lands. These Palestinian and Egyptian refugees were not as isolated as the Palestinian refugees in the Gaza Strip had been in the past, and they now were in a position to spread their militancy directly to the Egyptian masses.

The Arab governments again pressed the UN to enforce those General Assembly resolutions calling for repatriation or compensation. They again urged the UN to appoint a custodian to administer and protect Arab refugee properties in Israel, but still to no avail. They also insisted—as in the past—that there could be no hope for a peaceful solution to the Arab-Israeli problem until some provision was made for a just settlement of the refugee issue on the basis of existing UN decisions.

Israel, on the other hand, reiterated her view that the refugee question could be solved only "in the broad context of peace." She suggested that the Arab states, Israel and the main contributors to UNRWA meet and "negotiate a five-year plan for the rehabilitation of the refugees and their final integration into the economic life of the region." She agreed to contribute to a "re-integration and compensation fund" and she expressed a willingness to consider repatriating a "token" number of refugees "on compassionate grounds." But she strongly opposed the setting up of a UN custodian for refugee property and the admittance of any significant number of Palestinian refugees.[19]

Recognizing the vital role played by the refugee issue in the overall Arab-Israeli dilemma, on November 22, 1967, the UN Security Council passed Resolution 242 which, among other provisions relating to an Arab-Israeli peace, affirmed the "necessity" for "achieving a just settlement of the refugee problem" in order to make it possible to attain a "just and lasting peace in the

Middle East." While this resolution did not attempt to define what it meant by a "just settlement", from 1967 to 1969 the UN General Assembly passed by nearly unanimous votes three resolutions which repeatedly reiterated all prior resolutions dealing with the Palestine Arab refugee problem, expressed regret that the repatriation or compensation of the refugees had not been effected and requested the UN Conciliation Commission to exert continued efforts towards this end. The Assembly also reiterated Security Council resolutions of June 14, 1967 and the General Assembly Resolution of July 4, 1967 calling upon Israel

> to take effective and immediate steps for the return without delay of those inhabitants who fled the areas since the outbreak of hostilities

and endorsed the essential efforts of UNRWA

> to continue to provide humanitarian assistance, as far as practicable, on an emergency basis and as a temporary measure, to other persons in the area who are at present displaced and are in a serious need of continued assistance as a result of the June 1967 hostilities.

After the June War, the United States voted for the UN resolutions noted above and generally supported the return of the 1967 refugees and the principle of repatriation for the 1948 refugees. In a major speech delivered on December 9, 1969, Secretary of State William P. Rogers revealed a deep understanding of the refugee issue when he remarked,

> There can be no lasting peace without a just settlement of the problem of those Palestinians whom the wars of 1948 and 1967 have made homeless . . . We believe that a just settlement must take into account the desires and aspirations of the refugees and the legitimate concerns of the governments in the area.

> The problem posed by the refugees will become increasingly serious if their future is not resolved. There is a new consciousness among the young Palestinians who have grown up since 1948 which needs to be channeled away from bitterness and frustration toward hope and justice.[20]

As of early 1970, while nearly all members of the UN continued to support the principles of repatriation or resettlement with compensation for the Palestine War refugees and the early return of the Arabs displaced in 1967, these same members remained unwilling to implement their own resolutions in the face of Israeli opposition. The Arab states, meanwhile, remained too weak and divided to bring about a solution on their own which would satisfy the desires and demands of the impatient refugees, who now yearned more than ever for a return to their homes and "homeland." As a result, large numbers of refugees, having lost confidence in the Arab governments and the UN, began to feel that they must organize, mobilize and even fight on their own if they were ever to attain their cherished political goal. Many no longer felt any great loyalty to the Arab countries that sheltered them, and at times, they even seriously challenged the authority of the governments of the host states. They reserved their primary loyalty to their own national cause. In addition, they increased their pressures on the Arab governments and their own acts of violence against Israel—even though these acts usually precipitated Israeli retaliations that frequently caused greater damage to their host countries than had been inflicted on Israel by the Palestinian commandos. The June War and its aftermath had thus greatly complicated the Arab refugee problem and made it an even more formidable obstacle to peace than before. Only some constructive action to "channel" the Arab refugees "away from bitterness and frustration toward hope and justice," as Secretary of State Rogers has put the matter, can provide any hope of reducing the tension and violence which the unresolved refugee question continues to generate in the Middle East to the point where the Arabs and Israelis can peacefully resolve their differences.

ANALYSIS OF ISRAEL'S POSITION

Israel shares responsibility with the Arabs for the refugee problem, as well as for the failure to resolve it, since there is evidence that deliberate efforts to expel the Arabs were made during the two wars. Israelis have claimed that the Palestine Arab leaders had ordered their people to depart until they could return with the victorious Arab armies, but the Arabs deny this. Erskine B. Childers, a British Journalist, made an effort to find some proof of the existence of the alleged orders. After checking the monitored record made by British and American sources of Arab radio broadcasts during the months in question and asking Israeli officials to show him whatever tangible proof they had supporting their claim, he reported in the May 21, 1961 issue of The *Spectator* that he had found "not a single order, or appeal . . . about evacuation from Palestine from any Arab nation, inside or outside of Palestine, in 1948"; and that, in fact, there was "repeated monitoring record of Arab appeals, even flat orders, to the civilians of Palestine to stay put" and not to leave.[21]

Israeli charges that many Arab officials had played politics with the refugee question have some validity. Nevertheless, certain other factors must also be taken into consideration. While various Arab leaders had at some time or another exploited the refugee situation, it would be incorrect to conclude that they were unconcerned about the plight of the refugees, that they were responsible for refugee demands for repatriation and that for purely selfish reasons, they did not really want to see the refugee problem resolved. UN and other neutral observers repeatedly emphasized in their reports that most of the refugees had on their own initiative desired and demanded the right to return to their homes and that this desire remained "unabated" over the years and even increased after the June War. In fact, the position of Arab officials on the subject of repatriation has been determined far more by the actual feelings and pressures of the refugees than by any other internal factor. Having kept alive for 2,000 years their desire to return to Israel, Israeli Jews should not find it difficult to understand the strong yearning of the Palestine Arabs to return to their homes and "homeland." Moreover, UNRWA reported that

> over the years, the . . . four host countries have shown deep concern in the well-being of the refugees. They have . . . given substantial direct help to the refugee community in the form of educational, health, administrative and other services and the provision of building sites, water, and security protection [at the cost of millions of dollars each year. The host nations have also] carried a burden no less real or costly, even though less tangible, in the form of the complex political and social

problems that stem from the presence of the refugees within their boundaries.

Actually, most Arab officials would have felt relieved of a heavy burden had the refugee question been satisfactorily resolved. Israel has played her own share of politics with the Arab refugees; Israeli officials had not hesitated to use the Arab refugees as a lever for acquiring more land (Gaza Strip) and for bringing the Arabs to the negotiating table. Finally, it was most unrealistic and unreasonable to expect the Arab governments to insist that the refugees give up the right to repatriation when year after year nearly all UN members, including Israel herself at one time, had voted for resolutions clearly providing for this right.

Israel was justified in being concerned about the possible harmful consequences of any large-scale repatriation. Yet she failed to weigh adequately the even greater long-range harm that could result from allowing the refugee situation to fester and grow more dangerous. Israel has contended that the acceptance of repatriation would result in a mass movement of one million hostile refugees determined to destroy her from within. Yet most neutral experts maintained, at least before the June War, that "probably less than 10 percent" (or roughly 100,000) of the refugees would actually have opted for repatriation once they were faced with a clear cut choice between repatriation to Israel and resettlement with compensation; and most of these would have come from those with family ties with Israeli Arabs and would generally have been the least likely to want to create trouble.[22] Besides, Resolution 194(III) already stipulated that only those refugees willing to live in peace with their neighbors would be allowed to return and any UN agency set up to supervise repatriation would carefully screen out security risks among those refugees asking for repatriation. Israel had already been able to integrate quite successfully over 200,000 Israeli Arabs; so another 100,000 carefully screened Arabs could also have been gradually absorbed without great danger. In fact, a full reunion of families would have enabled many Israeli Arabs to overcome any existing discontent and divided loyalties created by family separations; and the newly returned Arabs—especially if treated equitably and well by the Israelis—and the now more contented Israeli Arabs could have provided an essential bridge between Israel and the Arab world. Besides, in the long run, Israel's security would depend far more on the development of normal relations with and a general acceptance by her Arab neighbors than upon the actual number of Arabs living within her borders. Ironically, many of those same Israelis who had insisted, before the 1967 war, that Israel could never permit any significant refugee repatriation because of security reasons, are now insisting that Israel should annex the occupied territories, despite the fact that these contain more than a million Arabs who, if anything, are more hostile than ever before and could pose a far greater security problem for Israel than the one which would have been created by the repatriation of a considerably smaller number of much less bitter and militant Arab refugees.

Israel had apparently believed that, somehow with time, the UN would lose interest in the refugee situation and the Arab states would finally permit de facto resettlement—and the whole refugee dispute would just disappear. However, instead of disappearing with time, the unresolved refugee problem merely grew in scope and complexity, intensified Arab hatred, bitterness and frustration and caused more and more serious border strife and commando raids; these developments, in turn, made the Arabs less ready to accept Israel on any terms. Had Israel been willing to permit the return of those refugees opting for repatriation, especially in the early years when the refugee dispute was less complicated, then the biggest obstacle to Arab acceptance of her would have been removed and a peace settlement could very well have been reached. The Israelis cannot realistically depend on maintaining military superiority forever over the Arab world, which possesses considerably greater manpower and resources than they can ever hope to attain. By refusing repeatedly to abide by UN resolutions, Israel has helped to weaken the authority of the UN, upon whose future strength and effectiveness Israel's long-term security, like that of all small nations, ultimately depends. Moreover, if Israel does not make it possible for the refugees to achieve by peaceful means at least those rights established by UN resolutions, then the Arabs would become convinced that they are given no alternative to the use of force and war.

As a result of the June War, Israel found herself in control of one-half million Arab refugees, as well as over 700,000 Arabs in the conquered areas. Shortly after the June War, some Israelis urged their government to take the initiative in devising and carrying out a large-scale resettlement scheme in the Israeli-controlled territories which would help both to lessen the scope of the overall refugee problem and to show the world what the Arab states should have been doing. An official committee was created but, as of early 1970 at least, only very limited industrial and agricultural projects were actually provided by Israel to promote jobs and resettlement opportunities for the occupied areas. If she would help rehabilitate the refugees under her rule and allow many of the newly displaced Arabs to return to their homes and if the Israelis would give up their superior airs and begin to treat the Arabs on an equal basis and take Arab feeling more into consideration, then Israel could significantly reduce the scope and harmful consequences of the refugee problem and at least start building that vitally needed bridge of understanding with the Arab world. If she is ever going to complete that bridge she must, like the Arabs, be prepared to accept a final political settlement whose terms would be consistent with the UN resolutions.

ANALYSIS OF THE ARAB POSITION

The Arabs—because of their own overconfidence, ineptness, lack of flexibility and political, economic and military weakness—shared responsibility for the refugee situation. Many frightened and selfish Palestine Arab leaders fled at the first sign of trouble after the passage of the UN partition resolution in November 1947, leaving their people disorganized and an easy prey to rumors and fears. The intervention of the Arab armies on May 15, 1948 helped greatly to spread and intensify the existing conflict in Palestine, and this caused many Arabs to leave their homes; and, of course, the Arab defeat, as well as Israeli opposition, prevented the refugees from returning to their homes.

Whereas Israel tended to exaggerate the economic, social, political and security difficulties that would have been created for her by accepting repatriation, the Arabs tended to minimize them. Although some Arab delegates to the UN did, on a number of occasions, seek to allay Israeli fears regarding repatriation, many Arab leaders merely made bellicose statements which did not calm Israel's natural fears for her safety. Several Arab governments also began to arm and train thousands of refugees to form the nucleus of the Palestine Liberation Army. Arab officials at times spoke as if they expected the great majority of the refugees to be repatriated and the more extremist Arabs hoped that Israel could thereby be weakened, thus strengthening the Israeli claim that the repatriation of one million hostile refugees would undermine her very existence. The Arab leaders should have been aware that the more extreme they were in their demands, the more difficult it would be to persuade the Israelis to accept repatriation and the easier it would be for the Israelis to convince UN members that she was entitled to deny the refugees their right to return on grounds of security.

Arab officials should have made a greater effort to inform the refugees of the full meaning and implication of paragraph 11 of Resolution 194(III), particularly that it provided for the repatriation of only those refugees who agreed to "live in peace with their neighbors" in the state of Israel. While the Arab governments generally worked closely and constructively with UNRWA, according to UNRWA's own reports, in certain specific areas they did not cooperate as effectively as they should have, such as in the rectification of refugee rolls. The Arabs desperately needed UNRWA's assistance and they were the principal losers whenever the agency's position was weakened and its services hindered in any way. In fact as a result of the larger and more complicated refugee problem created by the June War, the Arabs found themselves in greater need of UNRWA, the UN, and the main financial supporters of UNRWA than ever before.

The Arabs should have had a greater awareness of the fact that, at least after the first couple of years, the refugee question could no longer be resolved in isolation from other Arab-Israeli disputes. The Arab defeat in the June War, however, did encourage some Arab leaders—such as those in Jordan, Lebanon and Egypt—to express more openly than before the realization that a final solution of the refugee question could be brought about only as part of an overall political settlement with Israel. These leaders indicated that they would consider accepting such a settlement but only if it was based completely on Security Council Resolution 242 of November 22, 1967 calling for repatriation or compensation of the 1948 refugees and return of all June 1967 refugees. But the less moderate Arab leaders have rejected this same resolution because it does not provide what they consider to be a "just" solution for the "Palestine Question." This serious division in the Arab world helps to undermine the ability of the moderate Arabs to press the UN to enforce its decisions on the refugees and other issues.

The Arab governments should try to close ranks and seek a lasting solution of all major Arab-Israeli differences on the basis of the November 22 resolution, for only this could open the way to a reasonably just settlement of the refugee question. However, from the Palestinian point of view, this solution will not right all the wrongs done to them; and the clear and public recognition of the existence of such wrongs and the initiation of serious efforts to rectify some of them are essential to any lasting settlement.

In the meantime, Arab officials could make every effort: (1) to seek UN and other outside economic aid to enable them to initiate large-scale development schemes which would improve the economic lot of their own nationals, as well as the refugees; (2) to be prepared to integrate economically and politically the greater part of the refugees who will ultimately prefer to be resettled in the Arab world rather than live in Israel; (3) to cooperate fully with all UNRWA and UN activities in the area; and (4) to avoid playing politics with any aspect of the refugee problem. It would be in the best interests of the refugees and of all Arabs if Arab leaders would try everything within their power to work toward alleviating the overall refugee situation.

CONCLUSIONS

Over the years, extensive and unnecessary misunderstanding of the basic factors and issues involved caused most UN members, including the major powers, to oversimplify the refugee problem, to overlook the human element which is most fundamental to the entire Arab-Israeli dilemma, to seek repeatedly and vainly for some simple economic panacea, to make the same costly mistakes over and over again and to waste much invaluable time. It would have been much easier to have resolved the refugee question in 1948 and 1949 when the whole issue was less complicated and when Arab-Israeli relations were not as bitter as they soon were to become. Unfortunately, no party took advantage of the relatively favorable opportunities which then existed for settling the problem.

It should now be obvious that, until the emotional climate in the Middle East vastly improves, until the Arabs and Israelis are finally ready to accept a just and lasting political solution of their basic differences and the UN and the big powers are prepared to apply effective pressures on the parties concerned, the Arab-Israeli dilemma will persist and a solution to the refugee problem will remain unattainable. Nevertheless, in addition to the actions by Arabs and Israelis noted earlier, constructive and helpful actions could and should, in the meantime, be taken.

UNRWA's mandate must be continued and the organization provided with sufficient funds to deal effectively with the old and the new refugee problems for as long as necessary. In the long run, it would be far less costly in lives and money for the United States (which has been the most important financial supporter of UNRWA) and other UN members to provide the additional funds desperately needed by UNRWA than to allow the already dangerous situation in the Middle East to deteriorate to the point where another war will become inevitable. In fact, UNRWA should be given adequate money not only to provide essential services to all types of refugees, but also to increase substantially its vocational and higher educational program so that increasing numbers of refugees will be able to acquire the skills and education required to enable them to find work and have some hope for a decent life whether they are ultimately repatriated or resettled.

Besides providing funds and other support to UNRWA, the big powers should: (1) seek a deeper understanding of all aspects of the refugee and other Arab-Israeli issues; (2) offer large-scale financial assistance to those governments in the Middle East that are prepared to initiate major development programs which would improve the economic well-being of the refugees, as well as their own citizens; (3) open their own gates to interested refugees; and (4) apply the required pressures on the parties directly concerned to encourage them to take those measures which would help, first, to reduce the scope of the refugee problem such as by pressing Israel, for instance, to allow the return of many more of the refugees from the June War) and, ultimately, to bring about an across-the-board political settlement. Such a settlement should be reasonably consistent with the principles set down by the UN resolution of November 22, 1967 and other pertinent UN resolutions which were passed unanimously or almost unanimously. Only in this way can a just and lasting solution of the Arab refugee and other Arab-Israeli issues be finally attained.

[1] A/648, II, Sept. 18, 1948, 1, 24; A/1905, Sept. 28, 1951, 1; Don Peretz, *Israel and the Palestine Arabs* (Washington, 1958), 6f; J.C. Hurewitz, *The Struggle for Palestine* (N.Y., 1950), 313f; George E. Kirk, *The Middle East, 1945-50* (London, 1954), 261, 263f; Menachim Begin, *The Revolt: Story of the Irgun* (London, 1951), 164f.

[2] Kirk, *op. cit.*, 264, 281; Kenneth Bilby, *New Star in the East* (Garden City, 1950), 31; Edgar O'Ballance, *The Arab-Israeli War, 1948* (New York, 1957), 147, 150, 171f; Harry Sacher, *Israel and the Establishment of a State* (London, 1952), 149; Jon Kimche, *Seven Fallen Pillars* (New York, 1953), 226f; Hal Lehrman, "The Arabs and Israel", *Commentary*, VIII, No. 6, Dec. 1949, 529f; John Bagot Glubb, *A Soldier with the Arabs* (N.Y., 1958), 162, 211, 251.

[3] S/1071, Nov. 6, 1948; S/1122, Jan. 26, 1949; S/1286, March 14, 1949; S/1286, March 14, 1949; S/1797, Sept. 18, 1950; S/2234, July 8, 1951; S/2300, Aug. 16, 1951; *NY Times*, Oct. 31, Nov. 1, 2, 7, 1948; March 11, 15, 1949; Glubb, *op. cit.*, 211.

[4] A/838, April 19, 1949, Part I, 1ff, 7; Part II, 7; A/992, Sept. 22, 1949, 4ff., 8.

[5] James G. McDonald, *My Mission in Israel* (N.Y., 1951), 175, 181, 184; Peretz, *op. cit.*, 41f; Bilby, *op. cit.*, 239.

[6] A/927, June 21, 1949, 4; A/992, 1-6; Peretz, *op. cit.*, 43ff; Kirk, *op. cit.*, 303; Bilby, *op. cit.*. 240.

[7] A/927, 7f, 11f; A/1367, 9, 45, 49; Peretz, *op. cit.*, 65; UN, Official Records of the Third Session of the General Assembly (UN, OR of 3rd Ses. of GA), Part II, 217th Plenary Meetings (PM), May 11, 1949, 330; UN, OR of 4th Ses of GA, *Ad Hoc* Political Committee, 44th Meeting, Nov. 25, 1949, 261ff; 49th, Nov. 29, 293ff; 59th, Dec. 6, 352ff.

[8] A/992, 9, 11, 13; A/1252, Dec. 14, 1949, 2; A/AC.25/6, Dec. 28, 1949, Part I, 3.

[9] A/1255, May 29, 1950, 2; A/1367, Sept. 22, 44; A/1451, Oct. 19, 20.

[10] A/2171, 1952, 2ff; A/2141/Add 1, 1952, 1f; A/2210, 1952, 5.

[11] A/2470/Add 1, 1; A/2978, 1955, 1-6; A/3931, 1958, 2; A/4213, 1959, 5; A/4478, 1960, 1.

[12] A/2171, 1-6; A/2470/Add 1; A/2712/Add 1, 1954, 1ff; A/2717, 1956, 1-6; A/2470/Add 1, 1; A/2470/Add 1, 1; A/4478, 1960, 1-5; UN, OR of the 9th Ses. of GA, *Ad Hoc* Pol. Com., 28th Nov. 16, 1954, 127.

[13] A/2978, 9; A/3686, 1947, 1f; A/3931, 1958, 1; A/4213, 1959, 2; UN, OR of 11th Ses. of GA, Spec. Pol. Com., 23rd, Feb. 11, 1957, 107; 12th Ses., Spec. Pol. Com, 64th, Nov. 18, 1957, 99.

[14] S/4270, Feb. 23, 1960; S/5401, Aug. 24, 1963; S/7573, Nov. 2, 1966; S/7668, Jan. 9, 1967; S/7673, Jan. 10, 1967; S/7675, Jan. 12, 1967; S/7680, Jan. 13; S/7843, April 7, 1967; S/7845, April 9, 1967; Maj. Gen. Carl von Horn, *Soldiering for Peace* (N.Y., 1967), 127ff; Fred J. Khouri, "Friction and Conflict on the Israeli-Syrian Front", *The Middle East Journal*, Winter-Spring 1963, 20ff; personal interviews with UN officials in the Middle East.

[15] Charles W. Yost, "The Arab-Israeli War: How It Began", *Foreign Affairs*, Jan. 1968, 305ff; John Badeau, "The Arabs, 1967", *Atlantic Monthly*, Dec. 1967, 109; Fred J. Khouri, *The Arab-Israeli Dilemma* (Syracuse, 1968), 242ff; Malcolm H. Kerr, *The Middle East Conflict* (Foreign Policy Association Headline Series No. 191, Oct. 1968), 11ff, 17ff.

[16] *New York Times*, June 12, 13, 25, 26, 1967, *The Economist*, June 19, 1967; S/8021, June 29, 1967, Annex I, 1.

[17] *New York Times*, July 3, 4, 15, Aug. 14, 21, 23, 25, Sept. 1, 2, Nov. 28, 1967; *Israel Digest*, July 14, 1967, 5; *The Evening Bulletin* (Philadelphia), July 3, 1967; A/AC.132/PV.1, Dec. 6, 1967, 6f; *The Times* (London), July 27, 1967; *Christian Science Monitor*, Aug. 1, 1967.

[18] *New York Times*, June 26, July 3, Aug. 14, 1967.

[19] A/SPC/SR.588, Dec. 18, 1967, 2ff; A/SPC/SR.594, Dec. 20, 2ff; *New York Times*, Dec. 22, 1969.

[20] *New York Times*, Dec. 10, 1969.

[21] According to George E. Kirk (*The Middle East*, 1945-50, pages 362f), "a subsequent Zionist assertion that . . . the Arab Higher Committee had 'called on the Arab population to leave the country en masse' should be treated with reserve in the absence of positive evidence to corroborate

it, but there can be no question that the publicity which the Arab press and radio gave to the massacre at Deir Yassin for the purpose of attracting sympathy greatly accelerated the demoralization and flight of non-combatant Arabs." According to Edgar O'Ballance (*The Arab-Israeli War*, 1948, page 171), the Palestine Arab strategy actually was "to wage an underground resistance campaign against the Jews in any areas where the Arabs were in the minority"—and this could be done only if the Arabs generally remained in their villages and not if they all left.

[22] *U.S. Foreign Policy: Middle East Staff Study Prepared for the Use of the Committee on Foreign Relations*, U.S. Senate, No. 13, June 9, 1960, 38f; Joseph E. Johnson, "Arab vs. Israeli: A Persistent Challenge to America", Address given before the American Assembly, Arden House, Harriman, N.Y., Oct. 24, 1963, 10; Institute for Mediterranean Affairs, *The Palestine Refugee Problem* (N.Y., 1958); *New York Times*, Oct. 20, Nov. 15, 1955; April 12, 1957; Morris Sacks, "Economic Illusions and Reality," *New Outlook*, March-April, 1963, 77; Z.K., "America and the Refugees," *New Outlook*, Feb., 1963, 9.

The Second Arab Awakening

JON KIMCHE

George Antonius completed his account of the first Arab Awakening 33 years ago, in 1937, with this significant passage.

> Jewish hopes have been raised to such a pitch that the nonfulfillment of the Zionist dream of a Jewish state in Palestine will cause intense disillusionment and bitterness . . . It would be an act of further cruelty to the Jews to disappoint those hopes if there existed some way of satisfying them that did not involve cruelty to other people. But the logic of facts is inexorable. It shows that no room can be made in Palestine for a second nation except by dislodging or exterminating the nation in possession.

In their way, these few sentences encompass the change that had come over the Arab dream as it appeared to the hopeful revolutionaries of 1917 and the disillusioned publicist of 1937; they also illustrate the anticipations of one of the most perceptive Arab nationalists in Palestine at a time when the Jewish fate in Europe and the Zionist dream in Palestine looked like certain lost causes. It is a passage that should serve as a warning to all of us inclined to make judgments about the next decade or two on the basis of existing circumstances.

We might therefore do worse than to begin with some reflection on the reasons for Antonius's false assumptions and for the failure of the first Arab awakening. These were not entirely

169

due to the defeat of Hitler's Germany in the war which Antonius had not anticipated; nor were they altogether a consequence of the subsequent erosion of British imperial supremacy in the Middle East. His greatest error—and that of many Arab nationalists in the 20 years between the Arab revolt in the Hejaz and that in Palestine in 1937—lay in the Arab preoccupation with Palestine at the expense of other no less vital questions, such as the future of Egypt and of the Fertile Crescent. It was a costly error, and one which Arab nationalists appear to be intent on repeating once more.

The Egyptian question, as we have seen, was soluble; so was that of the Fertile Crescent. Had they been settled first, then there would have been no difficulty in finding an acceptable settlement in Palestine without the conflict and bloodshed which befell its people. In fairness to the much, and wrongly, abused originators of the modern Middle East during and immediately after World War I, it must be emphasized that this was essentially their philosophy: Palestine was a secondary consideration in the shaping of the Middle East at that time by the British, the Hashemites and the Egyptian nationalists. Even for the Zionists of those years, Palestine was part of a much bigger scheme with which Syria and the Arab national movement were directly linked.

It is quite mistaken to assume, as Phillip Knightley and Colin Simpson have done in their recent book on Lawrence of Arabia that the first Arab awakening and the Paris settlement represented a conspiracy by the British or the Zionists against the Arabs. We shall never begin to understand the present situation if we persist in this approach to its origins. We have enough documentation available now—if it is honestly used, which is not always the case—to show that the British were openly pursuing British interests rather than those of the Arabs or the Zionists. By the same token, Chaim Weizmann and his colleagues were pursuing essentially Zionist objectives and King Husain and the Arab nationalist leaders were concerned with their own aims. But unlike many of the leaders who were to follow them, these men were statesmen, realists and consummate political opportunists.

A model example of the diplomacy of realism (compared to that practiced nowadays) can be found in the papers dealing with the meeting which took place between the Emir Faisal and Weizmann in June 1918, and Weizmann's subsequent discussions with members of the British "Arab Bureau"; and particularly relevant to this are the papers which have only recently become available of the ad hoc Jerusalem Committee of Palestinian Arabs formed by Mussa Kazem and Amin al Husaini (who was to become the Mufti of Jerusalem) which also held talks with Weizmann and the Zionist Commission.

We have now a full account in the minutes of the meeting near Aqaba on June 4, 1918. According to Colonel Pierre C. Joyce, who stood in for Lawrence—who was ill and could not make the journey—Faisal was greatly impressed by Weizmann's promise of Jewish support for the establishment of an Arab kingdom in Syria with Faisal as monarch. Weizmann also assured Faisal "that the Jews do not propose setting up a Jewish government but would work under British protection," but Faisal was much less interested in this assurance than were the British, who had insisted upon it. Faisal did not want to discuss at this stage the future of Palestine because he feared Turkish and German propaganda, but, speaking for himself, he told Weizmann that "he accepted the possibility of future Jewish claims to territory in Palestine."

Palestine was, however, only part of a larger settlement in both Weizmann's and Faisal's appreciations. On July 17, six weeks later, Weizmann wrote to Lord Balfour about the meeting and stressed that much would depend on the manner in which the British dealt with Faisal, who would have need of much support. "We shall come to his help," Weizmann added, "not as exploiters or concessionaires, but with sincere desire to co-operate with a race which is destined to hold an important position in the Middle East."

Understandably, every senior British official concerned with Middle Eastern politics wanted to know if this was really the Zionist intention or whether it was no more than an opportunist Zionist sprat to catch the Arab mackerel. Accordingly, the director of the Arab Bureau in Cairo, Colonel G.S. Symes, arranged to see Weizmann on his return from the encounter with Faisal. They met at Ramleh on June 9, 1918. Weizmann formally repeated the offer which he had already made to the British military governor, General Clayton, that the Zionist organization was prepared to recognize King Husain as the head of the Arab national movement and, acting as a private organization, offer substantial financial aid (the sum of $40 million was mentioned) for the development of the Hejaz; they would also undertake to organize support in America and in Europe for Syrian independence against either French or Turkish intervention. As soon as circumstances would permit, the Zionist organization would call a Jewish congress in Jerusalem, request a British protectorate over Palestine, declare a Zionist alliance with the Sharif of Mecca and give full support to the Syrian nationalists in their struggle for independence.

After talking with Egyptian and Syrian nationalist leaders, and discussing the Weizmann-Faisal encounter with them, Symes noted in a privately circulated memorandum to his superiors and colleagues that by paying lip-service to the ideals of (future) Arab unity and of Zionism, Britain might secure "the substance while formally renouncing the shadow of ownership and sovereignty over Arab lands; and by this renunciation strengthen our hands against the French political penetration in Syria, and allow Syrian prejudice, Moslem partiality and Zionist opportunism to combine and operate on behalf of pro-British and anti-Hun influences throughout the Arab countries."

This was politics in the grand manner, the only way in which it can be practiced effectively. Each of the principals, Faisal, Weizmann and the British were at this stage prepared to support the greater concept of an alliance from which each would draw some important benefits, and for which each one of the partners was taking a calculated political risk by making concessions to begin with. It might have worked, but it did not.

The British were the first to take fright. In a "secret note" written by Commander Hogarth while he was in Jeddah, either in August or September 1918, he counselled the British Government to "most strongly oppose any meeting between Weizmann and

King Husain." What the reasons were for this British objection is not absolutely clear, but they can be gauged from this and other reports. Hogarth was of the opinion that notwithstanding any assurances that Weizmann had given to the British and to Faisal, "Dr. Weizmann hopes for a completely Jewish Palestine in 50 years ... " He also expressed concern at the possible consequences (for the British, presumably) of the combination of American and European Jewish capital and Syrian and other Arab enterprise. Be that as it may, there was no further British encouragement for too intimate Arab-Zionist collaboration; the French followed the same course.

But, curiously, the strongest support for this British policy of counteracting these initial attempts to reshape the Middle East by means of a combined Arab-Zionist approach, came from the Jerusalem committee of Palestinian Arab nationalists. The committee had been alarmed by the return of Amin al-Husaini from the Hashemite camp where he had acted as a liaison officer. He told the members of the committee that the Hashemites had become "a servile instrument of British imperialism;" he advised them, therefore, to pursue an independent Palestinian policy and to play off the British against the French, and the Jews against both. Unless they managed to drive a wedge between the Jews and the British, he argued, the Jews would win control over Palestine. He urged the committee to establish contact with the Zionist commission so as to find out more about Jewish intentions. The chairman of the committee, the venerable mayor of Jerusalem, Mussa Kazem, advised General Clayton of these supposedly secret talks with the Zionists; Sir Ronald Storrs and Colonel Waters-Taylor (a strong opponent of the Zionists) were also kept informed by Kazem.

It was largely due to this Palestinian intervention that the British were successful in their opposition to the more imaginative concepts of Faisal and Weismann. Amin al-Husaini effectively managed to drive the desired wedge between the British and the Jews. But his calculation was wrong: without this "wedge," which forced the Zionists to take independent action in Palestine, it is questionable whether a Jewish state would have been possible.

This, then, is one of the principal lessons of the first Arab awakening: without the British opposition to the wider collaboration between Zionists and the Arab nationalists, there would not have been this concentration on the Palestinians as the central factor; and without the Palestinian attempt to drive a wedge between the British and the Zionists, the extreme solution of 1948 would not have happened.

There is however one further aspect of the first awakening that needs to be emphasised before we can turn to the problems of the second awakening: in the years after World War I, and indeed during the war, none of the nationalist groups involved in the Middle East had imagined that it could achieve its objective against the will of the Great Powers concerned. The Arab nationalists in the Hejaz, in Syria and in Egypt sought an acceptable arrangement with the British or the French; and, similarly, the Zionists. All they were concerned with during the war was to be on the winning side, otherwise their cause would be lost. And, in a sense, this was also true of the subsequent negotiations at the Paris Peace Conference. It was a crucial distinction from the events that were to shape the second Arab awakening.

No new Arab—or for that matter, Zionist—awakening accompanied the outbreak of the second world war. As in 1914, the major protagonists in the Middle East looked to one side or the other for victory and linked their cause with that of the British or the Germans. The Jews in Palestine had no choice; they had to go along with the British. But across the board of Arab politics many differing variants of political consideration dictated local policy. Strangely, though, the British now made a classic miscalculation: they assumed that Arab support against the Axis could be purchased by concessions to the Palestinian Arab demands. Accordingly, they moved the Palestine question into the center of the political stage and angered the Jews by substantial gestures that were intended to convince the Arab leadership of Britain's intention to ensure Arab rights in Palestine. It was, in fact, this policy that persuaded George Antonius to write the passage that I quoted earlier. Britian's policy had convinced him that the cause of Zionism in Palestine was doomed.

But then, as now, concessions in Palestine or to the Palestinians did not guarantee Arab support for the British and their allies. It did not work in Iraq or Syria; it did not affect the nationalists in Egypt or King Ibn Saud. Palestine, the British discovered, was one thing; the national interest of the separate Arab states was another. So long as a British defeat at the hands of the Germans seemed certain, few hands in support of the British were raised in the Middle East. The Emir Abdullah of Transjordan was one of the few, the Wafd leadership in Egypt was another. But by and large, the Arab leadership in Palestine and Iraq, in Syria and Lebanon doubted that the British would be on the winning side; they remained either on the sidelines or they joined the Axis.

This illustrates that the political standards of World War I still prevailed during the first years of World War II. None of the leading nationalists spoke of upsetting the social structure or of revolution. Although the Paris settlement of 1919 had been undermined and the process of liquidation begun as soon as it had been completed, in another sense, perhaps the most telling one, the framework set in Paris was retained even after World War II. The League of Arab States inititated by the British was merely one more effort to underpin the superstructure of 1919. The fact that Egypt, Syria, Iraq and Transjordan were now independent countries did not alter the basic pattern of the Middle East, except that French influence had lessened and that of the British increased.

The British first broke the Paris pattern and gave continuing impetus to its liquidation, which began in 1947 and reached its climax 20 years later in 1967. When the British Government sought in 1945 an accommodation with the Arab League, and then, after the war, refused to implement the partition of Palestine and to align itself with the Americans and the Soviet Union, Amin al-Husaini's "wedge" became fully operative: British policy forced the Jews in Palestine into an act of open rebellion against the Middle Eastern system established by the British.

Indeed, looked at from the narrow confines of the Palestine problem, this rebellion in the immediate postwar years could have been described as the natural conclusion of the Paris settlement— the implementation of the Balfour Declaration, the last outstanding act of the Paris peacemakers. But to consider it only in this light is again to fall into the trap of viewing the Middle East from the point of view of Palestine—a false center.

For the real significance of the 1947 Palestine settlement was that it was legitimized by the United Nations and, even more important, that it was initiated and backed by the two Great Powers that had not been a part of the Paris settlement, the United States and the Soviet Union. The entrance of the Soviet Union signified the real change that had taken place. The Paris settlement of 1919 had been predicated on keeping the Soviet Union out of Europe and the Middle East. The 1947 settlement marked the beginning of the return of the Soviet Union, but still no more than a beginning. Had the Arabs and the British then prevailed against the Israelis, the process of revolution and change in the Middle East would have been considerably delayed, though not averted. But it would have certainly taken place within the old Paris framework. In fact, after the Israeli success of 1948 it seemed that the Soviet Union also would be unable to change the basic Versailles pattern.

The principal reason for this was the British attitude to any possible Arab-Israeli compact. One of the unmentionable precepts of British policy in the Middle East was the prevention of a possible alliance of Jew and Arab against the British. It was never spelled out in so many words, but the record is indisputable. We have already discussed the Faisal-Weizmann talks of 1918; there had been other opportunities in Egypt and Iraq for an arrangement during and immediately after the war but these foundered because of the fundamental opposition of the British and also because of the singularly inept approach of the Zionists at the time. In 1947, King Abdullah was prepared to initiate negotiations with the Jewish leaders in Palestine, but he was firmly dissuaded by the British Foreign Office and warned not to isolate himself from the other Arab countries.

By 1950, however, King Abdullah was prepared to risk British ire and the consequences of isolation. He agreed to negotiate a nonaggression pact with Israel. He was again warned not to proceed and in July 1951 he was assassinated. At least one prominent Palestinian—one of the counsel engaged for the defense at the subsequent trial of the alleged assassins—has since maintained that Abdullah's death was not unconnected with his persistence in seeking a negotiated settlement with Israel. There is no conclusive evidence, only the lingering suspicion that the accusation might be justified.

There was another fleeting opportunity in 1953, initiated by Ralph Bunche, but lost in the sands of the Negev and the perambulations of British officials. The full story of this interlude remains to be told on another occasion. But the pattern effectively set in 1918 continued to impress itself. So long as the British had a role to play in the Middle East, they wanted no influential partners, not the French, not the Americans and certainly not an Arab-Jewish alliance. It was not machiavellianism, only the most basic self-interest. And during the years from the first Arab awakening in 1916 to the Suez shambles in 1956, one central factor keeps recurring in the British calculations: the Palestinians, or, to put it in another way, the Balfour Declaration. Both—taken together—guaranteed continuing Mid-Eastern disunity and British hegemony.

The entry of the Soviet Union into the Middle Eastern arena in 1956, for the second time in the company of the United States, changed the situation substantially. On this occasion, the British were again opposed to the Russians but so were the Israelis. The policy changes so effectively carried out by the Soviet Union between 1947 and 1956 established the Russians in the position previously occupied by the British. They had a foothold in Egypt but little else that was effective: to expand Soviet influence they had to take a leaf out of the British book. In doing this the Russians needed patience and the assistance of Israel's unperceptive foreign policy. The Israelis had assumed since the end of the war in 1948 that time was on their side, and were strongly reinforced in this belief by the Sinai campaign of 1956. The ten year's peace, from 1957 to 1967, seemed to bear out this Israeli assumption, all the more so in the light of the outcome of the Six Day War in June 1967. Once more, however, this is true only if viewed in strictly Palestinian terms, or as merely one more encounter in a continuing war.

But in another sense, it marks a return to the familiar British pattern. Only now the Soviet Union had taken the place of the British, an advancing imperialism practicing a forward policy in place of a retreating one seeking a progressive disengagement. And just as the British used the Palestinians to provide the divisive factor in the conflict with the Jews and to justify their continuing presence in the area, so are the Russians now using the Palestinians, not only to justify their own expansion into the Middle East but also to keep the Eygptians, the Iraqis and the Jordanians in a dependent position that will make any Arab-Israeli settlement impossible.

The first victim of an Arab-Israeli settlement on whatever terms would be the Soviet presence in the Middle East, and the immediate beneficiary would be the United States. As long as the Palestinian leadership remains, aligned with the tight ruling group of Fatah and the other smaller Palestinian groups associated with the Syrian and Egyptian governments, the Soviet position in the Middle East is assured: no terms which the United States government or the Israeli government can offer would be acceptable to the Palestinians and therefore to the Soviet Union. It is the Soviet Union which has been the ultimate arbiter, not President Nasser, not King Hussein, not Yasir Arafat and not Golda Meir. We are back with Hogarth in 1918, with Anthony Eden in 1944, with Ernest Bevin in 1950, with the frustrations of the first Arab awakening: the exploitations of the Palestinian issue to maintain an imperial presence; the prevention of an Arab-Jewish rapprochement at all cost. Then the British, now the Russians.

In short, the second Arab awakening has not yet happened. On the contrary, the decolonization of the Middle East and North Africa has turned sour. In its place, there is a new form of recolonization in progress. The Americans in Morocco and Tunisia, the French in Algeria and Libya (where they may turn out to be no more than the pace-makers for the Soviet Union, as in Iraq), the Russians in Egypt and the Sudan, in Syria and in Iraq, in Southern Arabia and East Africa, are poised for the penetration of the Persian Gulf states. Jean-Jacques Berreby has estimated that before 1980, Soviet interests will directly or indirectly control most of the oil in the Middle East. By the end of 1970, the Middle East and North Africa will have arms contracts with the Soviet Union, the United States, France and Great Britain in excess of five billion dollars, a form of recolonization that has no parallel in the heyday of imperialism in India or Africa. All this has to be paid for in oil concessions, in strategic commitments, however defined or described, and by direct political dependence. This is the price the Arab countries of the Middle East and North Africa, Israel and also Iran have to pay for the continuing Arab-Israeli conflict.

The alternative is the second Arab awakening, a task infinitely greater than the first awakening, requiring not only leadership but also imagination, and demanding not only a second Arab awakening but also a second Israeli awakening. Against the forces now mustered against them, the whole economic and diplomatic weight of the superpowers backed by the lesser European powers, only a combined effort by all the countries of the Middle East and North Africa can avert their total recolonization.

It is much easier to tabulate what needs to be done than to find ways of doing it. But at least we need to see the priorities in proper order against their background of 50 years of conflict and regression. In the first place, there is the time factor. There is no need to overdramatize this; there has already been too much of the "unless there is a speedy settlement" talk with its dire predictions, of imminent catastrophe. As things are, there is still time enough to seek a settlement without the outbreak of another major conflict. What, then, can set the stage for the second Arab awakening?

In the first place the recognition that the continuing Arab-Israeli conflict will make it impossible for the countries of the Middle East and North Africa to halt the process of recolonization with all the attendant risks of a clash between the superpowers and the entry of China into the arena before long. It is thus of primary importance that Israel, Egypt, Jordan and the Palestinians find a political way towards a peace settlement. It will also require a new policy on the part of Israel and the Arab countries toward any elements, be they Palestinians, Israelis, Maoists or Muslim brethren, who seek to perpetuate the conflict.

The Israelis have missed the very real opportunities they had after June 1967 to reach a separate peace with a Palestinian national entity and it is unlikely that the opportunity will recur. Similarly, the divisions among the Palestinians, the intransigence of Fatah, and the timidity of most of the leaders of the West Bank, rule out even the prospect of an Arab-sponsored Palestinian entity. The rigid policies of the Israeli Government and the extreme formulations of Fatah and other Palestinian organizations may well mean that the possibility of establishing a Palestinian Arab state has been lost once more—largely by the Palestinians themselves.

This leads us to conclude that the second Arab awakening will not be able to take place within the political and geographic framework of the first Arab awakening, that of the Paris Peace Settlement of 1919. Somehow, the new Middle East will have to reconstitute itself to absorb the full implications of the coming changes, partly by natural evolution as may now be happening, as between Egypt, Libya and the Sudan; partly by revolution to unite Iraq with the Gulf States and join Northern, Central and Southern Arabia in a natural unit.

The failure of the Israelis and Palestinians to agree on a politically viable solution that would link the two in some form of federated unit has raised the question again whether a more natural unit for the Palestinians would not be a state which links parts of the West Bank with Jordan and Syria in a federated republic which might also absorb the northern and Muslim parts of Lebanon. That leaves the possibility of establishing a "Levant Federation" comprising a part of Lebanon (including Beirut), Israel and the Sinai peninsula to the Suez Canal. Such units would have at least a chance of reasserting their political and economic independence, and also obtain a realistic relationship with the superpowers and the consumer-powers that are again increasingly interested in the oil resources of the region.

The essence of the second Arab awakening is not, however, confined to geography. In terms of a radically changing future, the relationship and possible association of the Levant Federation with the United Arab Republic of Egypt, Libya and the Sudan, will be of much greater moment than the real and imagined injustices of the past. For the peoples of the Middle East, especially Jews and Arabs, have been as much in chains to their political and philosophic traditions as they were to the ortho-doxies of their religions and the domination of foreign powers.

The question that now confronts the new generation of leaders—and this applies particularly to the Israelis and the Palestinians—is whether they can look ahead far enough without being dragged down into the past, whether they can liberate themselves from the legacies of the first Arab and Israeli awakening and from the thinking, politics and leaders who still thrive on it.

From *The Second Arab Awakening* by Jon Kimche. Copyright ©1970 by John Kimche. Reprinted by permission of Holt, Rinehart and Winston, Inc. and Thames and Hudson Ltd., Great Britain.

Demography and Geography
in Palestine

SAMUEL MERLIN

Palestine, especially during the last 200 years of the Ottoman rule, was plagued by the ancient custom of blood-feud between tribes, clans and families. Generation after generation, families kept up the vendetta for no plausible reason, as the precise cause of the original feud became either obscured beyond recognition—if not forgotten altogether—or no longer relevant to contemporary circumstances. Thus, the shedding of blood became self-perpetuating, with no clearly defined purpose. Of course, all this is not peculiar to the Arabs of Palestine or to Arabs in general. Indeed, history shows us that many religious wars, especially those waged by Christendom, took on the same senseless continuity.

I mention this irrational custom because there is a definite danger that present-day Israeli-Arab conflict is in the process of becoming self-perpetuating without due consideration of real issues involved. As the conflict grows wider, with new participants becoming embroiled and joining the fray, the aims, aspirations and claims of the original antagonists—the Palestinian Arabs and the Jews of Israel—become ever more blurred, confused and perverted.

It is often asserted that the conflict is between two nationalisms—Israeli and Palestinian Arab—over the rule and jurisdiction of the same country. Such a premise implies that two concrete national entities are claiming the right to self-determination and sovereignty within a concrete territory. This assertion appeals to our predilection for clearly defined and logical formula, but the realities are much more complicated.

Let us leave formula aside for the present and take a closer look at these realities. Who is fighting whom, and where? Who are the national entities involved and what is the geographic framework within which the conflict is waged? Who are the protagonists of the dispute, and what are its territorial dimensions?

We know that Pakistani, Iraqi and Saudi Arabian military units are stationed in Jordan, ostensibly to fight Israel. Yet, there is some suspicion in Amman that though they are now on the firing line against "the Zionist enemy," the Iraqis and the Saudis eventually may harbor designs against Jordan rather than against Israel. It is also known that Algerians are stationed on the Suez Canal fighting alongside the Egyptians. El Al airplanes and offices are attacked by Palestinians on Swiss, German, Belgian, British, Dutch and Greek soil. Black Panthers in the United States and New Leftists in Germany and a dozen other countries on the European continent are agitating for the liquidation of the state of Israel, and for the establishment of some kind of a "secular" Arab-Moslem, "democratic" Socialist state. A pan-Moslem summit conference held recently in Rabat, Morocco in December 1969, was originally convened in connection with the fire set to al-Aksa mosque by a Christian madman from Australia. The ostensible purpose of the conference was the protection of the Moslem shrines under Israeli occupation and control. But as soon as the conference was inaugurated, its participants unanimously proclaimed their solidarity with the Palestinian fedayeen (whose leader, Yasir Arafat, was honored and feted at the conference) and pledged moral, political, financial and eventually, perhaps, military aid—for the term Jihad (holy war) was used time and again during the proceedings.

The Soviet Union is, as we know, actively involved in the war. It extends almost unlimited economic, financial, political and military aid to the governments of the "progressive" Arab states—Egypt, Syria, Iraq and Algeria—but not to Jordan and Lebanon, although these are the main bases and fronts of the Palestinians. Perhaps as many as 8,000 Russian advisers are reported to be operating on practically all levels of the Egyptian army. In 1956, in the wake of the Sinai campaign, the Russians threatened to send "hundreds of thousands of volunteers" to fight against the Israelis. The question now is how long it will take the Soviets to replace their advisers with "volunteers?"

The fedayeen ostensibly fight for the rights of the Palestinian people, the right to self-determination in their own country. But from their literature and their public statements one gets the impression that Palestine is only an excuse, or at best an instrument for quite different aims, such as the unification of all the Arabs into one nation, social revolution in the Arab world ("the road to Tel Aviv passes through Amman, Beirut, Riad, Kuwait and even Cairo and Damascus"), and sometimes even world revolution of all the oppressed and downtrodden people on the globe.

So, we may ask, what are the fedayeen fighting for? For Palestine? For the "uma al-Arabia" (the Arab nation stretching from the Persian Gulf to the Atlantic Ocean)? Or for social revolution?

These questions are relevant, because if the dispute is over Palestine, then Israel can do something about it. If the Palestine issue serves other purposes, Israel can contribute little towards a constructive solution, except perhaps that its very existence may serve as some kind of a catalyst in the Arab world.

But what is Arab nationalism? What is an Arab?

In commenting upon the recent Arab summit Conference (of heads of state) and its dismal failure, Hassanein Heykal, the editor of the prestigious *Al Ahram*, and confidante of President Nasser, wrote, "Egyptian nationalism, which constitutes the keystone of the struggle against Israel, has to become stronger than Arab nationalism."

What kind of double-talk is this? If there is such a thing as an uma al-Arabia—a unified Arab nation—then there must also be Arab nationalism. And if there is such a thing as Arab nationalism, how could there at the same time also be Egyptian nationalism—a nationalism which claims precedence over Arab nationalism? It is as if a Brazilian journalist would proclaim that from now on we have to strengthen Brazilian nationalism at the expense of Latin American nationalism; as if there is such a thing as a Latin American nation. Perhaps in the future there will emerge a Latin American nation. But then there will no longer be Brazilian nationalism, as in the United States there is no longer a New York or a Rhode Island nationalism, though there still are various vestigial, local, parochial, regional interests, loyalties and customs. There is not yet such a thing as a pan-Arab nation; whether the various Arab peoples, tribes and religious communities inhabiting the approximately 14 states claiming Arabism will one day become one nation is yet to be seen. For the time being it is a myth.

Indeed, in the same article Heykal dismissed the whole Arab world as nothing but a conglomorate of selfish, materialistic people who have the means but not the will to fight:

> The hundred million Arabs are not just poor devils without means. Their aggregate revenues amount to more than 15 billion pounds per year. Their possibilities should have assured them victory, but they are paralyzed by the absence of a common political willpower.

Yet, the 100 million Arabs, or those who call themselves Arabs, *are* involved—to one degree or another, willingly or by coercion—in the Palestinian conflict. Now, when Arabs fight Israelis, what are they fighting for, geographically speaking; and for whom are they fighting? What precisely do they try to liberate, and whom?

We cannot and must not treat these questions exclusively on the background of the Six Day War. That war was not the beginning of the conflict, but only a phase of it, an eruption of a dispute that goes back to the years following immediately World War I, to the issuance of the Balfour Declaration and the promulgation of the mandate over Palestine. Hence, it is not enough to say that the conflict concerns the territories conquered in 1967. Of course, Egypt, Jordan and Syria are anxious to get back the respective territories that they lost to the Israelis. But regardless of the urgency of these territorial claims, in themselves they are not the cause of the conflict, nor would the return of these territories constitute a final solution to the conflict.

ARAB PROPAGANDA AND ARAB AIMS

Arab propaganda is being repeated daily from hundreds of platforms at university campuses, international and national conferences in various lands on all continents, in newspapers, magazines and other mass media throughout the world. This propaganda tries to convey that there was a land called Palestine, which was inhabited, since time immemorial, by a Palestinian Arab Nation, though it didn't enjoy the trappings of independence. Then, after World War I, the Jews came in successive waves, conquered the land, and exiled its people, as the Romans did to the Judeans, or even worse, as the nineteenth and twentieth century colonialists did in Africa and Asia. However, while the latter merely conquered the lands and exploited and subjugated the native peoples, the Jews exiled the Arabs, and made a whole nation homeless.

Though this picture is false in every respect, by force of continuous and practically unchallenged repetition, it is being increasingly widely accepted. This is primarily because precise terms of reference are never adhered to. The Arabs and their apologists use interchangeably the terms: Palestine, the Palestinian nation, the rightful owners of Palestine, the Arab homeland, part of the Arab Nation's fatherland, the home, the right of the Arabs to return to their homes, and most frequently of all, the cherished slogan, "the plundered fatherland."

Let us try to pin down some of these floating arguments. When the Arabs speak of liberating the plundered fatherland, what precisely do they mean, geographically speaking? What was the fatherland that now has to be liberated? Liberated by whom? From whom?

To listen to Arab propagandists—and the whole war, though bloody and cruel, is essentially a war of propaganda on both sides—one gets the impression that by 1948 the Palestinian Arabs had lost, territorially, everything. The rhetoric of their territorial claims did not change for the next two decades; Israel's conquests of 1967 only accentuated them. The Arabs speak now of regaining the plundered fatherland, or whatever other term they use interchangeably, exactly as they have spoken ever since 1948.

But this claim, and our impression of it is, of course, erroneous. It was false after 1948 and is false even after 1967. For the territory of Israel is not equal to the territory of mandated Palestine on both sides of the Jordan: it constitutes only a part of it, and though substantial, territorially it is nonetheless the minor part. Israel proper, that is, without the occupied territories in 1967, covers an area of less than 20 percent of mandated Palestine containing, however, about 60 percent of the population of Palestine. [1] (Again exclusive of the population now under Israeli jurisdiction in the occupied territories).

For the Arabs to claim that Israel is territorially the same as the whole of Palestine, is like Mexico asserting that California is the equivalent of the whole of Mexico; or a Frenchman between the wars to claim that Alsace-Lorraine is the equivalent of France. It is true that California was a province of Mexico, and Alsace-Lorraine a province of France. So what is now Israel was part of mandated Palestine.

Whether from the point of view of justice and human progress it would have been preferable for California to remain Mexican, and for the Israeli part of Palestine to have remained Arab, is a different question and a matter of complicated evaluation. At this stage we are talking about facts, definitions and matters of reference. We should keep in mind, however, that Israel did not come into being by conquest but as a combined result of both resistance to the British occupier, and the United Nations' sanction of Jewish national aspirations by voting for the partition of Palestine into two states.

When the Arabs assert that they are fighting for the liberation of Palestine—and this they proclaimed from the very moment they took up arms against the partition of Palestine in 1947—one should always keep in mind that this is a misnomer. They cannot possibly fight for the liberation of what they already possess. For after the British relinquished the mandate and withdrew, in 1948, from what was left of mandated Palestine (west of the Jordan River), the bulk of that country was already under Arab jurisdiction, and only the smaller part became the territory of the state of Israel. Hence, the Arabs fought and continue to fight not for the liberation of a country as a whole, as, let us say, the Algerians fought the French, or the subjugated peoples of Europe fought the Germans during World War II, but to recover a part of what they consider to be their country; namely, that part of Palestine which became the state of Israel.

True, the Six Day War and the Israeli conquests brought about a substantial upset in the equilibrium that prevailed practically since 1948. This equilibrium was shattered not so much because Israel conquered the vast territories of the Sinai peninsula, but because it occupied the West Bank. Though territorially it involves only about 2,000 square miles, demographically, the relationship between the two parts of Palestine— Israel and Jordan— underwent a radical change and created a most confused situation. If the occuupation continues for a protracted length of time, the demographic character of the two parts of Palestine may become so confused that no constructive solution may be possible for decades to come. It therefore stands to reason that the occupation of the West Bank by Israel is only temporary and transient. There is little doubt that regardless of what Israeli politicians have proclaimed about retaining Shkem, Hebron, and other places, in the end Israel will relinquish the entire West Bank, against firm security guarantees and built-in safeguards to which she is entitled. But the Palestinians and their sponsors, supporters and apologists don't say they are fighting to recover the West Bank. They use the same slogans that Ahmed Shukairy used before 1967, and Fawzi al Kaukji used before 1948: the liberation of Palestine, as if Israel is equated territorially to Palestine.

There is something contemptuous on the part of those who relentlessly use this slogan, and it is an affront to those who know anything about the political history of the Middle East. Palestine, after all, is not a geographical abstraction, or a terra incognita sunk under the sea. It is, in modern terms, a territory with defined frontiers and an internationally recognized identity. It is the country on both sides of the Jordan River that was administered by Great Britain under the mandate of the League of Nations between 1922 and 1946. Originally the mandate included the whole of Palestine as the territory for the implementation of the Jewish national home (whatever that term might have meant). But as a result of big-power intrigues the

British quite arbitrarily decided in 1922 to withhold the application of the mandate's clauses concerning the Jewish national home in regard to the territory East of the Jordan. But the mandate itself was not abrogated over Transjordan, and the same British High Commissioner was responsible for the administration of the whole of Palestine—both East and West of the Jordan River. The High Commissioner submitted an annual report to the League of Nations that covered the entire area of Palestine, and not only that concerning the Jewish national home. This, as mentioned, lasted until 1946 when the League of Nations was dissolved and the British, under the circumstances, felt obliged to grant Transjordan the status of a quasi-independent state. Clearly, the fact that the Jews were forbidden to settle in Transjordan, and after the war of 1948 also in the West Bank (occupied by the Arab Legion) made these territories all the more Palestinian-Arab.

Against this background, and within the prevailing geopolitical realities in the Arab world, the term "liberation" as used by the Palestinians and their apologists can mean only the liquidation of the state of Israel and the mass slaughter of her people. One should not view lightly the danger of genocide. It is real: the Arabs heartily slaughter each other in Iraq, Yemen, in the Sudan; and feuds have occurred between fellow Palestinians in Gaza and in Jordan, and between Palestinians and fellow Arabs in Lebanon. Why should we doubt that genocide against the Israelis is possible if the opportunity presents itself. The concept of liberation is also misused by many Israelis. One does not liberate inanimate objects, stone, land or the desert. One either liberates or subjugates people, the territory being incidental. The Israelis would not consider themselves liberated by Fatah, nor do the Arabs of the West Bank consider themselves liberated by the Israeli army.

At any rate, the Palestinians and their fellow Arabs from the neighboring countries will sooner or later have to make up their minds as to their precise territorial objective. If it is the liquidation of Israel, then they should not expect Israel to acquiesce. One does not invite a nation to commit suicide. Israel certainly has enough military power to continue to inflict defeat, humiliation and suffering on her enemies as long as she feels that she fights for her very existence. Both the Arabs and the Israelis (who are no less vague than the Arabs) will have to introduce some rationality into their thinking concerning the territorial delineation of their respective states. Until they do, all their talk about a political solution or peaceful settlement is nothing but deceit, or, at best, a dialogue of the deaf.

PALESTINIAN SELF-DETERMINATION

There is an inner consistency in Arab mythomania: if Israel is territorially synonymous with Palestine then, of course, the Arab population was exiled and made into refugees. The plundered fatherland and the homeless people driven into exile, by Zionist colonialism backed by American imperialism, are the two inseparable aspects of the Arab propaganda package. This is not to belittle the human tragedy of the displaced Palestinians, or to deny them their birthright in the whole of Palestine. It is only an attempt, probably futile, to put things in a more realistic perspective. If in checking propaganda against facts we find that Israel is not territorially synonymous with the whole of Palestine, then we must conclude that the assertion that a whole people has been made homeless and driven into exile also misrepresents reality.

It is true that as a result of the war in 1948 hundreds of thousands of Palestinian Arabs fled from that part of the country that became Israel. But they did not flee into exile as let us say, did the Hungarians who fled to England or America after their revolt was crushed in 1956, or the Czechs who now find themselves as refugees in Europe and in America. What happened to the Arabs of Palestine during the war in 1948 was that most of them fled from one part of their country, Palestine, to another part of the same country. Hence, they became what one might call displaced people in their own country. Individually and humanly this may not diminish the tragedy, the sufferings, the anguish, the bitterness of having lost their individual homes, fields, factories and places where they lived and felt at home. But this tragedy is not of a nation but of a large number of individuals.

After the war in 1948 four-fifths of the refugees still found themselves inside Arab Palestine (West Jordan, Transjordan and the Gaza Strip). Well over half of all the displaced Arabs became subjects of the Hashemite Kingdom and until the war in 1967 played an active and sometimes a decisive political role in the country. Practically all of the Palestinians and Jordanians, to my knowledge—and I have spoken personally to hundreds of them—consider the state of Jordan (east and west of the river) as synonymous with Palestine. There are differences, rivalries and animosities between the Bedouins of Transjordan and the Palestinians from Western Palestine; between the king and some leaders of the Palestinians; but these are normal differences and much more manageable than in many another country. The dispute is not whether Jordan and Palestine are the same, but who should have the decisive policy-making power in that country. Hussein and his loyal advisors believe in the legitimacy of the Hashemite rule. But many Palestinians (it is impossible to evaluate their number) especially from among the intelligentsia, consider themselves intellectually superior to the Bedouins of the East Bank and, therefore, feel justified to rule the country. But these are, so to speak, family rivalries and not a conflict between two nationalities. That is why most of the notables on the West Bank, now under Israeli control, when interviewed about their wives and desirata as to the future of the occupied territory, declare that first of all it should be returned to Hussein. They add that after that perhaps plans will be discussed about the internal and constitutional relationships between the Palestinians and Jordanians.

This attitude is shared both by King Hussein and the fedayeen leader, Yasir Arafat. The former declared that after the recovery of the West Bank he will let the Palestinians decide for themselves whether they choose to administer the recovered territory as an autonomous province or to revert to the previous constitutional arrangements. Arafat has resisted the mounting pressure from various non-Palestinian Arabs to proclaim a provisional Palestinian government, either clandestinely and symbolically in the West Bank, or in "exile." He rejects this idea not only to avoid an open conflict with Hussein but also, to forestall any belief that the fighting Palestinians limit their territorial claim only to the territories west of the Jordan River. He is determined to avoid another partition of Palestine. Arafat, like the previous head of the Palestinian Liberation Organization, Ahmed Shukairy, considers the territories east and west of Jordan to be one country. As far as these patriots are concerned, history knows only one Palestine, extending from the Mediterranean to the Iraqi and Syrian deserts. Hussein also considers the parts of Palestine on either side of the Jordan River as one country, and all its inhabitants as one people. That is why he granted full citizenship en masse to the refugees, though they outnumbered more than two to one the autochthonous Bedouin Jordanian population. In line with this reasoning Hussein seemed to have decided to completely liquidate the refugee camps as soon as possible. Of course, the Six Day War interrupted the rehabilitation and integration of the Palestinians into the Arab part of the country. But there is no reason to doubt that after Israeli withdrawal from the West Bank, this process of rehabilitation and integration will be renewed with greater vigor and effectiveness, probably with Israeli and international assistance.

ARABS AND JEWS IN NINETEENTH CENTURY PALESTINE

There is one more part of the Arab propaganda package that requires analysis. In countless books, pamphlets, articles, not only those of pro-Arab bias but even those of impartial or objective content, dealing with the Palestine conflict and its origins, one invariably finds comparative population statistics. How many Arabs and how many Jews were there in Palestine in 1917 (at the issuance of the Balfour Declaration); in 1920 and 1922 (dates concerning the mandate of the League of Nations); then in every consecutive year dealing with one aspect or another of the Palestine situation; and lastly in 1947, when the United Nations decided about partition and in 1948 when the state of Israel was proclaimed and the Arab-Israeli war started in earnest? These statistics show that at each of these consecutive dates the Jews were few and the Arabs many. Thus, in 1917 on an estimated population of 700,000 people in Palestine, there were only about 70,000 Jews—a mere 10 percent.

I am not going to cavil about the reliability of these statistics. They are probably approximately correct. But all these statistics refer to dates in the twentieth century. To my knowledge, it has never occurred to anyone to ask the simple question: why begin with these twentieth century dates, and not earlier? If the reason given is the genesis of the Hebrew and Arab national movements, these started not in the twentieth but in the second half of the nineteenth century, when both nationalisms first began to express themselves in literature and in organized collective efforts. In 1869 the Alliance Israelite founded the agricultural school in Mikveh Israel; Baron Rothschild and Baron Hirsch became interested in promoting plans to settle Jews in Palestine. What kind of a country was Palestine then? What was its population? What were the demographic trends not only 50 years ago, but also 100 years ago? But even if in 1917 there were about 600,000 Arabic speaking people in Palestine, were they direct descendants of an ancient, autochthonous population or were they, some or most of them, first and second generation newcomers?

Of course, when the Arabs present their case one gets the impression that the Arabs in Palestine have been living there since time immemorial. No argument is too improbable to prove that point. On the one hand Arab propagandists and apologists have invented the theory that the contemporary Jews are not descendants of the ancient Hebrews but of the Khazars, a Turco-Mongolian people of the lower Volga region who converted to Judaism—and hence have no historic rights to Palestine. On the other hand, they claim that the contemporary Arabs are in fact descendants of the ancient Hebrews who remained in Palestine after the destruction of the Temple, and in the course of time became Arabized; hence, it is the contemporary Arabs who have historic rights to Palestine.

All this is, of course, sheer fancy.

The Institute for Mediterranean Affairs has recently undertaken a study on the demographic history of Palestine in the nineteenth century headed by Kemal Karpat of the University of Wisconsin. The reason we have tackled this question is simply that so far no one has bothered to find out what kind of a country, demographically speaking, Palestine was 100 years ago, though every stone, nook and wadi has been studied in minutest detail. It seemed to us that knowledge of the demographic background of Palestine in the last century might contribute to a better understanding of the conflicting claims in that country and put the Arab-Israeli dispute in a better historic perspective.

Our preliminary investigations into the archives of the Public Records office in London and the Basvekalet Arsivi (Prime Ministry Archives) and Foreign Office archives in Istanbul with a view to determining the demographic transformations of Palestine during the Ottoman administration in the nineteenth century have produced extremely interesting material concerning the migrations and settlement of various Arab and non-Arab tribes and ethnic groups in Palestine. But from the first interim report it seems that it is fair to assume that about the middle of the nineteenth century Palestine was, comparatively speaking, a depopulated country. There were few Jews, but there were not many Arabs either. In the whole of Palestine—on both sides of the Jordan, including some portions from what is now Southern Syria and Southern Lebanon—there lived, according to the preliminary and tentative findings of Karpat, about 200,000 people of whom probably 40-60 percent were Arabic speaking, 20-30 percent Turkish or Circassian, and 8-15 percent Jewish, etc. How and why the Arab speaking population increased so drastically in the next 70 or 80 years is not within the purview of this paper. Suffice it to say that one of the factors, but only one, attracting Arabs to Palestine was the beginning of Hebrew settlements and economic development of the country.

To point to these figures is not to deny the historic rights of the Arabs, but rather to indicate that whatever the respective historic claims of Arabs and Jews to Palestine, the important fact is that the two people are there today, and not how many were there 50, 100 or 1,000 years ago. Both Israelis and Arabs are, comparatively speaking, newcomers in the country. But both are there and both have rights, and the question is how to reconcile the legitimate claims of both peoples.

This in itself would not constitute an impossible task were the two parties to the conflict to state these legitimate rights in concrete geopolitical terms: but this they refuse to do. It seems that they are mostly driven by mystical motivations and indulge in extravagant illusions and delusions, much to their own detriment and to the confusion of the world at large, even some of their most patient and forbearing friends and supporters.

ISRAELI EXPANSIONISM

We have seen the fantasies, the ambiguities and the imaginary claims of the Arabs, both territorially and demographically. But the other side of the firing line is not much more reassuring: Israel is becoming more and more oriented toward world Jewry, following a pan-Judaic policy and considering itself not just a nation attending to its own interests and striving to national self-sufficiency, but rather as a vanguard as well as the guardian of all Jews the world over. It is now engaged in a vehement campaign against Russia, not just because the Kremlin is actively committed to the Arab side, with all its ominous political and military implications, but rather in order to compel the Soviets to permit their millions of Jews to leave the country and settle in Israel. Otherwise, some spokesmen declared in the Knesset, the Russian Jews will explode the regime from the inside.

The Arabs have a strong case when they argue that the Israelis, as the Zionist leaders before them, have never made clear what their ultimate aim is. They are always for something that they previously denied to have been their design. They were for a Jewish state after they for decades refused to proclaim it as the official aim of the Zionist movement; the man who actually took the history making step and proclaimed the state of Israel—its first Premier, David Ben Gurion—in the 1930s denounced the very concept of a Jewish state as something chauvinistic and even racist. They were for partition within the borders of the United Nations Resolution of November 29, 1947; then after the war of 1948, they were for the Armistice borders; now, after the Six Day War they are generally speaking for the present borders. They are always for the present, after victory and conquest.

The Arabs sometimes argue that when one demands that they recognize Israel as a state, within "secure" frontiers, they are confused about exactly what Israel is, both from the point of view of the people who make up the nation and concerning Israel's territorial aspirations. What is the merit of this argument?

The late Israeli Premier and Foreign Minister, Moshe Sharett, declared in a speech before the Press Club in Washington (1953):

We are often asked what are our peace conditions. There is but one condition—and nothing can be more simple and element-ary. It is that we should be accepted as we are, with our territory, population, and unrestricted sovereingnty . . . .

Thirteen years later another Foreign Minister, Abba Eban, spoke in the same vein:

. . . . If Arab minds were able to make peace with Israel at all, they would be able to go a step further and make peace with Israel *as it is*: not with Israel as it was not and is not and will not be."

This sounds like a fair claim if only the Arabs and for that matter anybody else could decide exactly what Israel actually is—demographically and geographically, not at a given moment, but basically and ultimately.

When Sharett and Eban made the statements just quoted, Israel was of a geographic shape that the Israeli leaders accepted without protest. Indeed, it was much greater than what they enthusiastically accepted in November 1947. But when the Israeli leaders repeat the same formula in 1970 as a condition for peace, we have to remember that the geographic shape of the country is quite different now; indeed it is four times greater than it was before June 5, 1967, and all the indications are that Israel is no longer to be satisfied with the territorial boundaries considered satisfactory in 1953 or 1966.

So what *is* Israel "as it is?" The Israeli Prime Minister, Golda Meir, declares repeatedly that she is not going to draw any maps before the Arabs come to the conference table. But in the meantime the map or maps are being drawn by creating new facts, geographically and demographically and politically. Indi-vidual ministers are ever discovering new reasons why this or that territory conquered in 1967 should be retained. Mystical reasons: Moshe Dayan says that if the Israelis don't exercise their claim to Hebron or Shkhem, how can they claim their rights to Tel Aviv or

Petakh Tikva? Economic reasons: the oil in Sinai. Agricultural reasons: to make the "bika" in the Jordan Valley bloom as they have done in the "Arava," south of Beersheba; strategic reasons: the Golan Heights are strategically more important than Jerusalem; and Sharm el-Sheik is more important than the Golan Heights.

The Israelis seem to have great difficulty in making up their minds about an official name for the newly conquered territories; and they have consecutively changed the designations from "occupied territories" to "administered territories," and after that simply to "territories." What do they mean? Do the Arabs or at least a substantial number of them consider themselves liberated by the Israelis? As I said when talking about Arab terminology, only people can proclaim whether they are liberated or not. Territories are silent. Under the circumstances the Arabs ask: How far do the Israelis intend to go in liberating territories? There are indeed voices in Israel, articulate and loud, though isolated, who claim an Israeli empire from the Euphrates to the Nile.

Yet, I should not venture to say that Israel is expansionist by nature or intent. When the late Premier Levi Eshkol declared at the outbreak of the war in June 1967 that Israel has no territorial designs of any kind, I believe he was sincere, though after the war he declared no less emphatically that the armistice borders are null and void and that henceforth the Jordan River will remain Israel's "security" border to the East. He probably meant it in both instances. It is both true that Israel has no premeditated plans for conquest and expansionism, and that in fact it is expansionist and rules by conquest. The paradox is that the Arabs force them to fight, to conquer and to expand; and that they are addicted to what they gain even though they got it, as it were, against their own will, in the sense that it was imposed upon them. The Israelis seem to be overwhelmed by their own military victories; they regard the "new" status quo with sanctity, whatever it may be at a given point in history. And what is most disturbing is Israel's lack of any creative imagination that there might be advantages in changing the status quo, even though it will entail concessions and withdrawal.

With the Arabs it is the other way around: they are always for what they refused in the past. In 1948 they waged war against partition. After suffering humiliating defeat and being forced to sign Armistice Agreements accepting the borders that resulted from the fighting, they expressed a willingness to agree to the Partition boundaries. Now, after their 1967 defeat, on occasion it seems that they might be willing to settle for the Armistice borders.

Yet there is a difference. It is my impression that the Israelis would, were they to agree to certain frontiers, consider them as permanent. The Arabs, however, even when they speak of agreeing to a settlement, like the Security Council Resolution of November 22, 1967, remain nonetheless evasive and elusive. On certain cardinal points, they give the impression that they don't really mean what they say but consider the settlement only a first step in a process of reversion, with the ultimate aim still the liquidation of Israel as a state.

This does not mean that the Arabs should trust Israel and that Israel should not trust the Arabs. On the contrary. The Arabs should demand from Israel plausible safeguards, while the Israelis should test the intentions of the Arabs by clarifying what security guarantees they could obtain for concessions and withdrawal.

WHO IS A JEW?

Israel's ambiguities and contradictions concern not only the territorial dimensions of the state but also, if not mainly, its demographic character and composition. The leaders of Israel never tire of proclaiming that the aim of Zionism was and remains a Jewish state, that is, one so predominantly Jewish that it will not only provide security but also enable the Jews to develop their peculiar genius and fulfill their unique destiny, whatever this may mean. I don't want to argue about whether this was really what the Zionists proclaimed in the years and decades before the state was established. For the sake of our survey it is enough to say that the present leaders of Israel believe that this is what was asserted. Immediately after the Six Day War, Moshe Dayan spoke in the same vein before a CBS panel of reporters interviewing him for the television program Face the Nation. On this occasion he intimated that Israel is not interested in keeping the West Bank because the integration of these territories would transform Israel into a binational state, while Zionism insists on the Jewish character of the State. This interpretation of Zionism has made Israeli leaders reluctant throughout the years to accept any sizeable number of the Arab refugees. One may well ask how the Israeli leadership expects to preserve the Jewish character of their state if they intend to keep the newly occupied territories that contain an additional million Arabs?

However, confusion is much greater than that. It isn't only a matter of numerical relations between Arabs and Hebrews or between Jews, Moslems and Christians. The confusion relates to the very concept of Jewishness, to what it means to be a Jew. Is it religious affiliation? Is it ethnic origins? Is it language, culture? Is it self-determination? When asked what is a Jewish state, Israeli leaders show impatience. They consider such questions either stupid, ignorant or motivated by unfriendly bias. Yet, they would do better to crystallize in their own minds what the concept or term "Jew" means legally, constitutionally—and hence what is meant by "a Jewish state." For the time being confusion is rampant. The judiciary and the legislative are split on the question. There are passionate divergences of opinion among Israelis. After the High Court's decision ordering the Ministry of the Interior to register Benjamin Shalit's two children as of Jewish nationality, though their mother was not born of Jewish parents, the Knesset quickly passed legislation to void and nullify the decision of the High Court. The initiative was taken by a Government predominantly Socialist. And Prime Minister Golda Meir insisted with some finality that there could be no differentiation between Jewish religion and nationality. In a sense this is a double misunderstanding because the bulk of those who identify themselves as Jews today are neither religious nor are they citizens of Israel. Former Prime Minister David Ben Gurion remarked that he was rather surprised to learn that Golda Meir defends the Halakha interpretation of Jewishness: because according to Halakha (the Rabbinic law) not only would she be barred from occupying any governmental position, let alone the premiership, but she wouldn't even qualify as a simple witness.

True, Golda Meir rushed through legislation in the Knesset perhaps not so much out of deep conviction and knowledge of the intricate matter, but rather because of political considerations: to keep the present coalition government intact and not to antagonize the religious parties represented in the government.

Though the religious parties represent but a small minority in the country, their views prevail and are imposed upon everyone. Israel, in its majority, is a secular society living in certain respects under a theocratic regime. When a crowd of demonstrators gathered before the Knesset to protest against the repeal of the Supreme Court's decision the incongruities of such a regime were made explicit. At that gathering a letter was read from a young man from Holland who came to Israel, was drafted into the army, was wounded on the Suez Canal and had both his legs amputated. But he is not recognized as a Jew because his mother is not Jewish. A woman was interviewed on TV in Jerusalem. She is from Poland, born into a Jewish family and, under Hitler, was sent to Auschwitz. She survived and came to Israel to discover that she is not recognized as a Jewess because her mother was not one. She broke out in tears before the TV and declared: "I'll emigrate. I'd rather live in the diaspora as a Jewess than as a gentile in the Jewish state." On the other hand, two terrorists imprisoned in Israel for murder, are sons of Jewish mothers. Are they Jews, while the boy from Holland is not?

Orthodox Jews pretend to follow in the tradition of the Pharisees in preserving the unity of the Jewish people. Yet the Pharisees, despite the "bad press" they have had throughout the centuries due to the New Testament and its apologists were, in fact, imaginative and far-reaching reformers rather than petrified conservatives. The present day Pharisees try to freeze customs, laws and traditions enacted more than 2,000 years ago.

The Khok Hashvut, the law of redemption, or the law of the return, as it is variably translated, had its justification with the establishment of the state. One had to give the Jews of the world a chance of free option, in the face of that unique, awe-inspiring historic event which the reestablishment of the state of Israel constituted. But for how long should this option be left open? At the time when the law was enacted I was a member of the

Knesset, and I suggested in the committee where it was discussed prior to submitting it to the plenary session of the legislature that the law should be enacted for 25 years. After that, it should be amended so that only Jews in distress (finding themselves in trouble because they are Jews) should benefit from the law. I was not opposed, I was shouted down. I still think that the relationship between the state of Israel and the Jewish communities in the world should be better and more clearly and distinctly defined and normalized. Of course, immigration is a prerogative of a sovereign state. And any diktat from the outside of how to regulate quantitatively or qualitatively the immigration to Israel would be an infringement upon Israel's sovereignty. But the law of return seems to transcend immigration policy. It expresses the essence of the state. It marks its character. But far from crystallizing its character, it blurs it and confuses both friends and foes. Very few Jews now apply for entry into Palestine, and there is very little chance that masses of Jews from the free countries will—unless, of course outbreaks of anti-Semitism occur. But if such a law is necessary, it should be based on the humanitarian criterion of practical needs rather than on mystical and symbolic considerations. Israel must sooner or later become normalized, and become in basic respects "kmo kol Hagoyim" like other nations, not from the point of view of compromising her unique personality and destiny and heritage, but from the point of view of international conventions as practiced and understood by modern man. Having achieved the common status of all, Israel will better be able to pursue its unique destiny—but not the other way around.

GUIDELINES TO A JUST RESOLUTION

Our survey has shown that both parties to the conflict demand not exactly the right to self-determination but rather the right to self-indetermination: the right to conceal and mystify; the right to self-contradiction and absurdity; the right to extravagant, often incongruous, claims, transcending conventional notions of legitimate national aspirations and precise territorial delineation;

the right to surrealistic subjectivity and exclusivity, without any regard to the legitimate and inalienable rights and interests of their opponents. All this with an amazing lack of respect for the common sense and sensibilities of their respective friends and well-wishers, let alone public opinion at large.

Of course, one should have empathy and sympathy. But on the other hand, scholars render little service by being indulgent or tolerant of the irresponsibility of leaders and nations—of the threats of the Arabs to destroy Israel and slaughter her people or, for that matter, tolerant of the heartless indifference of the Israeli leadership to the plight of the displaced Arabs in Palestine. Nor do scholars render any constructive contribution to knowledge or to the advancement of peace by apologizing for one side or the other: by declaring, for instance, that when an Arab leader speaks of the liquidation of Israel, he really doesn't mean it, but says it only for internal consumption. Likewise it does little good, when Israeli leaders follow a policy of creeping annexation of the conquered territories by creating ever new *faits accomplis* (refusing even in principle the use of the term "withdrawal"), to assert nonetheless that Israel is ready to negotiate with the Arabs in good faith and without any pre-conditions.

When it comes to the Middle East and the Israeli-Arab conflict we tend to share in the mysticism and the fatalism, if not obscurantism, of the parties involved. Above all, we take things for granted. We accept or tolerate such terms, phrases or statements as "Pan-Arabism," "a Jewish state," "the Uma al Arabia" (the Arab Nation), "Jewish nationalism," "Palestine," "Nasser is the leader of all the Arabs, or at least of what is called 'the progressive' Arabs," "the fedayeen fighting for the liberation of their country," "Israel wants peace, but the Arabs sabotage it (or vice versa according to our individual predilections)." But rarely do we make an honest intellectual effort to understand what these terms stand for, what the motive force is in each particular case, and what are the long range implications. Under such circumstances to take things for granted is tantamount to becoming accomplices to the obscurantism, irresponsibility and mischief that wreaks such havoc with the peoples involved and possibly endanger world peace.

Is it possible through this maze of confusion, contradiction and mythomania, to perceive the countours of a solution? Perhaps one should begin with the underlying principles of the Balfour Declaration, the mandate and the United Nations partition plan. These international acts of statesmanship and international sanction all contain three principles which may serve as a basis for a solution. One is territorial delineation; the second, recognition of the existence of two peoples who have rights within the contested territory; third, that these two peoples should cooperate.

If ever a peaceful solution is to evolve it will in all probability be on the basis of these three principles. In concrete terms the solution would probably entail some kind of at least symbolic reunification of Palestine on both banks of the Jordan as a loose confederation of two separate national states; Israel, within, roughly speaking, the armistice lines of 1949, and the Arab state within the rest of Palestine; with Jerusalem as the capital of the confederation.

Only within such a confederate arrangement could economic cooperation be achieved and the problem of the displaced Palestinians solved on the principle of free choice while safeguarding Israel's security requirements. Internationally such a confederation could be neutral in the sense that neither Israel nor the Arab states would become part of a military block or alliance without the consent of the other.

Whether this is practical at this stage of emotional surcharge I do not know. Probably not. But it seems to me that any of the other plans suggested by one party or the other, or by neutrals, stand even a lesser chance because they do not take into consideration the legitimate aspirations and rights of both parties. Within a confederate system in originally mandated Palestine these aspirations may yet have a realistic chance of fulfillment.

---

[1] The area of the original mandate over Palestine was, roughly speaking, some 44,500 square miles. Before the Six Day War the area of Jordan

(including the West Bank) was about 36,500 square miles (the West Bank covered a little more than 2,000 square miles). Israel covered an area of 8,017 miles.

The population distribution was: Jordan (and the West Bank): 2,059 people; Israel: 2,841,000.

The census taken by Israel in September 1967 showed that under Israel's jurisdiction in the occupied territories were 994,735 people (the West Bank, the Golan Heights, Gaza and Sinai, East Jerusalem).

DISCUSSION AT THE SECOND PANEL
February 15, 1970

The panel was opened to questions from the floor:

Question: These discussions usually center on the Palestine question. That is natural, because the Palestine question and what is happening with the Palestinians is perhaps what is most dynamic in the Middle East. My own view is that Palestinian statehood is inevitable, that those who try to negate it are whistling in the wind, and have to come to terms with it. But I think that very often the problem is discussed in a vacuum, as if the rest of the Arab world somehow didn't exist, as if there weren't power struggles within the Arab world. I would like to ask the members of the panel to comment on the following questions. What effect do the power struggles within the Arab world, particularly in the Egyptian government and the Algerian government, have on the dynamic of the Palestinian question and Israel? And what effect do the great powers, especially because of their interest in oil, have on the whole situation?

Kimche: Oil is a key factor in the situation. There is a formal recolonization going on in the Middle East. It is in some ways the most significant single development, aside from the possibility of a major clash, which is perhaps not as great a danger as the implications of recolonization. By recolonization I mean that during the last two or three years, certainly since 1967, there has been an evident failure in the Middle East of what we used to call decolonization elsewhere. In the Middle East some of the great powers have come back. The British have largely left. In their place have come the Russians and the Americans, taking an increasing interest in and gaining direct influence over the oil areas, of Arabia particularly but also of Egypt and North Africa. The oil of the Middle East has had a fluctuating influence on Western Europe in particular, but now also on Eastern Europe. This is so because the trend is that there is no single European source that can so cheaply and effectively meet the increasing requirements for oil energy as the Middle East. So oil remains a major political factor, now also for the Russians. For the first time, the Russians need additional oil sources. During the last few months, they have concluded major agreements with Iraq, with three other Arab governments, and they are beginning to show a very considerable interest in the Persian Gulf. There is no doubt that, as far as oil, recolonization will keep the great powers in the area.

Arms supplies to the Middle East have become the other aspect of recolonization. During the last year alone, something like $5 billion of arms have gone into the area. Now, this is quite fantastic—$5 billion. It creates a link of obligation between the recipient and the donor, or the seller, on a scale that never existed during the heyday of imperialism in Southeast Asia or in Africa. And the answer to your point is that the great powers, whatever they may say, are not vegetarians. They are in the Middle East for understandable national or imperial interests, whichever way you'd like to put it, and one has to bear that in mind. This is not something that can be argued away; it is a fact, and it's a fact that the Middle East has to live with.

Khouri: Actually the questioner has a very good point. There is a Palestine Arab problem and there is an Arab problem. And they have become much more distinct since the June 1967 war. Before the war the Arab governments would have been able to make a peace settlement without seriously taking the Palestine Arab national goals into consideration. They are much less free now because of the great influence of the Palestine Arab movement in the Arab states. They are much less free to act, even though they have in a sense tried to act—for instance by accepting the November 22, 1967 Security Council Resolution. This resolution in some sense solves the Arab-Israeli problem, but it does not solve the Palestinian Arab problem. And this has been the crux of the matter, especially as regards the Palestinian Arabs who do not accept the resolution and do everything they can to prevent such a solution. The Egyptian and Jordanian and Lebanese governments, for example, would like a political solution on that basis. The Palestinian Arabs and their supporters in Egypt, in Lebanon and in Jordan are the elements that want satisfaction. The feelings and aspirations and the influence of the Palestinian Arab movement have burgeoned in the Arab world, especially since the Karameh incident. They have separated themselves from the Arab governments in fear that they will make a solution that will not satisfy the Palestinian national goals. And Syrians and Iraqi officials are taking a similar position. Their primary opposition to the November 22, 1967 Resolution is that it does not provide a just solution to the Palestinian Arab problem. And it doesn't. It is true that the Palestinians have certain rights and legitimate aspirations, that are being to some extent ignored. And as long as they are ignored, they are going to keep fighting and causing difficulties.

Question: I would like to make two observations. I was in Israel in 1948 interviewing Jews and non-Jews in connection with the Arab exodus. Professor Khouri will perhaps be interested in knowing that as far as the Jews were concerned, they were bewildered by the Arab flight. I mention this particularly because he indicated that expulsion took place. There isn't time to go into the statistics, but surely Professor Khouri is aware, for instance, of the startling example of Haifa, to which the British, not friends of the Jews at the time, attest. They themselves bear testimony to the fact that at first, after the fall of Haifa to the Jews, the Arabs had agreed to stay, but they started a mass exodus from Haifa after instructions from the Arab high command. I should like to remind Professor Khouri of the statement that the Jordanians themselves made, which sums it up: "They told us to get out, so that they could come in. We got out but they did not come in." And as for the fact that the Arab refugees have been used as a tactic, only very recently Nasser and others have declared that when the refugees come in, Israel will cease to exist.

I want to make one other observation in connection with what Professor Merlin and others have suggested. It seems to me that, if you bear in mind that up to 40 years ago, Palestine was essentially the state on both sides of the Jordan River, that the state of Jordan was set up in 1922, that the West Bank was separated from Palestine in 1948, that Gaza under Egyptian rule was essentially a part of Palestine, that the bulk of the Arab refugees are in Gaza, the West Bank and Jordan, it would appear to be a logical conclusion to say that the Arabs never left Palestine. For the first time in history a village attachment has become a sacred national cause. This, I believe, is unique in history. As far as I know, there is no other such instance. And though one can respect attachment to a village, isn't it more just to speak of the dislocation and separation and loss of a home town, and not to speak in terms of the loss of a homeland. There exists this crucial distinction; the Arabs have lost no homeland, they are in Palestine, whatever name you give it, whether you call it West Bank or whether you call it Jordan. They have lost villages, and that is hard, that is difficult. But if one thinks in terms of peace, and of solutions for great problems, when the dislocation of villagers can take place for the Aswan Dam, surely in order to resolve a profound and difficult national question involving two peoples, attachment to a village might be subsidiary to the attachment to the homeland itself.

Khouri: In my paper I indicated I had copious footnotes documenting the statement that large numbers of the Palestine Arabs were in fact expelled. As one of the factors involving the exodus, I didn't say it was the only factor, I said one of the major factors was deliberate. This talk about Haifa and several other limited areas only is valid; some Jewish officals had encouraged Arabs not to leave. There are incidents of that kind. But, no matter what you might say, I did not see this as typical. I'm taking the opinions of responsible officials, of responsible students. I have references here to Jon Kimche's *Seven Fallen Pillars*, George E. Kirk's *The Middle East 1945-1950*, Kenneth Bilby's *New Star in the East*, Edgar O'Ballance, Harry Sacker's *Israel and Establishment of a State*, Hal Lehrman's article "The Arabs and Israel." I could give you a slew of other eye-witness, responsible sources that this took place. So I personally think it is incorrect to deny that such involuntary exodus occurred, especially after the Israelis took the offensive in the second stage of the Palestine war. They were largely on the defensive in the first part; from April 1 to May 15 they were on the offensive, because the Palestinian Arabs were too weak. And this is where a lot of the exodus took place. Even Menachim Begin himself takes credit for this tactic. In his own book, he argues that in the first period of the fighting the Israelis were primarily on the defensive, and consequently the Arabs were the ones moving primarily in Arab-controlled areas. In the second period after the first truce, the Israelis had built up their forces and were considerably more powerful than the Arabs by that time and they took the offensive. You cannot give me any incident after the Palestinian war in which Israeli officials asked the Arabs to stay. To deny a fact of history is no way of getting at the truth and no way of solving this particular problem.

Merlin: Of course, the Arabs fled not for one reason, but for a variety of reasons. I just don't believe that it's very important to analyze all the reasons as well as their interconnection. What is important is the question of what to do with them now, not why they became refugees. I don't think that Israel, and the apologists for Israel, should be so sensitive about the argument that some were encouraged to leave. I agree with Miss Syrkin that in many instances the Israelis appealed to the Arabs to stay and not to go, but there were also other instances. If Israel is not responsible at all for the Arabs having left, why doesn't she take them back? This is very central. It is true that the Arabs are not refugees as the Hungarians after 1956 were refugees in the United States. Most of them are still in Palestine, in their own country. But it is not exactly comparable to the situation of the tens of thousands of villagers in Egypt who were evacuated in order to build the Aswan Dam. In the latter case the evacuation was undertaken by the government, but in the case of the Palestinian refugees it was undertaken by an Arab government but by a government that they considered their enemy. The Arab refugees definitely have a right, a birthright, and in principle they demand to be given the choice to decide where they would like to be rehabilitated. It seems to me that Israel just has no way out of it, and it's going to be a plague forever, as we say in Hebrew, as long as this problem is not solved. I actually believe that it is manageable, because most of the Arabs are still in Palestine, because the vast majority would not hope to live under Israeli rule. But in principle, I believe that Israel has to offer the Arabs a future.

Question: I was a little surprised by the statement of my colleague, Professor Syrkin, who pointed out that there is a distinction between national aspirations and village aspirations. I'd like to point out, as an economist, that a large series of villages would constitute a state, in terms of aspirations. So you can't isolate the difference between a village and a state, if a sufficient number of villages and a large enough population exists in terms of living in villages. I have been trying to integrate in my own mind everything that I heard yesterday and today. I want to use a technique that is well known among scientists, that I have found very fruitful in seminars and in graduate discussions, and that is to start out with some assumptions that apparently are unrealistic and even fantastic, and see where they lead us. For example, with the question of historiography pointed by Merlin, I'd like to indicate that before we had the holocaust in Germany, which was a solution of expulsion, Hitler asked the international world to accept the Jews, and when there was either indifference or refusal on the part of any state to provide a place for the Jewish resettlement, genocide occured. From the historical point of view, we may very well be inviting another holocaust unless recognition is given to the aspirations of two different peoples, namely the Jews and the Arabs in the territory. And so I want to suggest an unrealistic, perhaps impractical, perhaps chimerical or fantastic assumption. I was very much impressed by Professor Kanvosky in connection with the question of economic development. It seems to me that you cannot divorce, at least in the Middle East, economic development from psychological attitudes and aspirations for political sovereignty. I'd like to ask this question: Suppose, as economists frequently do, that all resources now devoted for war purposes or the further preparation for war, were allocated for economic growth of the territory, and that the leadership of the United Nations were exercised in terms of creating capital as well as resources for purposes of economic development. If so, would the refugee problem, which is now considered mainly in terms of political aspirations, fall into a jigsaw settlement?

Khouri: One of the most important lessons that I've learned from the Arab refugee problem (that I have been studying, incidentally, for about 15 years) is that it is a human problem. It is first a psychological, emotional problem, then a political problem, and. then an economic problem. It's not something that's going to be solved by economic means. Nor is the Arab-Israeli problem going to be resolved by economic means. It's just not going to work, for the Israelis will not accept an economic solution and say, "Well, let's create a bi-national Palestine-Arab state and we'll pour into it a billion dollars in aid—they're not going to accept it. Neither are the Arabs going to accept an economic solution, until this problem is dealt on a human, psychological and increasingly, on a political level. It can't be done without the economic factor also being involved, but this will require billions of dollars and many, many years of effort. I suggest that economic aid be given to the Arab states so they can improve their economic situation and improve the economic lot of the Arab refugees. I also suggest that Israel could develop economic projects to help resettle the refugees. But this is not going to solve the problem, though it may be helpful. Unless this problem is dealt with on a human, political, psychological level, taking into account the strong feelings and emotions and nationalist feelings that exist, and until there is recognition of the feelings and aspirations of both sides, there is not going to be a solution. The Israelis must understand the Arab position and recognize certain of their rights, and vice versa. One must recognize there is not all right on one side and all wrong on the other side. When I'm in the Arab world, I try to make harsh criticisms of some of their attitudes and positions; and I did the same thing when I was in Israel. There must be greater understanding. This is the key to solution of the problem. All facts, all sides, must be taken into consideration and put into a proper perspective. To swallow one side of the story does not help peace, does not help Israel, does not help the Arabs and does not help our own country, the United States.

Question: I think all of us here are interested in a realistic appraisal of the situation, but I wonder whether some of the assumptions and some of the assertions that have been made here are realistic. For example, is it realistic to assume, as apparently you assumed in your paper, Professor Khouri, that a country— and a new one at that, with great internal as well as external problems—can be expected to accede to the repatriation of a large group of refugees, to accede to a request made by those who do not recognize the country's right to existence? This seems to me, at least in terms of historical experience, highly unrealistic. Is it realistic to ignore the enormous job of absorption of refugees, which you mentioned only in passing, that Israel performed, in accepting immigrants? They are not necessarily Zionists—I think that is the great misconception here. Most of the Jewish refugees from the Near and Middle Eastern countries were not Zionist at all. I recently had an opportunity to talk to a Jewish community in an Arabic country. They're anything but Zionists, but I think they find no other solution than to become refugees in Israel. I think it is not realistic to ignore this particular problem or to pass over it in one sentence. But my main question refers to the Palestine entity problem.

You talk here about national aspirations, but what about the social implications of this allegedly national and perhaps truly national movement. You referred briefly to the Palestine-Arab problem, as well as the Palestine-Israeli problem. Is not one of the keys to the whole business that the Palestine national entity, as it were, represents a social protest against the continued autocratic, post-feudal social arrangement that exists in most of the Arabic countries, regardless of the official designation of what the social system might be?

Khouri: It has been the view of United Nations, American, neutral experts and I even have references to two Israeli experts, that if, before the June 1967 war, the Arab refugees had in fact been given a clear cut choice between repatriation and resettlement with compensation, and had it made clear to them that they were going to Israel and not to a Palestinian Arab state, that no more than 10 percent, which would be roughly 100,000 would opt to go to Israel. Some experts even suggested that many of these would go there and become unhappy and actually leave and would only want to see what had happened to their property. And those that would return to Israel, would in the main, be those who are members of families already existing in Israel, those who could be integrated into Israel and were least likely to cause difficulty.

Another thing, so far as security is concerned. The United Nations resolution, as I read it, in Paragraph 11, indicated clearly that the refugee has to go back and live in peace with his neighbor. It has been clearly indicated that the United Nations body set up for this purpose would clear each individual. Obviously, troublemakers would not be allowed to come back. The process would have been gradual; consequently if some refugees did go back and cause problems, I'm sure there would be no difficulty in calling a halt to this process.

I'm not trying to say there is no security problem, and I indicated that Israel is logically concerned about it. I'm merely saying that the problem is grossly exaggerated. Israel has successfully incorporated 200,000 Arabs already, so another 100,000 would not constitute a gross danger. There are risks, but there are greater risks in not solving the refugee problem. Because the refugee problem has been concentrated in a few host states, there was only limited influence, especially in the earlier years, on the host government. Palestinians had not gone yet to Kuwait, Saudi Arabia and Libya spreading their hatred and bitterness. The hatred and bitterness has now spread to parts of the Arab world where it didn't previously exist. Even in places like Egypt, the feeling toward the Palestine question when I went there in 1958 and saw quite a number of important people, was very reasonable on the part of the whole Arab problem. They were willing to accept a political settlement, one that their people could accept and that would not be humiliating. Consequently, the situation within the Arab world was much more favorable. Taking 100,000 Arabs into Israel is not so important for security as not being accepted by the Arab world. This is the dangerous situation for Israel and this is the situation that has been perpetuated. Some

Arab states, Syria and Jordan specifically, and possibly Egypt also, said they would accept those refugees who would not opt for repatriation. The United Nations conciliation commission stated clearly that the Arabs in 1950 and 1951 were receptive to the idea that most of the refugees would have to be repatriated.

I recognize there are risks. But to ignore the much greater potential long range risk is very unrealistic. There was much better opportunity for peace and security years ago, especially before the June War, than there is today. And with all Israel's expanded borders the fact is there will be no peace and security until she gets acceptance on the part of people who have great advantage over them in population size and resources, and sooner or later will overcome their technological backwardness. With the potential resources the Arabs have, can Israel expect to remain forever militarily dominant, and allow concern for immediate short range security to endanger their long range security?

Kimche: I'd like to say just a few words, because I happen to have been virtually a participant and eye witness to so many of the events that are now quoted from documents. To some extent I had this in my mind when I spoke earlier about the fallacies that can very easily be deduced from official documentation of this period.

I don't want to go into too many details, but the whole question of the refugees, as it was, and the question of the refugees as it is today are two entirely different things. I think one can now write the history of the refugee problem up to 1967. That was one thing. Since 1967 there isn't really a refugee problem. And when we talk so passionately about doing this and that for the refugees we are really talking about a problem that doesn't any longer exist. There *is* a Palestine problem, and you cannot today settle the refugee problem without first considering the Palestine problem. In terms of numbers and position, various humanitarian schemes are open to the government of Israel today. It doesn't have to ask anybody's permission, it doesn't have to go to any do-gooders anywhere in order to be told what to do. It can act if it so decides. But this doesn't resolve the pre-1967 refugee problem. That is now the Palestine problem, and therefore, to discuss these two problems so completely separately, the Palestine question and the refugee problem, is merely to perpetuate a fallacy at this stage, which will not really help us to solve the central problem, the Palestine problem.

Question: I'd like to address the comment to Mr. Kimche. You said that with the stroke of a pen a new fact, a new territory can be established in the Middle East. But is there a receptive voice among Palestinian Arabs who would accept the Palestinian state and the existence of the state of Israel? I don't think it's meaningful to talk about creating a new fact if there is no one there to accept it. Is there some organization or group of individuals among the Palestinian Arabs who reject the ideas of Fatah but do want to see a Palestinian nationalism created that coexists with Israel?

Kimche: It must be borne in mind in history, as in weather, that it always rains on both sides of the frontier. And when you have the divisions and differences of opinion that have been shown in Israel, you similarly have the same kind of differences of opinion on the other side. In other words official Israeli policy seems fairly monolithic. Those of us who know the situation in Israel, know perfectly well that it doesn't fairly reflect the seething discussions that go on down below. In the same way, Fatah statements and Palestinian statements also appear to be monolithic and extreme and unbending. And in the same way they do not reflect the same position among the Palestinians. I know, in my own case, I have had during the last days and weeks, discussions and contributions from a number of representatives, Palestinians from the West Bank, from outside the West Bank, who have been concerned with just this one point; whether the extremist Palestinian position should be the only one that can represent the Palestinians, whether the time has not come. And I think this is the biggest decision now within the Palestinian movement—whether the time has not come for a representative body, perhaps a government in exile, that will reflect Palestinian, not only one Palestinian opinion, but varying Palestinian opinions, that will be a representative body and that will provide an address to which the Israeli government can go if it decides that it must talk to the Palestinians.

Political Dynamics and the Arab-Israeli Conflict.

Political Systems of the Middle East: Opening Remarks

IRVING LOUIS HOROWITZ

Before I open this session on the dynamics of political power in the Middle East, I should like to interject some cautionary remarks. There is a presumption of some kind, whether warranted or not, that I am an expert on Israel and the Arab system. But in all frankness, while I am concerned about the Third World and developing areas, my knowledge of Middle East politics is limited. My interest in the question of political dynamics of the Middle East and the crisis therein, stems from an overall concern with the Third World rather than with geo-politics as such.

That said, there are certain linkings between Israel and the Arab nations, whether they like to think they share commonalities or not. One commonality is their shopping-center attitude toward political systems. The entire area is rich in religious and cultural tradition, but the Middle East is new in nation building and sovereign political rule. For example, although there is a long and rich tradition of Arab political theory and practice, the problems of modern rule have been complicated by an ill-defined class structure and an ill-defined type of socioeconomic development. Thus, while there exists a rich variety of political analysis and political theory, the Arab world, because of the colonial experience, did not really have a nation-building problem until the twentieth century.

What has also happened is that the Israelis and the Arabs have purchased their political model from different places. The Israelis bought a multiparty system which is in fact a uniparty kind of government, whereas many Arab states reveal a tendency toward uniparty rule and multigovernment activity. Israeli political parties fight their political battles yet they maintain a relatively strong degree of internal control, whereas the Arab states tend to have single-party apparatus but very severe inner-party struggles, in part derived from the socialist model. Therefore, one large scale commonality of the area is the purchase of political theory and political systems from abroad.

Another common problem is legitimacy itself. The problem of legitimacy for Israel is that, in theory or in fact, Israel views itself as a ghetto surrounded by states that do not recognize her sovereignty. Israel is the only nation in the world that has common borders with other nations, not one of which recognizes her sovereign right to exist. On the other hand, the Arabs have the problem of establishing legitimacy in a more grandiose form. The Arab states represent a long and large land mass which is being constantly humiliated by the "ghetto" for its military impotence, its polymorphous political systems, and more pointedly by the loss of three wars to the Israelis. Thus both sides in the Middle East struggle consider themselves subject to political and military indignities; and both sides view themselves as the true source of area-wide liberation. The fact that within the Arab World a "third force" Palestinian view has arisen only sharpens the intensity of feelings, but does not lessen the common legacy of defeat.

Then too, there is the staggering problem in the area of politics and religion. It is impossible to talk about the Middle East or the Near East without recognizing that at one and the same time one is talking about problems of religion and problems of the state. A recent Israeli Supreme Court ruling, and the countermaking of those rulings by the Knesset, indicate that the question of identity both on a personal level and at a national level is a very serious and very sobering one. The quality of secularism in Israel, the character of the state and the integrity of its people, are constantly at stake and constantly being reviewed.

Similarly, the problem of religion in politics plagues many Arab states. The Ba'athist party is perhaps a classic example of the relationship between religiosity and socialism in the Middle East; between the socialism of a whole people, based on certain religious premises, and the character of socialism which, after all, involves a kind of highly secularized and modernized process.

The integrity of the area and the characteristics of the problem are in fact defined by the interaction of Israel and the Arab states, and not just by the inner mechanisms or inner workings of these nations. It is a question of the politics of nationalism and the agonizing problem of Third World peoples and Third World nations: the problem of dependency itself shared by Arab nations and Israel alike.

In a nutshell, the relationships between the Arab states and the Soviet Union and Israel and the United States are certainly questions of agony and high moment for all nations in the area, because they define the thirdness of the Third World as the problem of nationalism: that is, the right of these nations not only to exist as sovereign states but as autonomous states, in their own development process. The deepening of the military crisis stimulates a political crisis of identity and a crisis of who rules and the terms of rule in these nations.

It is important, especially in a time of enormous exacerbation over questions that affect people so profoundly, that we recognize the common problems of the Middle East. Unless this recognition becomes a paramount consideration, then the possibility of unity between the Arab and Jewish people in the area will never materialize. My own belief and hope, one that is shared by many, is that the unity of the Jewish and the Islamic peoples, the unity of Israel and the Middle Arab states, will in fact materialize over time, no matter how harsh and recriminatory the present moment in history appears to be.

The Fiasco of Anglo-American Middle East Policy.

AMOS PERLMUTTER

American Middle East policy during the last two decades has clearly demonstrated the role and impact of the United States' national, imperial and moral style. The United States has been imperial in that it has made itself central to the international system, although it does not necessarily dominate or occupy the lesser members directly. Instead, America's international role has been carefully designed in view of its moral posture. Thus the United States disguises its intrinsic national interests and international goals in terms such as "the extension of freedom," "self-government," "a representative political system," "freedom for the oppressed," and, since 1945, "social and economic justice" (although the latter term is less often used than the former ones).

The rationale for entering the Middle East was expressed in moral terms—the need to maintain order and to protect the above American ideals. In fact, the United States was acting in blatant self-interest, seeking to exploit the oil resources of the area and to dominate—or prevent the Soviet Union from dominating—land and water routes. Later, under the rationale of protecting the area from communism, America connived to displace the British.[1] Eventually, in the 1950s, United States oil interests were in fact subordinated to the establishment of a defense system for the Middle East against communism, styled after NATO and simultaneously contrived with SEATO. As the Truman Doctrine was universalized, what began as a European-centered policy was expanded to Asia. Accordingly, regional clients were developed and organized into a multinational association of lesser states shielded by American sponsored and dominated military alliances. A regional candidate for primacy over the system was sought to act as a surrogate for the United States; it was also hoped that this surrogate would bring other states into the alliance system.

The anachronistic assumptions of this global policy, which have been so obvious in Vietnam, were also manifest in the American approach toward the Middle East. However, the Middle East until recently received less attention than Vietnam, largely because United States military involvement in the area has been restricted to the supplying of arms and equipment. Even so, the errors, misconceptions and miscalculations in the Middle East are in many ways parallel to the ones that have been committed in Southeast Asia, as we shall see in the following examination of the Baghdad Pact and American posture toward Gamal Abdel Nasser of Eygpt.

IN DEFENSE AGAINST COMMUNISM:
THE STRUGGLE FOR MIDDLE EAST DOMINATION

American policy in the Middle East prior to the Truman Doctrine could be characterized as one of friendly noninvolvement. This policy was not wholly disinterested, for the scramble for oil had already begun; but not until 1950 did the United States become conscious that the defense against communism theory should be extended to the Middle East. Richard Nolte, an old Middle Eastern hand and short-term (one month) ambassador to Egypt, writes rather openly that "by 1950 . . . as the United States became *aware* of the Cold War importance of the Middle East to Western security, Arab good will might have been of immense value in furthering America's policies.[2]

In 1951, at a four-power meeting, the United States tried to persuade Britain, France and Turkey to cosponsor an allied Middle East Defense Command (MEDCO) that would eventually invite Egypt to be a founding member. This was perceived as an immediate challenge to British Middle East imperial policy, which then revolved around the Suez Canal. It also threatened Egyptian aspirations for a southern Arab hegemony (and this before Nasser's July 1952, coup). For these reasons, the United States MEDCO plan was shelved until Secretary of State John Foster Dulles, after returning from an extensive tour of the area, presented his Report on the Near and Middle East of June 1953, a report which marked the introduction of the Truman Doctrine to the Middle East. Dulles, learning on his trip (as he so writes)[3] of Iraqi-Eygptian antagonism, the Arab-Israeli impasse, and the Anglo-Egyptian dispute over Suez, proposed a "new" American plan to overcome all antagonisms. The idea was to establish an alliance of nations bordering on the southern frontier of the Soviet Union from Turkey to Pakistan—a Northern Tier defense system to substitute for the 1951 MEDCO plan. Dulles' plan included a mixed Arab–non-Arab alliance to surmount the Arab-Israeli impasse and to stabilize the area.

But while the Americans were thinking of a Western-oriented regional defense organization, the British were shaping a policy oriented around Iraq and its head, Nuri al-Said, to salvage Iraq's once prominent position in the Arab world. The American-British asymmetry became pronounced when Dulles, after meeting Nasser in 1953, decided to disassociate America from Britain's scheme, and began to espouse the elimination of Britain's role south of Suez. Dulles claimed that British withdrawal from Suez would "serve all Near Eastern and indeed Western security. Egypt stands at the threshold of what can be a great future."[4] Thus while Nuri al-Said of Iraq emerged as the chief agent for British-style imperial stability, Nasser's Egypt came to be considered by Dulles as the chief client for the Middle East military alliance against communism. Anthony Eden, the architect of Britain's Middle East policy had clear differences with the American scheme.

American policy in general seemed to be conditioned by a belief that Egypt was still the victim of British "colonialism," and as such deserving of American sympathy. It also appeared to be influenced by a desire to reach a quick solution almost at any cost and by a pathetic belief that, once agreement was reached, all would be well. These considerations, combined with a horror of unpopularity and fear of losing their influence with the new regime, particularly on the part of the United States Embassy in Cairo, and also an apparent disinclination by the United States Government to take second place even in an area where primary responsibility was not theirs, resulted in the Americans, at least locally, withholding the wholehearted support which their partner in NATO had the right to expect and which would have been of great, if not decisive, influence on our negotiations.[5]

But their rupture over Suez did not deter either Eden or Dulles from moving northward. Eden connived to tailor Dulles' northern plan into a British-Iraq design. Thus not only would Britain profit, but Nuri with Eden's help could isolate Egypt and mesmerize Dulles' "misunderstandings" of things Middle Eastern. Under the circumstances, Dulles considered it best that the United States participate only as a silent observer of the scheme, now supported by Britain-Iraq and Turkey-Iraq-Pakistan. Dulles had learned of Nasser's intransigence toward the scheme to establish Nuri as the leader of the Arab Middle East during their 1953 meeting, when he had told Dulles:

there would be no aggression from outside for the simple reason that methods of modern warfare with its nuclear weapons have changed the whole art of war, and rendered any foreign aggression a remote possibility. I then added that internal fronts were of highest priority as regards defence and security. I also told him that he could by his own ways and means exert pressure over any Arab Government, to join the Western camp and give them military bases on its own territory, but this would be of no avail when the decisive experience came. I also added that he would find that the Government which submitted to their pressure would be divorced from its popular support, and would be unable to lead the people. Leadership, therefore, would be leaders unknown to them. Besides, the military bases obtained under pressure would be of no use when they were needed. This was because there would be tens of bases working against this base.[6]

This must have impressed Dulles, who, on his return to the United States, reported: "In my view a Middle East defense organization was a future rather than an immediate possibility."[7]

However, on February 24, 1955, Turkey and Iraq signed a Pact of Mutual Cooperation, since known as the Baghdad Pact, which replaced the Turkish-Pakistani agreement of April 1954. This soon became the basic instrument of the Northern Tier, whose official members were now Turkey, Iran, Iraq and Great Britain. (The British ratified the Pact through the British-Iraqi Pact of April 4, 1955). What was missing, of course was a commitment on the part of the United States.

New light on this stage of British and American struggle for political and military supremacy in the Middle East has been shed in Harold Macmillan's third volume of memoirs, *Tides of Fortune: 1945-1955*.[8] As British Minister of Defense, Macmillan, in a meeting with Dulles in September 1955 at the United Nations, felt "obliged to stress the importance of some agreed Anglo-American policy [on the Northern Tier], if only to secure help to the friendly governments of Iraq and Iran."[9] What was not known (at least not publicly before Macmillan's memoirs) was the fact that although Dulles was suspicious of Baghdad because it had bypassed his plan to permit Egypt to join the alliance, he attributed his reservations about United States participation to "wretched" Arab-Israeli relations. According to Macmillan, "Dulles was now prepared to tell the Iraqis that America would agree to join [the Baghdad Pact], a full member, if a Palestine settlement could be reached."[10]

But far from resolving the Arab-Israeli conflict, the American-British and Dulles-Eden rivalries and contradictions exacerbated the hostility. By making only a vague commitment to the Baghdad Pact the United States allowed the Arab-Israeli conflict to serve as a rationale for its unwillingness to respond with direct and full support. The true intent of Dulles' proposal as described by Macmillan in his memoirs was as follows:[11]

It was to provide for the establishment of a sovereign Arab right-of-way to Eilat on the Red Sea. The idea was that Israel should cede two small triangles in the extreme south of the Negev, a few miles north of Eilat, one to Egypt with its base on the Egypt-Israel frontier, the other to Jordan with its base on the Jordan-Israel frontier. The points of the two triangles would meet on the Israeli road from Beersheba to Eilat; and at this junction, which might need mixed or international supervision, a road from Egypt to Jordan under complete Arab control would pass over (or under) the road to Eilat, which would remain under complete Israeli control. It was believed that this combination of diplomacy and engineering would be a novel, but perhaps decisive, feature in the settlement proposed. This plan, fantastic as it appeared, was Dulles' pet idea. Like the White Knight, he claimed it proudly as his own invention.[12]

Dulles' proposals for a "softer" Baghdad system (a non-Arab mixed assortment of northern states), were greeted with qualified approval by Israel but were straightforwardly condemned by Egypt, even though the Dulles proposal neither guaranteed the 1949 post-partition borders contended by Israel nor supported the Arab contention for borders based on the 1947 UN Partition Plan.

Eden, however, "accepted" the compromise plans for Israel, to redress the balance on behalf of Nuri. In his Guildhall speech of November 9, 1955, he made Dulles' plan even more palatable to the Arabs by proposing the United Nations Partition Resolution of 1947 as the beginning for Arab-Israeli negotiations, and by advocating division of the Negev between Israel and Egypt. Eden thought to reconcile Dulles and at the same time to bolster Nuri's position permanently by excluding Egypt from the alliance.

Dulles' scheme to divide the Negev and Eden's amendment, both under the official pretext of goodwill to both Arabs and Israelis, only had the effect of isolating Israel and aggravating the conflict on the Egyptian-Israeli frontier. They also encouraged Egypt in her inclination to make international bribery—the playing of East against West—her chief political contribution to the stability of the area.

To Macmillan and Eden, the Baghdad Pact meant a British-dominated Middle East presided over by Nuri al-Said. Only Dulles continued to believe in the value of the Pact as a military instrument against communism. Eden and Macmillan knew better; the Baghdad Pact was an insurance policy for the

British presence in the Arab East and a guaranteed wedge between Nuri and Nasser.

Anglo-American rivalry during this period could be summarized as follows. The British style of imperialism could have been successful if there had been no independent Israel and no new foreign policy orientation by Egypt toward the Soviet Union (which I will elaborate upon later). The new "moral" imperial style of the United States, as advocated by Dulles, had no chance from the beginning since the Arabs did not share his views on communism, materialism and Western spiritual superiority. British-American rivalry in the Middle East only made its people aware of the changing nature and meaning of imperialism.

INTELLECTUALS AND THE INTELLIGENCE
SYSTEM OF ANTI-COMMUNISM

In the early and middle 1950s, the ideologies of the State Department, the Central Intelligence Agency (CIA) and American social scientists began to converge with the inherently serious contradictions of Dulles' "moral" world view. Let's begin with the social scientists.

Inspired by theories which mainly evolved from anthropological concerns, Cold War social scientists devised a new theory of politics. This new value-free science, which they called Theoretical Comparative Politics, was institutionalized in the Social Science Research Council's Committee on Comparative Politics established in the middle 1950s. Comparative politics was applied to a study of developing politics, political development and political modernization in which Ghana and the Central African Republic were given the same attention (and sometimes more) than "classical" nations like England and France. (In fact, per capita we have now more data on the political systems of Ghana, Uganda, Gabon or the Ivory Coast than we have on France, Great Britain, Spain, Holland, Belgium or the almost "unknown" Switzerland.)

The Middle East unfortunately was not bestowed with the best of available theoretical comparative political scientists. Not until the United States brought the Cold War to that area was there even one significantly modern analysis of the area; until then it had been the domain of Islamic scholars, cultural anthropologists, linguists and travelogists. The first groups of modern Middle Eastern scholars came out with unabashed ideological support for progressive and national self-interest, for the "anti-colonial world." Among them were old Middle Eastern hands, State Department language and cultural officers, RAND Corporation and special State Department analysts, and assorted members of academia.

The "old Middle Eastern hands" held neo-Wilsonian, anachronistic beliefs in national self-determination and legalistic territorial integrity, mixed with optimism in the people, in the future of their politics and in the stability of the area. The American Protestant College, now the American University of Beirut—a harbinger of militant Arab nationalism since its formation in the 1840s—became a center for the American cadre of old Middle Eastern hands, as did the new American University in Cairo. New recruits were also made in United States universities.

While the State Department, the old hands, the bureaucrats, the missionaries and the Arabists did not exactly specify what a progressive middle class is, the pseudo-social scientists defined the military as the most effective stratum of the New Arab progressive middle class. According to a leading Middle Eastern expert of the comparative politics school

The new middle class has been able to act as a separate and independent force because: 1) prior to its seizure of power, it is freer than any other class from traditional bonds and preconceptions, and better equipped to manipulate armies and voluntary organizations as revolutionary political instruments; 2) once it controls the machinery of a modernizing state, it possesses a power base superior to that which any other class in the Middle East can muster on the basis of prestige, property, or physical force; 3) it is numerically one of the largest groups within the modern sector of society; 4) it is, so far, more obviously cohesive, more self-conscious, and better trained than any other class; 5) its political, economic and social actions, insofar as they come to grips with social change, are decisive in determining the role other classes will play in the future; and 6) it has shown itself capable of marshalling mass support.[13]

To another Cold War social scientist

1) the military is the most cohesive stratum of the NMC [New Middle Class], and the NMC is "at least" represented by the army when the army is "securely anchored in a well-organized movement;" and 2) the NMC's success in marshalling mass support depends on the army, as its most powerful instrument. The military plays an extraordinary role as the consolidator of the NMC because "[it has] served as national standard bearer when others who claimed that role proved irresponsible and ineffective." The army has been propelled into the political arena by its organization and, compared with the rest of society, was early in modernizing. The consequences are that "the more the army was modernized, the more its composition, [and] organization, spirit, capabilities, and purpose constituted a radical criticism of the existing political system.[14]

Thus an anti-colonialist and a "moral" anti-communist American ideology found new anchorage, as intellectuals and the intelligence communities converged in predicting the success of a progressive Arab middle class led by the ambitious colonels of Egypt and Syria. The convergence of moral ideals, enlightened self-interest and pseudo-social science supported the Dulles world view, even if the left hand of the system did not realize what its right hand was up to.

With the advent of Secretaries George C. Marshall and Dean Acheson, the State Department was infused with new blood; a younger generation, pragmatically oriented and schooled in modern organization, was recruited. These prototype whiz kids gravitated away from the old hands, who still supported Arab sheikhs and pashas. They preferred their own kind in the bureaucracy and the military of the modern Arab world. From this group came the doctrine of coming to terms with Nasser, or as Malcolm Kerr has put it, "a Western acceptance of Nasser's terms."[15] This doctrine conceived of Nasser as a progressive anti-communist, and accepted the army as the most effective, powerful and representative arm of the new middle class. Coming to terms with Nasser also meant that as the Arab Bismarck,[16] Nasser would unify a progressive Arab universe. This, of course, was an open-ended commitment to an overambitious Egyptian policy, which has had little or no chance of being fulfilled. To this end, which was to be reached by elevating obscure and erstwhile unpopular army officers,[17] the intelligence community applied itself.

The intelligence community was more active, vigorous and pragmatic than the new State and pseudo-social science groups. The postwar generation found State confining, highly stratified and intellectually petrified. Action-oriented intellectuals discovered a more flexible framework in the new Central Intelligence Agency (CIA). The CIA, established at the end of World War II and the beginning of the Cold War, soon became the most modern and efficient part of the intelligence network. Those who joined the CIA were dedicated against communist totalitarianism and conservative-reactionary regimes such as that of Chiang Kai-shek. They now opened up warfare against the Arab-Asian colonial powers. Engaged in clandestine support of military insurrections in the Middle East and elsewhere, and the overthrow of "old" regimes, the intelligence community became a decisive element in Dulles' Cold War plans.[18] Intelligence men were no longer restricted to cloak and dagger operations. They became highly sophisticated intellectual and political manipulators of men, resources and ideas for their "chosen" elites in foreign countries.

Not much has been written on the Middle East by former CIA officers but more is becoming known.[19] Miles Copeland, a low level, cloak and dagger type, closely connected (according to his own account, unchallenged as yet) with Kermit Roosevelt, the CIA chief in Cairo, has told the inside story of the making of Nasser by the CIA in his recently published *The Game of Nations.*[20]

What is significant about Copeland's story is that it is basically a true account of the CIA's meddling in Arab military politics. We know from other more reliable sources, such as the

Israeli intelligence, that Nasser was coopted and supported by the CIA, that the CIA infiltrated and manipulated the Egyptian Free Officers group,[21] that the CIA meddled in several Syrian and Iraqi army and Ba'ath plots, coups and countercoups (1949, 1961, 1963) and in Lebanon (1958), and even attempted some unsuccessful wedges in the Israeli defense establishment (1953-54).

Copeland claims that the CIA was in search for the "right kind of Arab leader", that is, a military leader. Copeland's description of Nasser's aggrandizement of police and military power at the expense of reform and social change is convincing, as is his analysis of the collusion between the CIA and Nasser. Also credible is his description of the new State-CIA types, Kermit Roosevelt and Ambassador Henry Byroade. These representatives of America were liberals dedicated to and searching for "progessive" anti-communist but non-radical Arabs among the military class. That the CIA was engaged in Cold War political engineering is by now a cliché, but true nonetheless. Copeland's motto, "If you cannot change the board, change the players" could be emblazoned on the CIA's Middle Eastern flag.

The Copeland appendix, "The Power Problem of a Revolutionary Government," by James Eichelberger, is a most revealing Cold War document on the CIA. Eichelberger, a State Department specialist on military regimes in the developing countries was invited by Ambassador Jefferson Caffery through the mediation of Kermit Roosevelt to write the American "constitution" for the "progressive" military regime in Egypt. In collusion with Nasser's journalist allies Muhammed Hassanein Heykal and Mustafa Amin, Eichelberger produced a document which, according to Copeland, was translated into Arabic for Nasser's staff to review. After being doctored by Amin and Heykal, the document was retranslated into English. The final version was published in English under the name of Zakariyah Muhi al-din, who was then a confidant of Nasser's in the junta. The document is written on the level of a high school senior's thesis in political science, but an analysis of its orientation is significant.

It says that the essence of government is power; that there are two types of power, repressive and constructive. The former is a simple tyranny; the latter a revolutionary regime. A true revolution must first be achieved through some repressive power, and the repressive action is unavoidable. This is the early stage of revolution from which government must inevitably move to a constructive phase; constitutionalism should be the constructive power base. During the revolutionary phase, the regime must eliminate opportunists, vested interests and political subversion; e.g., communists who wish to take over the revolution for their own ends. The police should receive the most attention from the revolutionary leaders during the early phases of the revolution. Intelligence is the nerve center of the whole security system of a revolutionary state (or of any state). The military must be loyal and efficient. These structures are the preconstitutional apparatus of a revolutionary government. Perfect security, control over police and military, and manipulation of the masses will establish the base for constitutional government. This is the institutional- ization of the revolution. Eichelberger concludes that "the revolutionary government must do *whatever is necessary* to actualize more power—repressive and constructive—than is al lowed to remain potential. It is hoped that this paper may serve as an introduction to the *art of doing the necessary*."

This position paper represents a practical derivation of pseudo-social scientific assumptions, a constitution to operation- alize the Cold War in developing areas. From the political theorist's point of view the document is trash, but governments do not operate on the planes of political philosophy. Thus, the CIA emulated Stalin's methods: the engineering of social and political systems by iron-clad rules. The CIA offered Egypt and other Afro-Asian regimes and rulers the benefits of the American political system by a *reductio ad absurdum* of American values and style packaged in a Neanderthal form of what would prove the foundation of Rostowism and nation building syndromes elsewhere.

Let me stress that there was no cabal among the CIA, social scientists and the State Department. Not only was the converg- ence unpremeditated, but the conflicts and disagreement between State Department advisors and Dulles were notorious. Further- more, in many cases no one pillar of the convergence triangle was aware of its relationship to the others. Indeed, there was a lack of coordination and even high tension and bitter antagonism between State and the CIA. For instance, the proposal to invade Lebanon in 1958 to save the conservative (so-called moderate) and unpopular regime of Kamil Chamoun was supported by the CIA while State was bitterly divided on invasion, though in the end, the latter's views prevailed.

The three converged, however, in their common political *Weltanschauung*; the more militant in State, like Dulles, opposing communism; the CIA pushing for aid to reformist, insurrectionist Arabs in the military; and the old hands supporting the progressive new middle sectors. The social scientists, by virtue of their "knowledge," legitimized United States foreign policy while abusing modern social science techniques. Except for the CIA, whose actions betrayed its real commitments, all three were dedicated to the international status quo, to area stability and tranquility and to mildly progressive regimes. But they brought about the opposite results; the breakdown of already shaky regimes, the intensification of tension, the destruction of real moderates by military progressive praetorians, and the breakdown of order.

This miscalculation resulted from a series of misconceptions held by all three groups. 1) The United States failed to recognize that the Middle East is not an exclusive Western sphere of interest. Because the Soviet Union was not invited to contribute to stability in the area, the Soviets have worked against this objective. 2) It was mistaken to assume that the Arabs' first nationlist or political priority would be to fight international communism. This was not even true of the most reactionary Arab sheikhs and monarchs. 3) The United States failed to perceive that Nasser's chief goal was to change the existing balance of forces in the Middle East. 4) The United States instrusion into Arab-Israeli antagonisms did not stabilize the conflict. Egypt's and later Syria's further involvement in the Palestine conflict enhanced Israel's isolation. Instead of seriously seeking the security of Israel, American policy played into the hands of Arab militants who exploited American goodwill to further Nasser's pan-Arabist ambitions and to aggravate the Palestinian conflict.

RUSSIA ENTERS THE MIDDLE EAST QUAGMIRE

What had begun as a rivalry between the United States and Britain over clients, strategy and influence ended with the Suez fiasco and a serious rupture in Anglo-American relations. By 1958 the Baghdad Pact had disintegrated and an era of intense American-Soviet rivalry over the Middle East began. The United States, attempting to redress an Arab-Israeli balance in the aftermath of Suez, adhered to the 1950 Tripartite Agreement (which also included France and Britain) on arms embargo and limitation in the Middle East. But when the British promised to deliver to Nuri some 50 Centurion tanks paid for by the United States[22] Egypt and Israel began to rearm, re-equip and modernize their armed forces. Egypt soon enough found an arms supplier in the Soviet Union, the only great power not a member of the 1950 agreement, while the Israelis connived with France to betray the agreement as Eden had done with Iraq.

Meanwhile the failures of Baghdad and the policy of coming to terms with Nasser, the Suez fiasco, and the worsening of Arab-Israeli relations were put by conventional interpretations on the shoulders of an overambitious Nasser and an armed prophet, David Ben Gurion.[23]. Dulles and the State Department made no realistic assessment as to whether the American and British machinations would threaten the independence, national integrity and forward-looking leadership of Israel and Egypt. Though bitter antagonists, both countries perceived that their national interests were being compromised and jeopardized by the British attempt to establish Nuri as a chief Arab leader and Iraq as a Central Western client.

Apologists for American policy in the Middle East have explained the failure in the area thus: Upset with a pro-Western, Nuri-Iraqi orientation geared to the interests of the Cold War, as exemplified by Dulles' reneging on United States support for the Aswan Dam, Nasser decided to move eastward. After concluding the agreement on the evacuation of British forces from Suez, where the United States played a key role in putting pressure on the British to conclude the Treaty, and which satisfied Egyptian aspirations for national independence,[24] Nasser "betrayed" the

Tripartite Agreement by buying weapons from the East. Another argument is that the militant Israeli border raid policy, culminating in the February 28, 1955 Gaza raid, pushed Nasser to buy arms from the Soviets. The 1955 Gaza raid is thus labeled as a decisive turning point in the Arab-Israeli conflict. It is said to have ruined the last chances for an Arab-Israeli diplomatic and political reconciliation, to have divided Egypt from the West, and above all to have forced Nasser to seek military aid from the Soviet Union. It is here that America supposedly "lost" Egypt.

The reinterpretation I shall offer here makes the above "facts" look suitable only for the Cold War *Weltanschauung* of the 1950s. According to my interpretation: 1) The Egyptian-USSR arms deal was a reaction to British-American machinations during Baghdad and not to Dulles' reneging on Aswan; 2) The Egyptian-Soviet arms deal was substantively a political transaction, not just a purely military deal; 3) The Egyptian request for arms both from the United States and Soviet Union predated the Gaza raid, which was actually irrelevant to overall Egyptian policy; 4) It was Nasser's pan-Arab policy, promulgated before Dulles reneged on Aswan and before the Gaza raid that was responsible for his search for a new ally, preferably one antagonistic to the West; 5) The policy of coming to terms with Nasser was obsolete from its inception and in fact contributed to American-Egyptian asymmetry and national misconceptions. Let us examine each of these propositions in turn.

Egypt and the Arab World

The Anglo-American connivance for a Middle Eastern defense system had persuaded Nasser that his approving Baghdad even in principle would be contrary to historical as well as new Egyptian ambitions. Historically, at least until 1945, Egypt's identification with the Arab world had been ambivalent and on the whole negative. Egypt refused to join the Arab League until 1945 and until 1956 did not officially consider itself an Arab country. When Sa'd Zaghlul, the leader of liberal nationalists and head of the first nationalist government in Egypt, was approached by Abdul Rahman al-Azm (the first pan-Arab Egyptian nationalist and later first secretary-general of the Arab league) in 1924 and asked why Egypt refused to join the Arab unity movement, he answered: "If you add one zero to another zero, then you add another zero, what will be the sum?"[25] But Nasser's own revolutionary ideology was proclaimed during the period when Baghdad was only a blueprint. In the 1930s the influential Muslim Brotherhood, which drew its power from the Egyptian middle class, the bureaucracy, the army and status-deprived individuals, succumbed to the antiliberal, proviolence and anti-Western doctrines of several ultranational groups. Nasser's philosophy of revolution was in large part the inspiration for the new wave of Arab nationalism that began in the decade beginning with the World War II. According to his world view, Egypt occupied the center, the Arabs and Islam second, and Africa the outer level of three concentric circles.

The doctrine of Egyptian hegemony in the Arab world, as institutionalized by Nasser's regime, was developed into an integrating national myth: romantic, messianic and universal, more similar to the concept of *Deutschtum* than any other political or nationalist philosophy. Its essence can be summarized in the following statement by Nasser:

From Egypt came the belief of the unity of God, the unified magnificent God, and with this Egypt shook the ground of every aspect of atheistic beliefs. She liberated humanity from worshipping the stones.

In Egypt medicine and surgery were developed to help relieve the sickness and pain of human beings ... Egypt was the ingenious nation which developed the art of geometry and building construction. Egypt's fleets crossed the seas carrying knowledge far out to her neighbors north, south, east, and west ... In Egypt different arts and fields of knowledge flourished. Literature thrived and sculpture and painting reached their peak ... Egypt protected Christianity from its birth and has preserved its features and characteristics. Egypt chose Islam as a religion—she protected it, kept it, and fostered Islamic scholars who developed new ideas and interpretations ... Because Egypt sustained the Islamic civilization when it was exposed to crusaders' threats, the Islamic world should express its gratitude to Egypt and consider her the leader of the Islamic nations. This is Egypt ... the African Egypt which lies on the Mediterranean and is the focal point of many civilizations . . . Egypt's glories in ancient history merit recognition by the world . . . She is the magnificent nation which firmly stood up to the power of the colonizing stream, kept her spirit, personality and structure.[26]

With such intense, nationalistic feeling, is it any wonder that Nasser regarded Egypt as the obvious choice for Middle Eastern leadership and could never join in a pact that guaranteed this to his chief rival in the area?

The Soviet-Egyptian Arms Deal

A revised interpretation of the prelude to the Soviet-Egyptian arms deal has recently been put forward by Uri Ra'anan, who has conclusively shown that, contrary to conventional interpretations, the deal was not a consequence of United States refusal to give Egypt weapons. In fact, Nasser had entered into negotiations with Moscow in January-February 1955, *before* requesting arms from Washington (and prior to Israel's Gaza raid of February 28, 1955). According to Ra'anan, the Soviets had decided, before any of these events took place, to engineer a political entry into the region. In support of his contention, Ra'anan quotes Soviet documents and contemporary Western sources which indicate that the arms deal was initiated between February 14 and 21, 1955, a full seven months before it was announced to the world.[27] The Soviet motivation was thus primarily a political foray into the area, not a simple military hardware transaction.

"From Egypt's point of view," writes Ra'anan, "as from Russia's, the freezing of the balance of power and the territorial status quo in the Near East was completely unpalatable.[28] In a session between the Egyptian and British Ambassadors on January 9, 1954, the purposes of Egypt's new foreign policy were made quite clear: "1) The establishment of an Arab bloc, free from imperialist influence, to protect the interests of Islamic, Arabic and African peoples; 2) the conclusion of a Treaty binding these peoples together; 3) the establishment of an African bloc which would include all African countries under the imperialist yoke."[29] A policy of nonalignment was proclaimed by Egypt to promulgate these principles. The Soviets, as a result of internal factional rivalries and their new policy of international involvement, were searching for a way to sabotage the Baghdad system.[30] "The Soviet leadership," writes Ra'anan, "was bound, therefore, to be perturbed by signs that the West was succeeding in laying down permanent, hardened lines to the south as well as to the east and west of the Soviet empire . . ."[31] Thus began the entente cordiale between Moscow and Cairo.

Adam Ulam writes that: "A pattern of dependence in the Soviet bloc was thus evolving, even though Nasser called the whole transaction a purely commercial one."[32] The realignment of forces in the Kremlin and the rise of Khrushchev[33] emphasized the political importance of the Moscow-Cairo entente. In fact, Ra'anan's detailed analysis of the Egyptian request for arms from the United States and Britain establishes the categorical fact that Egypt no longer desired an Anglo-American or Western Middle Eastern status quo.

Israel's Gaza Raid

This brings us to the debunking of another Anglo-American diplomatic myth: that Israel's February 28, 1955 Gaza raid upset the balance of power between Israel and Egypt, forced Nasser to request immediate arms supplies and, when the United States refused to comply with his long list of weapons forced Nasser to seek military aid from Russia. The rest is well known—Sinai-Suez, the collapse of coming to terms, the 1967 war and so on. The facts and the documents are there. But surprisingly, one is confronted with the carelessness of diplomatic historians, the lack of originality or curiosity or both of several "official" scholars of this era and area, and in the end, the muted complicity of policy-makers and the intelligence-intellectual community.

Ra'anan undisputedly establishes the fact that the Cairo-Moscow entente started sometime before Egypt requested American weapons.[34] His revised timetable reveals that the United States, never a main arms supplier to Egypt, had offered military assistance to Cairo earlier, but was cold-shouldered. Only at the end of January 1955, when the Baghdad Pact seemed to materialize with Iraq at its center, did the Egyptians indicate interest in American weapons. After the February 24, 1954 Turkish-Iraqi alliance, Nasser did not withdraw his request for aid. Why? Because during January and February of 1955, the

Cairo-Moscow entente was already being forged.[35] Nasser saw no point in continuing to seek a large arms supply from the United States, because he knew that under the terms of the Tripartite Agreement a large arms supply request would be rebuffed. He knew he could be supplied only by the Soviets. The Gaza raid, far from precipitating Egypt's request for arms from the Soviet Union, was actually an obstacle to an entente between Cairo and Moscow. Since the United States imposed a brief embargo on shipments to both Israel and Egypt after Gaza (all within the framework of 1950), how could Nasser have requested arms during this period or "turn away" from the West?

Furthermore, militarily speaking, the incident could have hardly been of direct relevance to Cairo's bid for heavy arms. Ra'anan notes that

Both sides increasingly relied on picked commando formations, using the traditional light equipment of such small, mobile units. Since Egypt's military request to the United States referred almost entirely to heavy armaments, it could have had little connection with the Gaza situation.[36]

In fact, the Israeli high command was so relaxed concerning the Egyptian front that between December 1953 and the middle of 1954, the new chief of staff, General Moshe Dayan, practically abolished the southern front by appointing a colonel in charge of it. Only with the increase of Egyptian organized fedayeen activities in the Negev and elsewhere was General Meir Amit, one of Israel's best officers, appointed to the command of the southern front.

Peace and the Great Powers

Another error is that the Gaza raid "destroyed" the last chances for an Israeli rapprochement[37] by upsetting delicate negotiations and turning Nasser's attention from peace to war.[38] The fact was that Egyptian-Israeli relations had already deteriorated with the rise of Nasser and his junta, enhanced by the great powers' machinations in the area. Nasser, a graduate of the 1936 era of militancy and Islamic-Egyptian nationalism, was imbued with fervent anti-Zionism and deeply committed to the Palestine question.[39] The radical Muslim-Arab nationalists could not reconcile themselves to an independent Jewish political entity—

not in 1936 and less so in 1953-54 when they were settled in power. In fact, it was David Ben Gurion who had great hopes that an Egypt engaged in socioeconomic reform would in the end be the Arab state that could extend peace to Israel.[40] According to Earl Berger:

> The Israelis' fundamental doctrine was that the Arabs would seek Israel's cooperation: this was 'a moral, a political, an economic necessity.' If the Arabs did not 'learn from us and labor with us' then they would have to do it with 'strangers, potent and tyrannous', the imperialists. The Israelis saw themselves as a bridge between the civilized West and the backward East. They would bring the social and economic revolution to the Arab world; they were the harbingers of the modern, progressive, and independent Middle East.[41]

The United States (especially Dulles) pressed Israel to make unilateral concessions in order to create an atmosphere of goodwill with Egypt. The Israelis were to pay compensations to refugees, provide a free port at Haifa for Jordan, sign a non-aggression pact with the Arabs, and, most importantly, provide a land link between Egypt and Jordan in the Negev. Egypt, however, wanted more and demanded a free zone in the Negev, without even promising to lift the blockade on Israeli ships in Suez.[42]

The history of Western attitudes toward Israel since the Balfour Declaration could not be better summarized than that Israel is: 1) the most negotiable item on any agenda which contemplates any level of Arab support, but that the inverse is never true; 2) that the security of Israel is never to be guaranteed fully. Except for a few years (1917-1920) no Arab ruler, group or state has supported the idea of a Jewish state, whatever its frontiers, size or type or regime. There was never even an official Arab attempt to reconcile the differences between them, although a few individuals and groups in the periphery of the Arab world tried, mostly before 1948. Today, the most reasonable and moderate Arabs accept at best a binational version of an Arab-Jewish polity, secular or otherwise. The rest, reactionary and revolutionary alike, are adamantly opposed to the idea of Jewish political independence. Nor do Arabs feel compelled to recognize Israel even after a resounding defeat such as 1967. Here the Arab argument is in my view quite rational: "We are 70 million, you are three; in the twelfth campaign we can lick you; our population is more expandable than yours. Israel, like the historical Crusader state, can at best last a century. In fact, the last Jewish state, the Hashmonite Kingdom, lasted less than 80 years. Above all, what we lose by war and violence can be restored by diplomacy, political pressure and political exhortation, and machinations between imperial and great powers, who in the end opt in favor of 70 million Arabs, oil revenues, United Nations votes, status quo and strategic-political considerations."

This is indeed a most rational contention. The cost that praetorian Arab regimes are willing to pay for a Hundred Years War are minimal if compared with the cost of Israeli survival. Also, Arabs have learned from experience that no imperial or great power fails to appreciate the fact that political and economic pressures on Israel can yield considerable headway in the Arab world at least for a brief period. The political vulnerability of Israel is an established fact. Why should Arabs try for less?

Let's make a brief historical survey of the above contention. During the 1930s fervent Arab nationalists courted Nazis and Fascists as allies against British-French imperialism and Zionism.[43] Ben Gurion suggested to Neville Chamberlain in 1938 that the British government's appeasement of Arabs at the cost of the Jewish community would not change the Arab attitude to Britain.[44] Although the British courted the Arabs by restricting Jewish immigration and purchase of land in Palestine,[45] the Mufti of Jerusalem, the most important political figure of Palestinian Arabs, became a Nazi Gauleiter in Yugoslavia in charge of extermination of minority groups; Rashid ali al-Gailani established a fascist regime in Iraq in 1941; King Farouk of Egypt made contact with the Germans before el-Alamein; and Nuri al-Said, Britain's most loyal ally, courted the Germans as well.[46] In addition, three future members of Nasser's 1952 junta (Hasan Iberiam, Abd al-Latif Baghdadi and Hasan Sabri) abortively attempted to smuggle the commander-in-chief of the Egyptian army (an old Germanophile), General Aziz ali al-Misri,[47] to

Rommell's German headquarters, hoping to set up a government in exile in the event Rommell conquered Egypt.[48]

When America entered the Middle East these lessons were unknown. Dean Acheson admits that he was opposed to Truman's policy of the recognition of Israel,[49] as were most of Truman's political advisors led by Secretary of the Navy (later Defense) James Forrestal.[50] Both Dulles and Eden went further than Nasser in imposing on Israel, as we have discussed earlier, by suggesting the division of the Negev to make an Egyptian corridor linking Egypt to Jordan.

In fact, though we have as yet no document to corroborate the following, the following extreme hypotheses seem quite plausible (in view of the author's interviews with key Israeli decision-makers in 1956): Eden's part in the collusion over Suez-Sinai was really part of the Baghdad-Nuri scheme. Eden hoped that once Israel and Egypt engaged one another they would be prepared to accept him as an honest broker between them. Israel would give a part of the Negev to Jordan, thereby completing the Baghdad system and Iraqi domination over Jordan, and the other half to Egypt, who would be "pacified" by another part of Israel. Eden admitted that he did not consider an Israeli–Egyptian war a chief danger, but the possibility that the conflict would spread. "A localized war between Israel and Egypt, while troublesome, should not be highly dangerous internationally. The same could not be said of a war which has spread to include Syria and Jordan, with Iraq morally compelled to take a hand too."[51]

American-Egyptian Misconceptions

American-Egyptian policy was strained by the protracted and complex character of coming to terms with Nasser. Dulles' idea was to treat Nasser and Egypt on their own terms, which took the form of placing great pressure on the British to evacuate Suez, in the belief that Egypt could become the key to a Middle East defense only if it joined the Turkish-Iraqi pact. To placate Egypt further, Dulles also offered to curtail the territorial integrity of Israel.

The evacuation of the British from Suez was already part of an Egyptian policy of independence from the West, and the opposition to Nuri stemmed from this as well as from the rivalry between the Napoleon and the Metternich of the Middle East. This was almost totally misunderstood by the Secretary of State. In retrospect Macmillan admits that:

> Nevertheless, the whole of this long dispute [on the British evacuation from the Canal] was painful in the extreme. We could not of course foresee that Nasser, once he had finally obtained supreme control, would turn to expansionist aims in the hope of creating a great Arab empire, or would move so rapidly toward increasing covert and open threats against Israel, while preparing to repudiate with complete cynicism Egypt's international obligations with respect to the Canal.[52]

The consequences of United States and Egyptian misconceptions bore their first results in the American rejection of support for Nasser's gigantic scheme on Aswan. When Dulles was finally informed (seven months too late) on how close Egyptian-Soviet ties were, he called off American and World Bank support for the Aswan Project. Nasser retaliated by nationalizing the Canal. This triggered Franco-British, Franco-Israeli designs on a joint venture contra Egypt. Enraged with Eden, Dulles retaliated by forcing Britain, France and Israel to withdraw from Sinai-Suez.

These policies were pursued even though the Egyptians were still inwardly uncertain of their national identity; neither they nor other Arabs were yet sure what it meant to them to be socialists.[53] But the coming to terms lingers on, even though Nasser has been relegated to a lesser status since 1958; since June 1967, when Egypt broke its diplomatic relations with the United States, relations have been at their lowest ebb. Secretary Rogers' speech of December 9, 1969 signifies a new type of low-key coming to terms with Egypt.

United States relations with Israel are less complex. The pattern of two decades seems clear. Israel, born out of an American-Soviet concert of interest in 1948, supported economically and even morally by the United States—especially by one segment of the American population, having no political interest to sell (at least not yet)—allied to none, and delivering an American victory by proxy in 1967, can be compromised to comply with wider American national (and global) interests. The Americans never contemplated guaranteeing Israeli security. At best Israel must fight on its own. At worst one can sell pieces of Israel to placate revolutionary Arabs or conservative sheikhs and regimes. In fact, both Badeau and Nolte agree that Israel was a liability and not an asset, a problem for the United States rather than an interest.[54] "The policy of support of Israel . . . was not undertaken for consideration of national interest . . ."[55]

The fact that Israel is a Middle Eastern power and a factor in the American national interest is not yet admitted in Washington. If the national interest is peace and the status quo in the Middle East, paying Arabs with Israeli coins is manifestly counterproductive. The failure to guarantee Israel's security is precisely why Arabs feel that it is still an open-ended question and that they can challenge peace in the Middle East without compunction.

What has been demonstrated could thus be summarized: 1) Arab leaders and local conflicts of the Arab-Israeli type were at a most tolerable level in the early 1950s only to change when the Middle East was chosen as a major area of contest in the Cold War; 2) a policy of even-handedness not buttressed by a guarantee of the security of Israel's territory and a firm, sustained arms embargo is futile; 3) If the Soviet Union is not made a partner to the balance of power in the area, it will become the leading power to upset the balance; 4) The strategic interests of imperial powers seldom coincide with the interests and ambitions of local powers, and no amount of intelligence-intellectual information analyses can overcome the basic dichotomy between the great powers and the small ones; 5) The asymmetry between the orientations of great and small powers make the latter bellicose while the former disrupt international stability.

THE FOUR POWER CONFERENCE:
SOVIET DUPLICITY AND AMERICAN COMPLICITY

The 1967 war resulted in a total defeat of Arab armies, but not of Arab rationale. The Egyptians accepted a cease-fire only as a respite and to reconstruct the 1956 scenario. How? First, by accepting a cease-fire and purging the army officers "responsible"

for the debacle. Then, by blaming the Anglo-American imperialists for the debacle; by reconstructing and re-equipping the
Egyptian army; speaking adamantly of nonrecognition and
non-negotiation; and beginning the war of attrition with Soviet
support, guidance and blessing. The climax will be reached when
the world is warned of an impending Middle Eastern powder keg
unless the Arabs are restored what they have lost by violence.

The Soviet entrance into the Middle East took the guise of a
Franco-Soviet sponsored four-power conference, in which American acquiesced. What was the Soviet rationale for working for
such a conference and practically engineering its agenda?

The Soviets stepped into the Middle East arena in the postwar
era with no emotional attachments of political legacies to
distort their realistic appraisal of the situation. Because they
were historically anti-Zionist and unsympathetic to the bour-
geois Arab leaders, they previously had stayed out of the
Arab-Zionist conflict. The Soviet Union originally sought to
eliminate the imperial power of Great Britain for strategic
purposes, and the Palestine conflict served its purpose well by
forcing the British to withdraw from the Middle East. Between
1947 and 1952 the Soviets supported Israel militarily because
they were primarily interested in British evacuation and sought
no other stake in the area. Because of the cold war, however,
they eventually opted for Arab allies, and since 1953 they have
deliberately sought to exacerbate Arab-Israeli tensions.

The errors of the Soviet New Outlook policy of supporting "national liberation forces" in anticipation of establishing
Cuba-like regimes in Syria, Egypt and Algeria placed Moscow
in a dilemma during the existence (1959-61) of the United
Arab Republic. The Soviets had chosen Nasser as their chief
client; as long as no other progressive Arabs competed with
him, Soviet Egyptian policy was successful and profitable. But
when Nasser in 1959 and 1960 clashed with the Ba'ath, the
supposed emerging New Middle Class of Syria, over the UAR's
internal policies, Moscow found itself in a situation common to
all imperialist powers in the Middle East, namely, which party
should be chosen as chief client. The Soviets adopted the
practice of British imperialism between the wars, i.e., *divide et*

impera, but discovered in 1967 that pursuit of this dangerous policy of oscillating between their Egyptian and Syrian clients could catapult them to the brink of war.

Soviet involvement in the Middle East is based on the geopolitical strategic foundations of historic Russian foreign policy: the security of Russia's southern flank and an open Bosphorus passage to the Mediterranean Sea. For these reasons a Soviet rapprochement with Turkey and Iran would seem more important than achievements on the Arab front. But Khrushchev's New Outlook policy plunged Moscow into what has become a costly involvement in inter-Arab and Israeli conflicts.[56]

The Soviet dilemma of whether gradually to abandon or to become more deeply committed to Egypt was not resolved so much by events in the Middle East as by a bitter Kremlin debate. The old guard ideologists argued that the Soviet Union as a revolutionary power must continue to support the forces fighting the imperialists. Thus, Moscow would support Syria and Egypt and their military in anticipation of the subsequent radicalization of Syria and Egypt after the 1967 disaster. A policy of vigorous support of the Arabs against Israel, the Soviets hope, will exclude them from involvement in the apparent contradictions between Egypt and Syria and will consolidate their interests more successfully in these countries.

The irresponsibility of the Soviets in their Middle Eastern adventure again illustrates the price the powers and their clients must pay for imperialism. The Soviets moving now for "spheres of influence" (an old time imperialistic device cloaked under theories of the balance of power) must pay the price of their success: the protection of a revanchist Egyptian regime, a police state dedicated to internal suppression and to a war of "iron and blood." The four-power conference hardened the position of both Israel and Egypt, encouraging Egypt's hopes to achieve concessions from Israel via American pressure, and Israel's inclination to resist pressures to a compromise in order to demonstrate that she is no longer subject to political exhortation.

The Soviet dilemma in the Middle East is how to prevent its Egyptian tail from wagging. The Soviet Union is in no position to prevail upon its client Egypt or upon Israel not to escalate the conflict or even to keep it on a manageable level without Israeli consent. Only the Israelis are militarily capable of avoiding a war. The Egyptians are in no position to intensify the warfare; their efforts since March 1969 to break the Israeli line on the Suez have been disastrous. The Soviet Union has been unable to guarantee the stability of the area. Soviet air and strategic protection of Egypt only whets the appetite of Arab extremists. As was demonstrated in 1967, whether left alone or with even a tacit American understanding, the Soviets cannot harness their clients.

The United States is in no position to pacify Nasser, whose Khartoum conditions of no recognition, no peace negotiation, and no free navigation rights for Israel in Suez and Aqaba prevents the United States from reaching a compromise with him. The United States cannot placate Egyptian revanchism and adamacy or Israeli stubbornness for nothing less than direct negotiation with the Arabs. An accommodation with the Soviets in the Middle East is possible if and when all parties to the conflict are sincerely interested in modifying their maximum aspirations and values.

The willingness to accommodate has been harnessed to the need to achieve maximum benefits for the United States and the Soviet Union. A four-power conference cannot succeed for the same reasons that the Anglo-American alliances failed. As long as the powers "negotiate" without a serious agenda and a list of particulars about which to bargain (multilateral disarmament, guarantees of frontiers, free navigation rights, joint economic programs, and the harnessing of guerrilla operations) there can be no serious or legitimate concert of powers and of interests mutually and multilaterally to close the cap on the Middle Eastern powder-keg.

---

[1] The most revealing analysis of America's oil machinations and the replacement of British oil and strategic interests is found in Gabriel Kolko, *The Politics of War* (New York: Random House, 1968).

[2] Richard Nolte, "American Policy in the Middle East," *Journal of International Affairs*, XIII (1959), p. 114.

[3] See text of Dulles' Report in J.C. Hurewitz, *Diplomacy in the Near and Middle East: A Documentary Record*, 11, Document 100 (Princeton: Van Nostrand, 1956), p. 338.

[4] *Ibid.*

[5] *The Memoirs of Sir Anthony Eden: Full Circle*, 111 (1960), pp. 256-7.

[6] Interview with Nasser by the *New York Times*, as quoted in Patrick Seale, *The Struggle for Syria, 1954-58* (London: Oxford, 1965), p. 188.

[7] *Ibid.*

[8] Harold Macmillan, *Tides of Fortune: 1945-1955* (New York: Harper and Row, 1969), pp. 504-504, 633-658.

[9] Eden, *op. cit.*, p. 630.

[10] *Ibid.*

[11] See Dulles' proposal in Hurewitz, *op. cit.* Document 198, p. 395-398.

[12] Macmillan, *op. cit.*, p. 631.

[13] Manfred Halpern, *The Politics of Social Change in the Middle East and North Africa* (Princeton: Princeton University Press, 1963), p. 59.

[14] Amos Perlmutter, "Egypt and the Myth of New Middle Class: A Comparative Analysis," *Comparative Studies in Society and History*, (October, 1967), p. 46-65.

[15] Malcolm Kerr, "Coming to Terms with Nasser's Attempts and Failures," *International Affairs*, XLIII (January, 1967), p. 65.

[16] Nolte, *op. cit.*, p. 118.

[17] When the Nasser junta staged the July 23, 1952 coup, it had no support except among some trade union leaders. In fact, the students, the professionals and the radical members of the Moslem Brotherhood in Al Azhar Islamic University rejected and demonstrated against the junta. On the student-professional opposition to Nasser's rise, see Keith Wheelock, *Nasser's New Egypt* (New York: Praeger, 1960), and Jean and Simone Lacouture, *Egypt in Transition* (New York: Capricorn, 1958)

[18] Dulles, *Ibid.*

[19] Among the following authors, some were connected with and some actually were members of the CIA: Tom Little, *Nasser's Egypt* (Praeger, 1958); Charles Cremens, *The Arabs and the World* (Praeger, 1963); John Campbell, *In Defense of the Middle East* (Harper & Row, 1960); Gordon Torrey, *Syrian Politics and the Military* (Ohio State University, 1965). See also, for fiction on the CIA in Egypt, *Kingdom of Illusion* (Panther Books, 1967). For a general account of the CIA and the Cold War, see Allen Dulles, *The Craft of Intelligence* (Harper & Row, 1963).

[20] *The Game of Nations* (Simon & Shuster, 1970).

[21] See the most comprehensive description of the Egyptian Free Officers in Eliezer Beeri, *Army Officers in Arab Politics and Society* (Praeger, 1969).

[22] Macmillan, *op. cit.*, pp. 633-635.

[23] For conventional interpretations see John Badeau, *The American Approach to the Arab World* (New York: Harper & Row, 1968); Richard Nolte and William Polk, "Toward a Policy for the Middle East," *Foreign Affairs* (July, 1958). See also the memorandum of Henry Byroade, Charles Yost, etc.

[24] Macmillan, *op cit.*, p. 63.

[25] Anwar G. Chejne, "Egyptian Attitudes toward Pan-Arabism," *The Middle East Journal* (Summer, 1957), p. 253.

[26] Hussein Mu'nis, *Misr Wa-Risaltuah (Egypt's Mission), Ikhtarna Lak*, No. 55 (Cairo, 1956). See also Abd as Star Kamal, *Misr al-'Uzmah (Mighty Egypt)* (Cairo: Government Printing House, 1954); Introduction by Minister of National Education, Kamal Al-Din Hussein.

[27] Uri Ra'anan, *The USSR Arms and the Third World* (MIT Press, 1969), pp. 69-129.

[28] *Ibid.*, p. 21.

[29] BBC, No. 431, January 15, 1954, quoted in Seale, *op. cit.*, p. 195.

[30] On the general trend of changing directions in the Soviet Union see the monumental study of Adam Ulam, *Expansion and Coexistence: The History of Soviet Foreign Policy, 1917-1967* (New York: Praeger, 1968), pp. 496-571. On the Near East see pp. 584-590.

[31] Ra'anan, *op. cit.*, p. 20.

[32] Ulam, *op. cit.*, p. 586.

[33] See for analysis Ra'anan, *op. cit.*, pp. 86-102.

[34] *Ibid.*, pp. 36-37-44-53.

[35] *Ibid.*, pp. 70-74.

[36] *Ibid.*, p.47.

[37] Nolte, *op. cit.*, Badeau, *op. cit.*, Ra'anan, *op. cit.*

[38] See also the apologist for the Arabs and old Eden protege, Anthony Nutting, *No End of a Lesson: The Story of the Suez Crisis* (New York; C.N. Potter, 1967); and the fiery Irish pro-Arab writer Erskine Childers, *On the Road to Suez.*

[39] Four (Abdul Hakim Amer, Anwarl-Sadat, Kamal al-din Hussein, and Abdul Muneim Abd al-Rawf) of the original thirteen members of the officer club junta were affiliates of this movement; Nasser himself was an extreme follower of pan-Arabist, pan-Islamic nationalism. For details on Nasser's upbringing, political *weltanschauung* and Moslem Brotherhood's connections, see Richard P. Mitchell, "The Society of Muslim Brothers" (unpublished Ph.D. dissertation, Princeton University, 1960), pp. 61-250; Ishak Musa Husaini, *The Moslem Brethren* (Beirut, 1956, pp. 125-130; Eleizer Beeri, "On the History of the Free Officers," *The New East (Hamizrah Hehadash)*, XIII, no. 51 (1964), 247-268; Kamil Isma'il al-Sharif, *al-Ikhwan al-Muslimin Fi Harb-Filastin (The Muslim Brotherhood in the Palestine War)* (Cairo, 1951); J. and S. Lacouture, *Egypt*, pp. 131 ff. On relationships between Free Officers, Egypt, and the Axis, see Lukasz Hirszowicz, *The Third Reich and the Arab East* (London, 1966), pp. 229-249.

[40] See Ben Gurion speeches in the period July 1952-February 1954 (when Nasser finally ousted Naguib) on their moderate tone toward Egypt. A detailed analysis is found in Earl Berger, *The Covenant and the Sword: Arab-Israeli Relations, 1948-1956* (London, Routledge and Kegan Paul Ltd., 1965), pp. 165-183.

[41] Berger, p. 169.

[42] *Ibid.*, p. 172-173.

[43] See Hirszowicz, *op. cit.* pp. 229-249. See also Mitchell, *op. cit.*, pp. 61-250.

[44] David Ben Gurion, *Meetings With Arab Leaders* (Tel Aviv, Am Ovid, 1966).s

[45] See the authoritative study of J.C. Hurewitz, *The Struggle for Palestine*, (New York: Norton, 1950), pp. 94-111.

[46] See the most revealing study on Nuri-Axis contact in Majid Khadduri, "General Nuri's Flirtation with the Axis Powers," *The Middle East Journal* (Summer, 1962), pp. 328-336.

[47] On al-Misri see Majid Khadduri, "Aziz ali al-Misri and the Arab Nationalist Movement," in A. Hourani (ed.) *Middle Eastern Affairs* (Oxford, 1965), pp. 140-163.

[48] See Anwar al-Sadat, *Revolt on Nile* (London, 1954). See also Beeri, *op. cit.*, and Abd Latif Baghdadi, Memoirs (arabic) (Cairo, 1956)

[49] Dean Acheson, *Present at the Creation* (New York, Norton, 1969) pp. 169-170.

[50] James Forrestal, *Forrestal Diaries* (New York: Viking Press, 1951).

[51] Eden, *op. cit.*, p. 588.

[52] Macmillan, *op. cit.*, p. 505.

[53] Kerr, *op. cit.*, p. 67.

[54] Badeau, *o. cit.*, p. 21.

[55] Nolte, *op. cit.*, p. 115.

[56] Perlmutter, "Sources of Instability," Orbis, *op. cit.*

The Middle East
and the Great Powers

F. H. HINSLEY

Of a famous nineteenth century crisis, just over 100 years ago, the third Marquess of Salisbury once said that only three men had ever understood the issues involved—and that the other two were dead. In one respect today's crisis in the Middle East is different: everybody understands the issues only too well. In another respect it is like many serious international struggles: In the Middle East both sides have an equally arguable historical, political and moral case—it is futile to attempt to rate either as better than the other—and the obstacles which prevent both from considering any compromise are so insurmountable that the only possible settlement will be a settlement that is imposed.

In international disputes a settlement may be imposed in only three ways. The simplest of these is that which can be followed when one of the direct participants has the power to impose a settlement upon the other. In the case of the Middle East dispute, it may be taken as a starting point that the Arab states do not possess this power, and are unlikely to acquire it.

It is sometimes said that there will be revolution in the Arab countries if the Arab governments do not soon intensify the dispute by resorting to open war on Israel. The truth is the other way round. These governments would be toppled by revolution if they did launch an open war. So long as they confine the struggle to the level of attrition tactics, guerrilla activities and breast-beat-ing speeches made for domestic ideological consumption, they may survive; for their incompetence as governments is offset by the incoherence of the undeveloped body-politics in which they govern. But so long as they do this they must face the fact that they will not force Israel to a settlement. So great, on the other hand, is this incompetence, especially in the conduct of modern military operations, so lacking their ability to co-ordinate such operations between themselves, that if they resort to open war their defeat in another lightning campaign may be accepted as certain; and their prospects of retaining office after a repetition of the Six Day War may be taken to be negligible.

Is the ability of Israel to enforce an end to the struggle, to impose a settlement on the Arab states, any greater? This is the next question; and we must recognize that it can be answered in two ways, according to whether we are thinking in the short term or on a longer perspective. In the short term the answer is no. Faced with a recalcitrant opponent, and one that remains convinced of the rightness of its cause, a state can make it submit only by victory in a war; and the test of victory in a war is the power to follow up victory in battle with the ability to destroy the defeated side—if necessary by going to the lengths of occupying its territories. In this sense the Six Day War has been misnamed. In 1967 Israel won only a battle, at the most a campaign. Whatever the value to her of the prestige and of the conquests acquired in the battle, they have in no way made her capable of forcing the Arab states to negotiate by occupying them or by threatening to do so. Israel's incapacity flows partly from the risk that any attempt to extend hostilities would produce, as it would have in 1967, the intervention of outside powers. It flows partly from the fact that, by associating the Israeli cause with expansion and aggression, any such attempt would upset the fine balance that exists between the morality of the Israeli and the Arab causes in world opinion. It rests mainly, however, on Israel's limitations in resources and population. These impose such serious restrictions on the duration and the radius of her effective military capacity that she can no more force the Arab states to negotiate than they can force her to disgorge.

In the longer term, on the other hand, within the framework of a defensive strategy of retaining what she has acquired but not seeking to extend it, the probability is high that Israel could impose a settlement that rests so firmly on *fait accompli* that its negotiation would be a formality. The belief is widespread that time is not on Israel's side—that she cannot for long sustain a defense budget which consumes 16 percent of the economy, that she must succumb to the nervous strains of existence under siege: This belief underestimates the disparity, both material and psychological, that separates Israel from the Arab societies.

Materially Israel is a modern state, a product of the world that has emerged from the industrial and scientific revolutions of the European area since the seventeenth century—revolutions by which the Arab world has scarcely been touched to this day. This fact is already reflected in its gross national product. At 1,160 U.S. dollars per head this is not much short of that of the Netherlands (1,440) or East Germany (1,220), higher than that of Italy (1,030), and Czechoslovakia (1,010), markedly higher than that of the USSR (890), Ireland (850), Spain (640) or Bulgaria (620), and in a quite different category from the average for those of its immediate Arab neighbors, the United Arab Republic, Jordan, Iraq and Syria, which stands at 210. Absolutely, of course, its population, its territory and its other basic resources are limited. But it need not be doubted that these limitations will be turned into a positive incentive to reach a greater efficiency than would otherwise have been achieved. In all probability, the material disparity between Israel and its Arab neighbors will continue to increase.

All the more is this the case because in political and psychological terms Israel is not merely a modern state, by comparison with which the Arab states remain in outlook and organization somewhere about the European sixteenth century. It is a notably specialized and potent example of the modern state as that has evolved in Europe since that date. Its creation has been called by some the last great achievement of European nationalism, by others the concrete outcome of the workings of an older religious faith. In truth its unusual drive and thrust derive from the fact that it has amalgamated these two sources of loyalty and cohesion more completely, perhaps, than they have ever previously been amalgamated in a body-politic. It is difficult to point to any time in the history of any state in which religious belief and secular nationalism have been so totally fused as to be, as they are in Israel, indistinguishable. Certainly no nation has ever before succeeded in reviving a dead script and in making it, as Hebrew has been made, into a living and an expanding language that is adequate for all secular purposes.

But just because Israel incorporates this unusual cohesion, in this special form, a grave risk will infallibly arise if she decides to adopt the course we have just been considering. Should she ride out the struggle, holding what she has acquired and rejecting any settlement that falls short of her demands, she will probably succeed, materially and politically, in time. What would happen to her morally and psychologically, however, with the passage of time, if this were to be her decision? In the course of converting even her material limitations into a positive incentive to greater efficiency, and on the basis of her already extraordinary degree of social cohesion, she would run the considerable danger of degenerating morally and psychologically until she became, on the margins of the European and the Arab worlds, the Sparta of the Middle East.

For Israel herself, let alone for the peace of the Middle East and for the conscience of Jews everywhere, this would be an unfortunate outcome—so unfortunate that it is desirable to consider the two remaining methods by which a settlement of the struggle might be imposed. Of these the next most simple and direct would be that by which one or some of the world's leading powers enforced a settlement upon the participants without consulting the other leading powers. Until a few years ago this would have been within the capacity of the western powers. Of late, however, the retreat of those powers from the Middle East has been accompanied by the advance of the Soviet claim to be at least indirectly involved there. It is a measure of the success of this advance that, while Russia herself cannot contemplate the imposition of a unilateral settlement, neither, now, can the United States or even NATO as a whole. The Middle East has joined Central Europe, hitherto the only place in the world where a unilateral attempt to alter the balance of the spheres of influence of the great powers would be the certain occasion for a great power war, as a second such area.

This being the case—and there can be little doubt that it is—no single leading power, and neither side in a divided group of leading powers, will intervene to the extent of attempting to impose a settlement. The balance between them is so fine, their fear of war between themselves is so pronounced, that both major powers are already hesitating even about the less direct form of intervention which has hitherto led them to try to contain or to decide the struggle by supplying arms to one or the other or both contestants. For the same reasons, the policy of the leading powers in the Middle East, as also in relation to difficult situations elsewhere, has recently undergone a development which suggests that both sides are tired of the dreary and profitless posturings of the Cold War. I refer to their willingness to undertake four-power and two-power discussion of the Arab-Israeli struggle.

This development indicates that the preconditions are beginning to emerge for an attempt to impose a settlement on the Middle East by the third and sole remaining method. The leading powers, recognizing that they are all indirectly involved by virtue of being great powers, but recognizing also that none of them can afford to be more directly involved than the others and risk widening the conflict, can move jointly to impose an agreed settlement and agree jointly to guarantee it. These preconditions could not begin to form until both sides in the Cold War had grown weary of it. They could not form until the Western powers had retreated from the Middle East, where they had filled the vacuum for a hundred years; and until the Russians had recognized that, in backing the Arab states as the means of replacing the Western powers there, they have, to borrow another famous phrase from the third Marquess of Salisbury's many comments on the Eastern question, "backed the wrong horse." The necessary preconditions are now in the process of being established, however, because all these changes and realizations have come about. On this account we have already had the initiation of talks. On this account also we should, if we possessed a wholly rational and intelligent international system, soon be witnessing the reconstitution of the nineteenth century concert of the great powers; and the imposition of a jointly guaranteed settlement in the Middle East would be its first achievement.

Even in the nineteenth century, however, when the concert was working well, agreed action by the great powers was never easily taken. Even in situations where the preconditions for agreed action existed, it was by no means always possible for the powers to agree. And in the present situation, when the revival of the concert is in its early stages and when effective joint intervention in the Middle East requires considerable resolution, it is unlikely that we shall see any immediate progress along these lines. We know little about the four-power and the two-power discussions as they have proceeded to date. What we do know supports all that we have been able to learn from history about how great powers behave. Though disposed to act jointly, they are now as always being held back by their real problems and their imaginary fears, by their understandable lethargy and their less forgivable poverty of imagination and anticipation, which prevents them from taking in advance of a further deterioration of the conflict the step they will bring themselves to take when this further deterioration arrives.

Must we wait for that step, then, until the situation gets worse—until the direct participants to the struggle either fight another inconclusive round, or have degenerated gradually to the point at which their antagonism has become an intolerable obstacle to the wider programs of the great powers? What, alternatively, can be done by those who do not wish to wait? Well, they can stress in all quarters that the only practicable settlement will be one that is imposed, in the hope of dissipating the wishful thinking that still leads governments to talk only of mediation. They can insist at every opportunity that an early imposed settlement is beyond the abilities either of the Arab states or of Israel or of any one of the great power camps. They can add—and can do so with every confidence that in doing so they are teaching another of history's lessons—that an imposed settlement could be brought about both soon and effectively if all the great powers would recognize that they must compromise, settle on what they want, and agree to enforce and to guarantee it jointly. And it would matter very little, incidentally, whether they did this as constituting the core of the Security Council of the United Nations or by reconstituting the concert of the great powers; whichever of the two courses they pursued the result would be a return to the concert. But they can profitably be active in yet a further direction—in bringing the merits of this solution to the attention of Israel.

Until now, the Israeli government has consistently opposed intervention by the great powers, regretting the four-power and the two-power discussions. Equally consistently it has insisted that a settlement can be achieved only by face-to-face negotiations that are limited to itself and the Arab states. Israel is perhaps beginning to realize that this demand is unattainable. What it still shows no signs of realizing is that, even if it could be achieved, a settlement negotiated directly with the Arab states, and signed, sealed and ratified by them, would leave the situation exactly as it was before. Exactly like the Treaty of Versailles with Germany in 1919, the resulting treaty, if not actually a *diktat* would necessarily be regarded as a diktat by Arab states which, exactly like post-1918 Germany, would have neither the intention nor the ability to abide by it. This is only another way of saying that the only means of reaching an early settlement of the Middle East is by means of the arbitrary, agreed intervention of the great powers. But it is also only another way of saying that it is by this method only that Israel can obtain reasonable security at a reasonably early date.

I have conceded that Israel could probably obtain security in the long run by riding out the struggle. But I have warned that the long run might be very long, and that the consequences for Israel's moral and psychological well-being as a body-politic might be very regrettable. These are not idle warnings. The most useful thing that we can do here and now—it would be even more useful than an effort to remind the leading states of their opportunity and their duty—is to organize an effort to bring to Israel's attention that her own best interests require her to change her stance. Instead of opposing the intervention of the leading states of the world, she should begin to demand their intervention.

Instead of seeking by local agreement, which can be no more than formal, a local security, which would be bound to remain elusive, Israel should begin to demand that this intervention take the form of intervention to establish a settlement that is arbitrarily constructed by the great powers, jointly agreed by them, and by them jointly imposed and jointly guaranteed.

A final word. If Israel could bring herself to this position she would not merely serve her own best interests. She would also fulfill a valuable international function. For this change on her part would probably be the most effective way of ending the irresolution of the great powers and of thus initiating their return to the concert of the great powers—a return which is now overdue and which all who care for international stability must hope to witness before long.

Ending the Arab-Israeli Conflict:

YEHOSHAFAT HARKABI

In the fortnight before the Six Day War Arab leaders gave great prominence to the Arab objective of destroying the state of Israel. Today, realizing how damaging to their cause such rabid declarations have been, Arab spokesmen excuse themselves on the ground that they had only been carried away by their own exuberance. Examination of Arab declarations, however, indicates that their basic position has not changed. For instance, Hassanein Heykal, editor of *Al Ahram*, considered to be President Gamal Abdel Nasser's spokesman, has stated:

There is no room in the Middle East for Arab nationalism and Zionist nationalism. The struggle between them may be protracted without arriving at an accommodation. Let me make it clear: in the Middle East there is room for the Arab nation and any Jews who desire to live in its midst however in the Middle East there is no room for the Arab nation and Israel, with its aggressive and expansionist ambition. (*Al-Ahram*, February 21, 1969)

Many Arabs say now that they denounce Ahmed Shukairy, former head of the Palestine Liberation Organization, for his extreme pronouncements. Yet the difference between what Heykal says today and what Shukairy said in the past is merely in elegance of style and not at all in substance. Both have advocated the liquidation of Israel as a state. In the Middle East Heykal says

258

there is room only for Arab states and Arab nationalism, but not for Jewish nationalism and a Jewish state, which he declares must always be aggressive and expansionist.

History is full of cases of conflict, but in most of them the bone of contention was generally limited to competition for superiority or quarrels over a certain region; the sheer existence of the two adversaries as political entities was outside the conflict. So rare has been the objective of abolishing the opponent's political entity that there was even no term for it. Several years ago I proposed to name it "politicide".

ZIONISM AS POLITICIDE

Arabs usually justify their program of politicide by enumerating the historical evils of Zionism. Zionism certainly aimed to establish a Jewish state. Zionism was not, however, a plot to expel them, as Arabs are fond of describing it. Once Theodor Herzl failed to get an international charter allotting Palestine to the Jews, Zionism had no clear program for achieving the miracle of bringing a Jewish state into being. Thus Zionism concentrated its efforts on buying land, cultivating it and bringing in Jews. Land was not confiscated but sold by the Arabs themselves at high prices. Arab apologists, for whom this fact is disturbing, explain that only about 6 percent of the land in Palestine was sold. Yet in a country where more than half the territory is uncultivable desert and mountainous terrain, it was a considerable part of the arable private land,

The Zionist's idea of the possibility of buying out the Arabs cannot be blamed on them alone. As a popular movement Arab nationalism hardly existed. Some Arab leaders expressed their readiness to recognize the special interests of Jews in Palestine as long as they would be compensated politically elsewhere, and the Zionist leaders were willing to have a Jewish state as a member in an Arab federation. The Palestinian Arabs gave little evidence of being particularly attached to the country, and many of their leaders themselves sold land, even while protesting against it to the outside. Of course these Arab leaders are now branded traitors, but in those days they represented the Arabs and were their spokesmen.

On many occasions the British and the Jews suggested compromise solutions, though none satisfied the more extremist Arab demands. Had the Arabs accepted the Legislative Council offered in the 1920s, Israel would not have existed. Instead, they launched riots against the Jewish immigrants; Zionism became an imperative for the Jewish community in Palestine as it already was for Jews abroad. The Jewish community had to organize a defense organization, not because of inherent militarism or plans to seize the country by force, but for sheer self-defense. Arab intransigence forced partition and Jewish statehood. It is an irony of history that the Arabs should deservedly be counted among the founding fathers of the Jewish state.

The long tradition of intransigence reached a climax when the Arabs attempted to prevent, by force, the execution of the United Nations Partition Resolution. They described as just their effort to subvert a United Nations decision, yet they see no inconsistency in their demands that Israel adhere to all United Nations decisions. The Arab plans to converge on Tel Aviv and Haifa is described by them as a defensive action, while all the efforts of the Jews are described as offensive.

If the Palestinians were displaced, they mostly displaced themselves. The atomization of their society, the weakness of its social links, their lack of confidence in one another (the same reasons that are at the root of the debacle in the Six Day War) caused Palestinian society to disintegrate. Each man felt deserted, and consequently they all dispersed. Some acknowledged this truth. A nationalist like Walid al-Qamhawi in his magnum opus *Disaster and Construction in the Arab Fatherland*, has written:

> Four months passed . . . while most of the rich families and those of the leaders were quitting the country for tranquility in Egypt, Syria and Lebanon, leaving the burden of struggle and sacrifice to the workers, villagers and middle class . . . These factors, the collective fear, moral disintegration and chaos in every domain, were what displaced the Arabs from Tiberias, Haifa, Jaffa and scores of cities and villages.

Arabs now explain that their exodus came from the impact of one case of atrocity by the Jewish side: Deir Yassin. Interestingly, at the time (April 1948) Deir Yassin was scarcely spoken about or mentioned in the press. It was seized upon by the Arab press many months after its occurrence. At the time of its occurrence it was intertwined with the hundreds of cases of Arabs attacking Jewish villages and disrupting Jewish traffic.

Victory did not come easily. The Israeli army was an extraordinary improvisation, and unlike the Arabs, the Jews did not then possess a government, with all its instruments. Knowledge of what awaited them in case of defeat was at the base of their victories in 1948 and 1967, and victory was achieved through endless cases of heroism and sacrifice. Israeli dead in that short war in 1948 amounted to 6,000 (about 1 percent of the population—the total United States casualties in World War II were .25 percent of the population). The war was initiated by the Arabs' rejection, by force, of the partition resolution. They failed, but by continued adherence to an uncompromising position they vitiated, even in the eyes of many foreigners, their subsidiary demand that Israel withdraw to the 1947 lines. Had the Arabs succeeded in their design to converge on Tel Aviv and Haifa, would they have been ready to restore the prewar situation?

As W.C. Smith has explained: "The Arab writing of history has been functioning . . . less as genuine inquiry than as a psychological defense".[1] Thus, the usual Arab version of the history of the Arab-Israel conflict and its origins in Zionism seems motivated by a need to describe the present reality as if it had been imposed on the Arabs, so that they can revolt against it. Actually, it is to a great extent their own handiwork.

THE GROWTH OF ARAB INTRANSIGENCE

For the Arabs to admit their share of responsibility for the situation that has developed would be to undermine their cause. How much easier it is to shirk all responsibility and to externalize all blame. As S. Hamady, a Lebanese, has explained in *Temperament and Character of the Arabs*:

> The Arab is reluctant to assume responsibility for his personal or national misfortune and he is inclined to put the entire blame upon the shoulders of others.[2]

Hamady quoted the authority of F. Sayegh, who in his pamphlet *Understanding the Arab Mind*, generalized:

The Arab is fascinated by criticism of foreigners, of fellow countrymen, of followers, always of "the other", seldom of oneself . . . which accordingly serves to thwart collective and personal accomplishment rather than to stimulate creative efforts and bold enterprises.[3]

Arab nationalism and Zionism came into being at more or less the same time. Both tried in those days to enlist the support of the Western powers. Arab nationalism developed along political-nationalistic lines. Consequently many of the Arab states came under authoritarian military regimes. Zionism, on the other hand, gave a social content to its message, striving to build a democratic society based on social justice. Thus Israel despite all prophecies that it would become a garrison state, retains its democracy, and its social organizations are a model for many developing countries.

Arab criticisms of Zionism and Israel contain many ambi-valences. The easiest way for Arabs to avoid dissonance is to identify Zionism with colonialism. But if colonialism means living by exploiting others, what could be further from colonialism than the idealism of city-dwelling Jews who strive to become farmers and laborers and to live by their own work? Reviving a language and developing a culture requires the creation of a community, but that does not mean simple exclusivity. On the other hand, the contention that Jews should have become assimilated into Arab society only implies that the Arab stance is to domineer.

The Zionists were not "fiends", as the Arabs describe them to be. They were driven to the land of Israel by deep and powerful bonds, together with the pressure of the terrible sufferings of the Jewish people, culminating in the European holocaust. They had no intention of harming Arabs. They hoped only to settle among them, and to contribute to the progress of the Middle East as a whole. Faced with the horrors of the holocaust in Europe and the pressure of the need for a haven for the remnant left of European Jewry, they found Arab resistance to immigration the less important problem.

Zionism did not, and perhaps could not provide a solution for the Arab problem it created. This fact is a heavy burden, which Zionism must carry on its conscience. Members of the young Israeli generation in particular are aware that Arabs do have a case, though not as they themselves describe it. But acknowledging that the Arabs have a case does not mean that they are ready to restore the situation as it existed before, nor does it justify the barbarity of calling for the destruction of the state of Israel. The assertion that the coming of the Jews to Palestine and the establishment of Israel are the causes of the conflict is correct. The inference that, therefore, the destruction of the state, and still worse, the eviction of the Jews, is the only solution is mere casuistry. The Arabs are unwilling to admit that their demand that Israel disappear borders on the absurd. No state can be expected to commit suicide. The tragedy of the Arab case is that their grievance cannot be redressed to their satisfaction without perpetrating an even greater evil. Human destiny decrees that many misfortunes cannot be rectified. The Arabs' ruminating endlessly on past events and on the vices of Zionism will get nowhere. Israel's problem is that with the best will in the world she cannot meet the Arabs' demand, because it is unlimited and cannot be satisfied so long as Israel exists. Their vision is not peace with Israel but peace without Israel.

First, the Arabs explain that the very existence of Israel is, as a matter of principle, not acceptable to them. This is only a euphemistic way of calling for Israel's liquidation. They then proceed to enumerate subsidiary items of accusation against Israel. Israel would not let the refugees return, she retaliated against the acts of infiltrators and she launched attacks; she is expansionist, aggressive, callous and so on. The Arabs remain unaware that these accusations, whether real or fanciful, are the outcome of their basic position, which is that Israel as a Jewish state should be destroyed. Israel's responsibility to defend her people sometimes impels her to take measures that run counter to other values. The Arabs describe the conflict as a battle for survival, and they make it so for Israel. But they then expect Israel to behave as if the conflict was some kind of genial game.

Furthermore, these accusations are basically somewhat irrelevant. Even if Israel behaved impeccably, the Arabs' principle of unacceptability would still remain. Some even spell this out, asserting that even if the refugee problem did not exist and even if Israel shrank to the size of Tel Aviv, its existence would still be unacceptable. Whatever its size, they condemn it as a "cancerous foreign body" that must be exorcised. Thus the Arab position, centering on the principle of the rejection of Israel's statehood, becomes inelastic and impervious to any policy that might be adopted by Israel.

Some Arabs philosophize that Jewishness is a matter of religion, not nationalism. Therefore the Jews, as a matter of principle, do not deserve to have a state. Some would go on to assert that a Jewish state is a hybrid creature, doomed to collapse. It is true that some Jews sense their Jewishness as only a religion, but some feel otherwise. The Arabs need not pontificate to us on the nature of Jewishness. Finding "contradictions" in Israel and its society has become a pastime for Arab intellectuals. True; there are problems, both within Israel and in its relation to Jews abroad, yet no societies—including those of the Arab states—are free from internal difficulties and contradictions. Arab nationalism abounds in ambiguities, such as for example, its relationship to Islam, or the great gap between the ideology of Arab unity and the reality of Arab disunity.

ARAB ANTI-SEMITISM

The volume of anti-Semitic literature published in the Arab world has had no parallel in modern history since the demise of Nazi Germany. What makes this literature even more significant is that it has been put out by official government publishing houses—not from the fringes of Arab society but from its very center. The *Protocols of the Elders of Zion* (a forgery by the Russian Tsarist secret police, which "described" a meeting of Jewish leaders conspiring to achieve world domination by odious means, and is the basic writ of modern anti-Semitism) has been published by the United Arab Republic (UAR) Ministry of Orientation. President Nasser's brother has reissued it. The UAR government has gone to the extreme of publishing books like *Human Sacrifices in the Talmud*, in which Jews are accused of the ritual murder of Gentile children.[5] The Jordanian prime minister, Sa' as Juma', has published a book that explains Israel's victory as based on the Protocols.[6] An Arab newspaper has published a "Letter to Eichmann" pledging to avenge his death and to follow his example in destroying all Jews still left alive.[7] Rabid anti-Semitic themes, including excerpts from the Protocols, are found in textbooks for schools and in the indoctrination literature for the armed forces.

These are only a few random examples. No intellectual acrobatics can brush them aside. The argument that the Arabs being Semites themselves, cannot be anti-Semitic is only specious, for anti-Semitism means hatred of Jews and not of Semites. The fact that the Arabs could view the moral havoc wrought by anti-Semitism in Germany without feeling inhibited, indicates the vehemence of their anti-Semitism. True, the Germans destroyed millions of Jews, but after reading what Arabs write about Israel I cannot escape the impression that many Arabs also harbor just such a dream. It may even be possible that such desires are more prevalent and central in Arab society than they were in German society. The Arabs have gone far in their vilification of Israel and Jews, and the road back is not a short one.

There is now a tendency in some Arab quarters to give an Islamic form to Arab anti-Semitism. Many such examples are found in the monthly magazine of Al Azhar, which is the oldest and principal Islamic university in Cairo. In the magazine's October 1968 issue, a religious dignitary evokes a tradition (*hadith*) according to which Muhammed was said to have declared that a Muslim slaughter of Jews will precede the Day of Resurrection. The learned sheik asserts the authenticity of this tradition and its importance as gospel. He calls the slaughter of the Jewish minorities, whose position in the Arab countries was low, "unbecoming," (thus illustrating the basic Arab attitude towards Jews—the Koran decreed (KK,58,III,108) that they should be "in a low and miserable position"); God ordained that the Jews would develop an aggressive state and attain power, so that the *hadith* might be realized: thus the hidden meaning of this tradition, he argues, will henceforth unfold. A theological justification is, thus, given to politicide-genocide and a comforting explanation to Arab defeats. Had a similar article appeared in a Christian publication, it would have created an uproar of protest.

R.I. Al-Fruki has delivered a series of lectures to the Arab League's Institute of High Arabic Studies, entitled "The Origins of Zionism are in the Jewish Religion", in which he furnished a disparaging analysis of Judaism. Arab efforts to differentiate between Judaism and Zionism usually founder. Both are too frequently described in Arab writings as identical (sinwaan), or else Zionism is said to be only "the executive mechanism" of Judaism. "World Zionism" and "World Jewry" are treated as identical. Thus it is no wonder that anti-Zionist Jews are stigmatized as hypocritical and fraudulent.

I do not argue that Arab anti-Semitism has social or religious roots; its origins are mainly political. Nevertheless, this is no accidental growth on the Arab stand against Israel. The need to substantiate the evil of Israel, as a state that deserves a death sentence, produced an inclination to present this evil as profound. Only evil people could give rise to such a monstrosity as Zionism, could "usurp" a country and build an inherently aggressive state such as Israel is seen to be.

A PALESTINIAN STATE

For a long time the Arabs kept stressing that the Palestinian problem was a pan-Arab problem. To view it in the narrow framework of Palestinians versus Israel was stigmatized as anti-nationalist. It used to be a basic doctrine of Arab nationalism that national boundaries in the Middle East were the artificial fabrications of colonialism. Thus to acknowledge the existence of a Palestinian entity, precisely because of its colonialist parenthood, was considered a heresy. With the defeat of the Arab states, the Palestinian cause has been resurrected and sanctified. The Palestinians once complained that the Arab states were using them as instruments in inter-Arab bickerings and that they were being treated as pawns. These roles have now been reversed, and the tools have become the actors. It is explained that the Palestinian aspect is the major one in the conflict. Yet this had been left to hibernate for at least 16 years.

I do not doubt that the Palestinians share feelings of communality, for they have suffered a great deal. Their national aspirations could have been partially satisfied on the West Bank, in the Gaza Strip and even in Jordan, (which has actually been "Palestinized"). If they stick to their totalistic demand that their aspirations can only be fulfilled if Israel disappears, if they do not see a possibility of accommodation between Israeli nationalism and their own, they will probably lose out.

A new slogan that has recently appeared in some quarters urges that Israel be superseded by a "lay, democratic, pluralistic Palestine". It is easy, though, to show that this slogan is only politicide in a new, "humanistic" guise. Among themselves Arabs specify that this new state will be Arab and part of Arab nationalism, which stresses homogeneity. Fatah and the other organizations end their proclamations with the formula "Long live an *Arab*, Free Palestine." Fatah's position toward the Jews is enunciated in an authoritative document called the Palestinian National Covenant. In its original (1964) version it read that the *Jews of Palestinian origin*, (which could be interpreted as those living in the country before 1948), would be recognized as Palestinians—and permitted to stay. The Covenant was revised in July 1968, after the Fatah take-over of the Palestinian Liberation Organization, and the stand on Jews has now been radicalized. Now the corresponding Article reads that only those Jews who have been living in Palestine permanently "before the beginning of the Zionist invasion" (i.e. 1917), would be considered Palestinians; the rest would be considered aliens, and expelled. The need to reduce the number of Jews in the country by all and any means is understandable, for by now they form the majority of the population, and this fact undermines the claim that the Jews will only be allowed to exist as a minority in an Arab state. Unwittingly, perhaps, such a slogan implies a return to the fundamentalist Islamic stand. Islam recognizes neither independence nor equality for Jews. The Jews, like all the "People of the Book," have to be fought until they submit to the supremacy of Islam (Koran, IX, 29).

The Islamic aspects of the struggle against Israel have been accentuated as, for instance, by Fatah's repeated appeals to Islamic religious leaders to declare a *jihad* (holy war), and to delegate monetary contributions to Fatah as *zakat* (a religious obligation). Ironically, then, a holy war must be waged in order to establish an allegedly lay republic! The constitutions of all the Arab states (with the exception of Lebanon) specify Islam as the state religion. This, of course, does not restrain Arabs from branding Israel as a reactionary state based on religion. The advocacy of a democratic Palestine, too, is old, when one considers that the general trend in most Arab countries has been away from democracy.

In the past the Zionist leaders have called for a binational state. Now it is too late for that. The Arabs refuse to make peace, or even to meet us face to face, as though our very presence were contaminating. They seethe with desire for vengeance; they use the most abusive invectives against Israel and resort to anti-Semitic vilification. The veritable festival of hangings of Jews in Baghdad reflects the Arab mood and attitude much more accurately than does the synthetic Arab position portrayed by Arab professors at the American University of Beirut. The direct leap made from such a hostile stance to one advocating the intimacy of a common state must give rise to a suspicion of some ulterior motive—that the Arab call for a pluralistic Palestine may be only a euphemism for the destruction of Israel. The sublime sound of such a suggestion may bring self-gratification to its propagators, as proof of their own nobility of soul, but its true intent may be of a much lower order. The acid test of the Arab's peaceful intentions is their readiness to make peace with an Israel that is alive, and not with a ruin. When the conflict has been settled and when the mood in the Middle East has changed, integration may indeed come about, and on a higher level a union of Middle Eastern states, of which Israel is a member.

The Middle East is in the throes of the age of nationalism. To suggest at this point a solution to suit a post-nationalistic age demonstrates neither farsightedness nor idealism; it is at best irrelevant. Those who wish to suggest a political solution must have the humility to consider reality. However, the Arabs sometimes tend to downgrade reality, and give greater importance to the word: " . . . language, for Arabs, is not a means to describe reality, it is reality itself," writes H.E. Tutsch.[8]

Fancy and words, blurring reality, cause delusions and deception. Arab writers, when analyzing their society, often point to the extraordinary frequency of deception, lies and false communiques by governments as constituting a major social weakness. In the literature now being published in the Arab countries on the lessons to be drawn from their defeat, these flaws are described as one of the major causes of that defeat (1967). This is a subject I feel uneasy discussing. No society can claim to be blameless of distorting facts. Still a quantitative difference may have a qualitative significance. I find it baffling that the very Arab academics, who reproach their people for distorting facts, resort to such distortions themselves.

In order to understand the Arab position in the conflict one must learn their terminology. "A peaceful settlement of the present crisis" does not necessarily mean a peace settlement with Israel, but only the withdrawal of Israeli troops to the pre-1967 war lines. The meaning of "crisis" is limited to indicate the pressure put on the Arabs by the occupation; it does not mean the state of continuous tension between the both sides. "Liberating the occupied territories" may apply to the area occupied in the Six Day War and also to the liquidation of Israel, since Israel, prior to 1967, was already referred to in Arabic, as "the occupied territory." "Recognition of Israel's existence" may mean no more than an awareness that there *is* such a thing as Israel. Az-Zayat, the UAR spokesman, has reiterated to foreign journalists that Egypt had always recognized the existence of Israel. (Since Egypt has continuously called for the destruction of Israel, he apparently senses no contradiction between recognizing the existence of Israel and calling for its liquidation.) "Nonbelligerence" means that the Arab regular armies will not take military action against Israel, but it does not exclude support of terrorist action operating from Arab territory. Since the Arabs declare that they agree to nonbelligerence but not to peace, nonbelligerence must thus be interpreted as merely a pause in the war.

Strangely enough, the principle of Arab policy, (as agreed upon at the Khartoum Conference and as pronounced in Nasser's speech of June 23, 1968) of adherence to the right of the

Palestinians to regain their fatherland, is also a euphemism for politicide. For the Palestinian Liberation Organization and all the fedayeen groups repeatedly declare that they reject a political solution and that their aim is the liquidation of the "Zionist entity." The support of the Arab leaders of the aims of the fedayeen organizations is a blatant contradiction of their alleged acceptance of the November 22 Security Council Resolution. Such support implies endorsement of politicide, despite the Arab leaders' spokesmen's ambiguous expressions when addressing foreign audiences. Similarly "a pluralistic Palestine" may be no more than an elegant phrase for politicide.

REJECTION OF COEXISTENCE

The Arab rejection of Jewish statehood and of coexistence with the state of Israel lies at the heart of the conflict. The Arabs are demanding that their national aspirations for self-determination, (including those of the Palestinians), should be met while the national aspirations of the Jewish community in Israel should be rejected. The Jews, they say, notwithstanding the fact that they now form a political community, should not have the right to political self-determination. Herein lies the asymmetry that is basic to the Arab stand. Arabs may fight against Israel and do it harm, but if Israel fights back, she is aggressive. Israel must observe the ceasefire: the Arabs are exempt from its limitations.

The Arab attitude has caused an important change in the attitude toward statehood of many Israelis. It has come to acquire a great value, even to those for whom previously it meant but little. It became clear to those who would have been content with only a "spiritual center" for Jewry (like the cultural Zionist essayist Ahad Ha'am), that it could not be achieved without some guardian, in the form of a state. Statehood, to Israelis, has become the defense line for survival. "Zionism" has now come to mean that Jews possess a country and a state, as do other peoples. Thus "de-Zionization" of Israel is only a euphemistic expression for the destruction of Israel.

The Arabs acceptance of coexistence with Israel and of peace is possible and will come about one day. Yet the significance for the Arabs of such a change should not be underestimated. To the Arab states it may appear as a betrayal of the national cause and of their obligations toward the Palestinians. The United States did not have to change the Constitution in order to make peace with Japan, for the conflict with Japan was not enshrined in the American Constitution. The Arab-Israeli conflict and the non-acceptability of the existence of Israel are inscribed in Arab sacred writs, as National Charters. If in the West, people tend to dismiss Arab extremist declarations as stemming from exuberance, flamboyance or momentary hot-headedness, Arab writings are free from such notions. They are the result of long deliberation: the rejection of the existence of Israel has become an important component of Arab national thought. Though Israel's existence is not the sole concern of the Arabs, they have forged their national thinking on the anvil of the conflict to a much greater extent than could have been expected.

This applies particularly to Israel's neighbors. For instance, the conflict is referred to six times in the United Arab Republic National Charter, (this Charter is considered the most sacred writ in Egypt's national existence) and was hailed by The National Congress of the Popular Powers on June 30, 1962 as "the frame for our life, the path to our revolution and the guide for the future." In it, the liquidation of Israel is specified in unmistakable terms: I quote: "The insistence of our people on liquidating the Israeli aggression on a part of the Palestine land is a determination to liquidate one of the most dangerous pockets of imperialistic resistance against the struggle of peoples." Thus, the Arab position towards Israel is not only expressed in their diplomatic or political stand, but it is a basic tenet of Arab nationalism, practically ingrained in the Arab ethos. This development is extremely unfortunate, and many in Israel prefer to ignore it. Yet it is better to see reality, bitter and disheartening though it may be, than to indulge in illusions, which will only court disappointment.

Changing the Arab position on the acceptance of Israel would not involve a political or diplomatic act alone, but a national transformation. It would be a change not *in* but *of* the Arabs' stand; not of a *norm* but of a *value*. It would entail a modification of their educational system, with its many ramifications in national life. Of course, such a change could not be accomplished overnight. A political settlement might signal the first step to a change in the national stance. Yet any political settlement that did not entail a change in the national position would be only ephemeral. It could produce an absurd situation, comparable to that of a state making peace with its rival but continuing to sing the verse in its national anthem that calls for the destruction of the other state. Thus Israel, before foregoing the security advantages that the present borders afford, demands a manifestation of readiness on the part of the Arabs to change their national position by negotiating a peace settlement.

The Arabs reject direct negotiation, not because they prefer another procedure leading to peace but because refusal to negotiate directly has symbolized for them, their rejection of coexistence and peace. Israel's insistence on direct negotiations does not stem from procedural pedantry, but from recognition of what such negotiations symbolize to the Arab mind. So long as the Arabs reject direct negotiations, they have not given up the intention to destroy the state of Israel. A peace that contains the provision that the parties to the conflict do not meet is a contradiction in terms. It is without precedent in human history. Recognition, peace and direct negotiations were all lumped together and proscribed at the Khartoum Conference. The Arab contention that direct negotiations imply a surrender does not so much follow from psychological sensitivity about meeting with Israelis as from the realization that negotiations imply a renunciation of politicide.

Arab diplomacy is trying to achieve an arrangement that will snatch, from Israel, its present means of applying pressure on the Arab states to make peace, in order that the Arabs might be in a position to renew the conflict. What they want is at most an armistice, for which Israel, pressured by the big powers, will be made to pay as if for peace. Though a contractual peace settlement negotiated between the parties is not an absolute guarantee against resumption of the conflict, it is a step in the right direction. Having learned some bitter lessons from the armistice agreements concluded with its Arab neighbors in 1949,

Israel is resolved not to agree to any arrangement short of peace. Because the Arabs categorically refuse to conclude such a peace agreement, the conflict becomes a test of endurance.

PROSPECTS FOR PEACE

Arab leaders repeatedly declare that if Israel does not withdraw to the former borders, they will force her back by renewing the war. The urge for vengeance to wipe out the shame of defeat is strong among the Arab military. Yet memories of the Six Day War serve as deterrents. In such a situation there is always the danger of a flare-up and war, although it would appear that the Arab armies are not yet ready to engage in one.

In the meanwhile, the fedayeen will continue their terrorist and subversive activities. Despite Arab claims, the effects of these activities have been limited. In the period from the Six Day War to May 2, 1969, there were ten times more deaths from suicide and traffic accidents than from fedayeen actions in Israel. No society can be immune from terrorist activities. We shall have to treat them like the toll in road accidents paid by modern societies, and take them in our stride.

Fedayeen thinking is fuzzy, and no coherent action can flow from incoherent thought. They do not examine the relationship between means and aims; the suitability of guerrilla warfare to the circumstances. They claim that guerrilla warfare will bring about the liquidation of Israel, but—to use a parallel—while the FLN could induce the French to relinquish their rule in Algeria, no amount of terrorism could force the French to give up France. Yet that is precisely what the Arab fedayeen hope to do in the case of Israel.

The fedayeen organizations fill the gap between their pretensions and their accomplishments by false reporting. The new generation of Palestinians is now reproaching its parents for their evasion of reality, illusions, self-delusion and deception. In their misrepresentations, the fedayeen communiques surpass all description. It is not just rationalistic optimism to think that such fabrications are self-defeating. These fictitious reports create a certain problem of education in Israel. When the fedayeen claim, for example, to be responsible for the death of the late Prime Minister Levi Eshkol, it becomes difficult to expect people to have respect for an adversary who resorts to making such fantastic claims.

Educating the present Arab generation on vengeance and brutality, though it is directed outward, may rebound and take a heavy toll within the Arab states themselves. The fedayeen may well become a sect. Continued frustration on the Arab side may cause, at least for some time, greater radicalization. Latent disparities between the fedayeen organizations and the Arab states may come into the open and bring havoc to the Arab societies.

The Arab-Israeli conflict is not the source of all Arab problems. The Arab states suffer from instability in political life, the militarization of their regimes, from backwardness, the alienation of their peoples from public affairs, etc. This malaise has much deeper roots and may outlive the conflict; however, the conflict serves to aggravate the malaise.

The Arabs need peace no less than does Israel. Continuation of the present conflict may be a nightmare for Israel; but it is also destructive for the Arabs. International conflict is always a calamity, yet for Israel it has had beneficial effects as well, for it has promoted national integration, construction and creativity. For the Arabs the conflict has been a national disaster and an obstacle to modernization. Many Arabs stress that only all-embracing change can overcome the structural weaknesses of their societies, which were reflected in their debacle in the Six Day War. Presumably, such a catastrophe could be an all-powerful incentive to reforms that might usher in a national revival. It seems, however, that so far the defeat has had adverse effects, bringing greater social atomization, internal disintegration and hopelessness. The Arabs are caught in a vicious circle because their obsession with the conflict has had paralyzing effects. National reforms require collective effort, but it is precisely their failure to sustain a collective effort that thwarts them. This trend toward disintegration takes place in a parallel fashion on both the social and the state levels. The Arab states are now experiencing not political growth but political decay. For example, Iraq today is "less a state" than was the Iraq of Nuri al-Said, and the same holds true for the other Arab states.

The Arabs contend that the reason for their defeat in 1967 was the scientific technological gap between them and Israel. I cannot measure it, but it is my impression that this gap is widening. In the last few years, Israel has made extraordinary leaps in her industrial capacity. It appears that the Arab universities are frittering away a great amount of energy because students and faculty are so preoccupied with the conflict.

It is difficult to be optimistic about the settlement of the conflict in the near future, though developments not yet envisaged may emerge. One should never be too positive in predicting international events. I am most sanguine about Israel's ability to withstand the conflict, protected though this may be. A settlement that does not entail liquidation of the conflict may mean its perpetuation. Only the parties to the conflict themselves can end it. A solution imposed from the outside may be only a palliative, producing even more harmful after-effects. Third parties can contribute as mediators, but they cannot act as substitutes for the two sides.

Arab political literature often claims that if Israel is not liquidated, Arab states will be obliterated by Israel. On the one hand, this is an apocalyptic dramatization: on the other, it is an attempt to impose symmetry on a situation that is inherently asymmetrical. Between these two prophecies of doom there is a third possibility—much less melodramatic but more practical and humane—the coexistence of Jewish nationalism and Israel with Arab nationalism and the Arab states.

Though the conflict originated with the coming of the Jews to Palestine, its resolution rests more with the Arabs. We Israelis find ourselves in a morally awkward position, for we appear to put all the onus for a solution to the conflict on the Arabs. Yet until we are accepted as a partner in the Middle East community of nations, we must stay put. This is our predicament. In any conflict, the side that wants to change the status quo is dominant while the side that tries to preserve the status quo is respondent and most reactive. Before 1948 the Zionist position was the primary factor in the conflict. Since then the roles have been reversed.

Of course Israel must not resign itself to a waiting position. It must do its best to explore and initiate steps and policies to facilitate a change in the Arab position and a resolution of the conflict. Nevertheless, so long as the Arabs maintain that any concession by Israel that leaves its existence intact is too small, Israel's latitude to make concessions is very limited. Israel cannot compromise the principle of its statehood. A compromise could take place, on a higher level, by Israel's gradual transference of some attributes of its sovereignty to the central authority of a Middle Eastern Confederation or Federation. Such a union, though pluralistic in nature, would be predominantly Arab, and that may reassure the Arabs and calm their fears about Israel.

If the Arabs had been ready for a real peace settlement immediately after the Six Day War, Israel would have withdrawn from almost all the occupied areas. The longer the wait, the stronger grew the feeling in Israel that our only course of action was to strengthen ourselves and to settle the strategic areas. If we cannot belay Arab hostility, and since they will not give up the tenet of the inevitability of war, preparation for war becomes for us an overriding imperative. The possibility of the radicalization of the Arab regimes, with all that may entail for the radicalization of their policies, even if it is, for them, self-defeating, looms on the horizon. The contingency of war becomes real, and volunteering to forego the margin of security that the present borders give is tantamount to madness. Furthermore, Israel cannot allow " . . . every area . . . Israel will evacuate (to) serve as a firm base for fedayeen action" (as the Egyptian *Ruz al-Yusuf* May 12, 1969 explained was Arab intent and strategy). Thus in the present circumstances Israel has no other alternative than to sit tight. Both sides are caught in a vicious circle. Arab hostility has driven Israel to enlarge its grip and that action is interpreted by the Arabs as expansionism and has aggravated their hostility. The only escape from such a predicament is peace.

It is to be hoped that the cumulative effect of the repeated failure of the Arab efforts to liquidate Israel will eventually induce the Arabs to resign themselves to Israel's existence and thus spell the end of the conflict. Then a period of collaboration may start. Raw wounds will heal, hostilities evaporate and problems now outstanding will be solved constructively. The day may still be far away—but it will come.

[1] W.C. Smith, *Islam in Modern History*, (Princeton University Press, Princeton, 1957) p. 20.

[2] S. Hamad, *Temperament and Character of the Arabs*, (Twayne, N.Y. 1960) p. 43.

[3] F.A. Sayegh, *Understanding the Arab Mind*. (Organization of Arab Students in the United States, New York 1953) p. 28.

[4] Series of "Political Books," No. 5 (Ministry of Orientation, Cairo, 1957).

[5] "National Books," No. 184 (Ministry of Orientation, Cairo, 1962).

[6] *The Plot and the Battle of Destiny*, (Dar Al-Kalib, Al-Arabi, Beirut 1968).

[7] *Jerusalem Times*, April 24, 1961.

[8] H.E. Tutsch, *Facets of Arab Nationalism*, (Wayne State University Press, Detroit, 1965) p. 116.

Clashing Horizons:
Arabs and Revolution

ABDUL AZIZ SAID

The task of analyzing revolution in the Arab world initially appeared to me to be a simple one. Literature on Arab revolutionary phenomena is both rich and abundant, and my training as a political scientist had prepared me to handle a wide spectrum of analytical tools. However, things did not work out this way. My mind kept wandering back to memories mixed with pain and tears, for revolution was as much a part of my formative years as Captain Kangaroo and Ranger Hal have been part of my son's.

I was only six years old when the wise men began tampering with my childhood. As my elders resisted French designs to separate their province of al-Jazirah from the rest of Syria, French airplanes leveled Amouda, my hometown. My family escaped to Damascus, where the French caught up with us and sent us into exile in Aleppo. In the French school, where my brother and I were enrolled, we took to soccer, but World War II and the bombing raids took care of that. We became experts at running into bomb shelters and stealing bread from military vehicles. We also became "revolutionaries." I was barely 13 years old when I began my career as a street demonstrator which lasted through my college days; our chant, "The army is our army and Paris is our horses' stable" still resounds in my ears. More family tragedies followed, and finally, an armed confrontation with the French to liberate Syria.

I remember our lengthy meetings in the street corners of Damascus, Beirut and Cairo, our heated debates in coffeeshops and our constant arguments over Arab unity and socialism. In the meantime, Israel defeated the Arabs. The Arab world was outraged. We demonstrated for the restoration of Arab honor. Colonel Husni al-Zaim answered our prayers with a military coup and a promise of Utopia. President al-Kuwatli, founding father of Syria, was declared a traitor. No sooner did we learn to dance to Colonel Zaim's baton, then he was executed for treason. We cheered our new messiah, Colonel Sami al-Hinnawi. But he too did not last. We demonstrated again. Arab streets are filled with the debris of frustrated dreams and abandoned schemes, as each new prophet attacks his predecessor with gay abandon.

Much has happened since then. The men in uniform have "redeemed" the governments of Iraq, Egypt, Yemen, Algeria, Sudan and Libya. Attempted coups have shaken Saudi Arabia, Jordan and Tunisia, and there have been more coups in Syria. The Arabs and the Israelis fought two more wars, in 1956 and 1967, and the Arabs were humiliatingly defeated. The Mediterranean has since become a crowded bathtub, littered with American and Soviet boats. Some of my classmates have become theorists of revolution, while others have become accomplished practitioners. Some are in prison, others have lost their lives. And I am in Washington, D.C., making a living teaching political science.

During the last two decades, I have visited almost every Arab state, from Morocco to Iraq, from Lebanon to Yemen. Much has changed, but more has remained the same. The Arabs are caught up in a "caucus race" which forces them to run faster and faster just to stay in the same place. Like the inhabitants of an island who have been promised that the ship of deliverance will soon arrive, they have buried their tools and packed their meager belongings; but when the ship arrives, it is a slave boat. Theirs is a tragic fate, painful for me because I do not hear their laughter; I see only tears. Paper and pen are often such an ineffective method to convey the impressions of eyes that have seen and endured more than paper can ever record or reveal.

BETWEEN TWO HORIZONS

The story of Arab expectations is a tragic one. It mirrors the enigmas of deserts, seas and mirages. The Arabs are clustered in isolated settlements, thrust between the sand and the shore, bound to a geographical inheritance of barriers to community and communication. There is much debate about the notion of revolution, and little concern with its content. The trimmings of revolution mask a non-revolutionary tradition; and unlike Asia, where there is a Mao Tse-Tung, or Latin America, with Fidel Castro, the Arabs have no dominant revolutionary who can personify the revolution. While such men as Gamal Abdel Nasser and Yasir Arafat have been symbols of conviction, Arab life-style favors conservative institutions such as the military and Islam. The Arab remains comfortable with his identity, making it difficult for him to entertain revolutionary ideas. Even when he does, he wages his revolution on the battlefield of rhetoric. In a region where there have always been appropriate audiences and garrulous orators, the faces are the same; only the masks are new. The structures have donned new colors and leaders have affected revolutionary postures, but there has been little departure from the old institutions.

In the Arab world, revolution is merely a medium, and the medium is the message until a new medium appears. As a medium, it is a justification for the rivalry of pretenders for power rather than a process of significant change. Rejecting the political messianism of Western philosophies of history and unwilling to abandon his life-style, the Arab is not easily won to radicalism in action. Imprisoned in seemingly hopeless economic and social conditions, his response is similar to the howling of a caged wolf, for it is less a demonstration of virility than a function of self-preservation and a release of frustration.

The Arab revolutionary glosses over the impotence of the present by idealizing the past. The messianism of his vision carries to the immediate present what was, in the past, the rewards of the other world. His quest for new faith and rebirth is transformed from the universality of Islam to the universality of such secular movements as Pan-Arabism and nationalism, and the latter has yet to cut the bonds that tie it to the underlying aspirations of Islam.

SEARCH FOR AN ARAB REVOLUTIONARY VISION

In the prenationalist years, from mid-nineteenth to early twentieth century, Arab revolutionary vision was exemplified by the expansion of the prophet Muhammad's thought by the reformers of the time: Rif'at al-Tahtawi, Khayr al-Din Tunisi, Abd al-Rahman al-Kawakibi, Jamal al-Din al-Afghani, Muhammad Abduh, Mustafa Kamil and Rashid Rida. These men conceived of Western superiority over the Muslim world as a function of superior Western political organization and systems, rather than Christian ethics, which they viewed as apolitical. Christianity, many of these reformers concluded, was not concerned with temporal and political matters, and it therefore represented no barriers to rationalism or secularism. Yet Islam, corrupted by non-Arab, superstitious elements that were unworthy of the Islamic message, combined worldly and religious matters under the one and only law, al-Shari'ah, (Islamic Law), thus inhibiting the Islamic trend towards rationalism and secularism. They argued for the establishment of secular institutions sustained by a purified and revived Islamic doctrine. Their writings served as a revolutionary Bible for the alienated Arab intelligentsia following the Young Turk Revolution of 1908.

Arab alienation found expression in Arab societies which turned from cage literary clubs to political groups such as Fatah and al-Ahd and to the Arab insurrection of 1916. The Arab revolt of 1916 has appeared highly symbolic in the eyes of Arab nationalists, as the first concrete manifestation in modern times of their desire to recreate an independent and unified Arab state. The insurgency arose not in the land of the intellectuals of Lebanon, Syria and Egypt, but in the desert of Arabia. A synthesis of Arab nationalist aspirations, dynastic ambitions and British strategic interests in World War I, the revolt sparked a movement which claimed the temporary liberation of Damascus, the ancient center of Arabism, from centuries of Ottoman domination. Amir (prince) Faisal's entry into Damascus for a brief moment made the dreams come true, but was soon smashed by the Western division of the area into the mandate system.

Certain geographic regions and religious groups in most intimate contact with the ideas and techniques of the West provided a disproportionate share of leadership in the process of change. The regional foci of westernization—Syria, Egypt, Palestine and Lebanon, and to a lesser extent, Iraq—assumed central roles in the first nationalist movements in defiance of the authority of the Ottoman Empire. These areas became centers for Western missionary and educational efforts and resource places for political leadership and nationalist movements. Consequently, until recent years, political boundaries in the Arab world did not coincide with the areas of strongest political sentiment.

Christian Arabs spearheaded the movement to define the emerging Arab personality. In Lebanon, in the middle of the nineteenth century, such Christian Arab scholars as Nasif Yaziji and Butrus Bustani, attempted to reform Arabic as a vehicle of change within the Arab community of the Ottoman Empire. From the Syrian Scientific Society in 1857 to the secret societies of the early twentieth century, literary groups became politically active.

The interwar developments added to the frustrations of the fledgling Arab nationalist, with his meager means and unlimited ends. Western concepts were introduced into a society just set free from scholastic theology, but ambivalent about the direction of its goals. While Arab nationalists called for rationalism and secularism, they did so not in repudiation of Islam, but rather to reform it. They maintained that Islam should return to its roots in its Arabic background. Aside from its remote possibility, this seemed an outmoded explanation of the ills of the Arab society. While it is true that thinkers of the time—Sati al-Husri, Abd Allah al'Ala'illi, Sami Shawkat, and Ali Yusuf Nasir al-Din, strove to advance concepts of Arab nationhood and nationalism, they made no lasting impact. Furthermore, parochial nationalisms so pervasive in Lebanon, Syria, Egypt and Iraq at this time, combined with a neo-Islamic revival to reduce these efforts to polemics.

The first victories in the Arab national struggle at the conclusion of World War II, the independence of several Arab states and the establishment of the League of Arab states in 1945, all helped to renew the search for an Arab political personality. The ideas of Abd Allah Abd al-Daim, Constantine Zurayk and Musa al-Ami became a new source of inspiration among Arab youth. It was recognized that Arab society had been weak and corrupt prior to the imperialist onslaught. Governments were urged to produce changes in the societal and economic spheres. While these men attempted to formulate new myths to sustain new structures, environmental changes lagged behind, rendering the new institutions mere empty shells.

IMPACT OF WESTERN THOUGHT

It has become a cliche among scholars of the area to view the Arabs as caught up in some vast social upheaval. The growing irrelevance of old established patterns and institutions, however, has resulted less from internal changes than from the impact of ideas from outside the culture. Indigenous intellectual developments have been sparse, despite those events purported to be a consequence of new mass political awareness. Fatalism and resignation to the will of Allah—that acceptance of the order of things and men—had indeed been eroded, but sociopolitical consciousness on the part of an overwhelmingly illiterate mass was slow to develop.

Ideological changes reflected, first and foremost, issues of faith and rebirth: faith that would endow human life with meaning; rebirth that would enable man to fit his altered environment. The revolutionary search for new bases of integration is compromised by the fact that old myths retain much of their vitality. In addition, the Arabs are not convinced that the traditional Western ideologies and institutions can provide such bases.

In the past century, the Arabs have been exposed to the force of democratic and industrial revolutions and to the drastic revolution signified in Western history by the Renaissance and the

Reformation. At the beginning of modern European history, Islamic Ulemas recoiled from heresy and innovation, preferring the shelter of authoritative doctrine and established hierarchy. When in the twentieth century, those hierarchic institutions which had been perfected to guard orthodoxy lost their effectiveness, Islam and Arabism had to pay the price of their earlier intellectual abdication by confronting within a single century that complex of ideas and techniques which Europe had developed in the course of 500 years.

At the individual level, the reaction to the incompatability between Islam and modern thought had been a rigorous compartmentalization of the mind, a reaction still evident in contemporary Arab political behavior. Lip service to Islam and to Western liberalism, combined with systematic failure to conform to the precepts of either, have produced duality of mind that characterizes the Arab intelligentsia. Thus, the Arab world is uncertain and insecure about the relationship between internal Islamic and external Western influences.

ARAB POLITICAL DEVELOPMENT

Nowhere else is the definition of an internal affair more anomalous than in the Arab world. Independence and anti-colonialism could perhaps be vehicles for self-determination and modernization, but they become conflicting ones in the milieu in which energies are channeled toward redefinition of the national policy. Consequently, there is an interaction over the major issues of nationhood and Pan-Arabism among movements, political parties such as the Ba'ath (Resurrection) Party in Syria and Iraq, and such prominent groups as the army, students and religious leaders.

Within this sociological and intellectual setting, political development in most Arab states during the early period of independence was stunted, thwarted and diverted into conspiracy, violence and personal interests. The nationalist parties that struggled for independence were generally non-doctrinaire parliamentary bloc parties. The Wafd and the Sa'dis in Egypt, the National and the People's parties in Syria, the Independence and National Democractic parties in Iraq, the Constitutional and

National blocs in Lebanon, the Destour party in Tunisia and similar parties in other Arab states were frustrated by internal struggles for power after independence.

The secular doctrinaire parties, the Syrian Social National Party (SSNP), the Ba'ath and Arab communist parties consisting mainly of Christians, Jews and other national and religious minorities all made a little ideological impact. The SSNP, founded by Antun Sa'adeh, a Christian, in 1932, represented an important development and departure in the ideological context. As the first doctrinal party in Syria, with the exception of the Arab communist parties, it ushered in the era of mass-party organization and well-defined social reform platforms. By advocating the concept of geographic Syria (based on the closer affinity of the peoples of Iraq, Jordan, Lebanon and Syria and a common historical era that preceded Islam) and by adopting a rational and positive approach to social reform (the corporate state, separation of church and state and the reeducation of the masses), it departed from Pan-Arabism and Pan-Islamism in its regional stance and cultural inspiration. Elite-oriented and opposed by all religious sects in the area, the SSNP failed to achieve power and is proscribed today in the Arab world.

While communist parties were established in the twenties, their influence remained negligible. During World War II and in the immediate postwar period, local communist parties gained some influence but never became an integral part of the mainstream of Arab political life. Today, Arab communist parties are hardly a factor to reckon with in Arab revolutionary activity.

The Ba'ath Party founded in 1941 by Michel Aflaq, a Christian, evolved into the most important secular doctrinaire party in the Arab world. Similar to the SSNP, the Ba'ath emphasized secularism, a mass-party organization, and social and political action programs. Unlike the SSNP, it advocates Pan-Arabism. While the Ba'ath has been in the ascendancy in Syria since 1956 and is presently ruling in Syria and Iraq, it suffers from serious factionalism and remains little more than a tool manipulated by the military elites of these two states.

The acquisition of independence revealed the latent differences and antagonisms among Arab states. The Arab response to their new challenges stimulated the rapid rise and equally rapid decline of competing unity schemes: the Fertile Crescent Plan advanced by Nuri al-Said of Iraq and the Greater Syria blueprint of King Abdullah of Jordan. The League of Arab States degenerated into a powerless debating forum.

The Arab defeat in Palestine in 1948-49 dramatized the need for change. Prominent Arab scholars such as Constantine Zurayk, Hasan Sa'ab and others termed it the great tragedy of modern Arab history. Along with many others they attempted to examine the ills of Arab society and the means best suited to alleviate them. But their pleas for a rebirth of nationalism and spiritualism, and the adoption of new attitudes to effect modernization merely served to reveal the moral bankruptcy of the Arab ruling elites, and the ideological power vacuum in the Arab world.

Arab political movements had failed to come to grips with the internal contradictions of Arab society. In many societies, the resolution of such contradictions had set free a dynamic spark, purging them from the shackles of parochialism with its attendant misconceptions, prejudices, biases and subjectivism. In Britain, the mechanism was the attainment of the Magna Carta; in France, it was the Revolution of 1789; in Germany and Italy, the wars of unification beginning in 1956; in Russia, the 1917 Revolution; in China, the revolutions of 1908, 1927 and 1948. Each of these societies achieved a higher level of internal cohesion following its revolutionary experience. This made possible the normal functioning of the governing institutions in the absence of priority restraints imposed by conflicting, minority group interest. Some of these experiences came from within the established institutions, others from without and some from a combined effort from both sides. But the objective understanding of the revolutionary goals preceded the swelling party membership and the revolutionary takeover of power. In the Arab world, however the takeover of power has always preceded an objective understanding and articulation of the revolutionary goals.

REVOLUTION AS PROTEST

Beginning with the early fifties in the Eastern Arab states, and the early sixties in North Africa, a new revolutionary wave swept the

Arab world. A political complex of norms and values, organization and aspiration, was hastily put together. A spectacular display of radical pronouncements of policy and showpiece projects was exhibited to attract popular support and justify the sacrifices needed to effect development.

The Ba'ath party in Syria and Iraq, the Neo-Destour (renamed the Destourian Socialist Party) in Tunisia, the Front of National Liberation in Algeria and the Arab Socialist Union in Egypt all competed for revolutionary leadership. Inspired by an amalgam of traditional and Western ideas, they have avoided defining or crystallizing their role from the outset. Their origins are not to be found in any homogeneous socioeconomic class, but in semi-secularized groups oriented towards control of governmental power. Ultimately, the various revolutionary models in the Arab world merged in the overriding context of the single-party state with an ever-widening public sector. No early solution to the problem of national identity is in sight for these revolutionary models. Public authority remains precarious, political personnel often untrained and inexperienced. A general impatience for political participation by certain groups is evident, but "the transformation" has yet to come.

In effect, every Arab revolutionary state still perceives itself to be weak, and protests through "revolution" the existing societal, inter-Arab and international stratification. As they are subject to subversion and internal opposition, their political insecurity functions in their mutual relations on a continuum between winning support from each other to countering violent attacks on their respective legitimacies. None of the Arab revolutionary models has been able to institutionalize itself firmly, to create lasting structures, to establish liberal or popular institutions, or to relax its vigil against subversion, real or imagined. Their overreaction to such forces constantly places these revolutionary models at the mercy of counter-productive developments.

Much of the revolutionary leadership is distinguished from the masses by the ability to articulate ideas rather than by their substance. Arab revolutionaries have failed to forge a potent force among themselves, let alone rally popular support among the people. They have developed goals of societal change, but failed to mobilize the internal resources, human and physical, to approximate such goals. With the exception of the Destourian Socialist party in Tunisia, all of these movements turned to the army, the country's sole cohesive force capable of any action. The Party-Army coalition provides a combination of force and intellectual theoretical criticism—the prerequisite for raising a movement to a revolutionary level in the Arab world.

Shifts in balance of the uneasy coalition are commonly recurring since both parties to the coalition are also themselves victims of the antagonistic sectional, religious and minority groupings. Every new shift produces moves for another "revolution" either to redress the imbalance caused by its predecessor or to create new alignments. Each new revolutionary vanguard maintains a set of societal goals, a collection of those promissory notes of rebirth considered long overdue, to justify to the masses and above all to the army—the main source of support—the concentration of power and the sacrifices called for. Although these revolutionary goals, be they land reform, industrialization or nationalization of foreign interests, are presented in the form of an ideology which holds little promise of galvanizing or cementing the population, they nevertheless became a vehicle of consolidation and perpetuation of the revolutionary elite. Their realization is indeed secondary; the goals become ends in themselves.

After every coup those revolutionaries who survive the internal consolidation of the ruling elite base their claims to continued leadership upon their past glories. The revolution, or more accurately the coup d'etat, is made a substitute for history; it becomes a national myth that ensures the "demonization" of the former regime.

If today Westerners burn what they worshipped at the end of the last century, the nation as a masterpiece of modern history, the Arab revolutionary's collective pride turns upon the assertion of his cultural superiority. Unconsciously seeking diamonds in ashes, he reinforces his drive by believing that the fate of his culture is to be decided on the battlefield simultaneously with the fate of his aspirations.

The resulting revolutionary doctrine in the national context relies on an eclectic pragmatic borrowing. Militarism, a Leninistdisciplined organization expressed in a one-party system, the long-range economic plan, token agrarian reform, superficial Western liberalism and fascism, are all adapted from this amalgam to perceived local needs. It is cloaked in terms of basic questions of social hierarchy and human purpose without providing solutions to the problems these questions raise. In a decade and a milieu in which the inherited institutions and customary relationships no longer appear natural, inevitable or immutable, that which is borrowed assumes an indigenous character for lack of alternatives.

In the search by those revolutionaries for new institutions and refashioned relationships, hierarchy and control remain as vital as they have been in the past. The complex coordination of human effort required to meet the promissory notes of the revolutionary leadership is attempted in an economic-demographic set of conditions that predicates a pessimistic result. These conditions make it plausible for the few to defy these principles during the democratic socialist experiment. The few must manage and foresee developments. The majority must obey, sacrifice and endure, as they are important to change or validate the direction of the society.

Bound together by their repudiation of the traditional political and social structures, the revolutionaries find themselves even more frustrated at the social aspect of the revolution. At least in the realm of rhetoric, the concept of revolution in the early sixties shifted the focus of ideological attention of the Ba'athist regime in Syria and the Arab Socialist regime in Egypt from political processes to the class structure and economic organization of their respective states. To the extent that parliamentary democracy was frustrated for the lack of a middle class, these regimes developed under army control and without the firm base of a working class.

The quality and quantity of social and economic change in these states, as well as in such "revolutionary" states as Iraq, Libya, Algeria and others, will inevitably be the result of the direction and effort embodied in various development programs and the extent to which the masses identify with the goals of the leadership in radical reform. Such development, it would seem, will not be prejudiced greatly by an ideological conception of the perfect society, no matter how revolutionary. When progress is realized in any given area, it will be clothed in such a garment, more for external benefit than for anything else. The further these ideals are separated from reality, the more frustrated and potentially explosive will become the political situation in societies which must run to stand still.

The manifestations of military regimes in the Arab states reveal that revolutions there occur mainly for military and political considerations and rarely for economic or social reasons. The legitimacy of these regimes is derived from their predecessor's inability to make good on their political and military promises: modernization, and the liberation of Palestine. The inability to fulfill promises results from a serious and recurring imbalance in the means-ends relationship of these regimes, whether they are military or civilian. Their recurring imbalance is mainly due not to the unavailability of means, but rather to Arab inability to deal effectively with operational modifiers influencing the flexibility of their means and the priority of their objectives.

PALESTINIAN LIBERATION MOVEMENTS

Their defeat in 1967 introduced a new outlook in the Arab world. There could be no excuses; and none were accepted as readily as were the excuses given in 1948 and 1956. The prestige of governments, as sources of leadership, reached a new low in the Arab world. The problem was increasingly seen to be not just the liberation of Palestine—a distant goal to which all Arab governments pay lip service—but also the liberation of the Arab states, revolutionary or otherwise, and the best methods by which to achieve it. The traditional approach has been proven to be fallible and a far more radical alternative is sought. The infatuation of Arabs with the Palestinian liberation movement is in part an appreciation of mass participation as the means to action and goal fulfillment.

Palestinians, aware of this new climate in the Arab world, and of the general weakness of the Arab regimes and their inability to restore their rights in Palestine, have moved on their own. For the first time since 1949, the Palestinians have been free and willing to act militantly, independent of their hosts. The success of the Palestinians, however, will depend on whether they can unite into a single revolutionary movement, and elicit the participation of the restive Arab intelligentsia. They must also overcome the restraints imposed by Arab regimes, and in some cases, the open hostility of those regimes.

Although the unity of the Palestinian liberation movement is not yet a reality, a radical hegemonic group may yet emerge and move toward the next stage, that of linking up with the Arab intelligentsia. Both Fatah and the Popular Front for the Liberation of Palestine realize their success will depend on their ability to spread the revolution to non-Palestinian Arabs. It is in this stage that they will encounter their greatest challenge. Linking up with other Arabs will require an ideology and the creation of what may be called "parallel organizations" supported by radical means.

Although ideologically uncommitted, Fatah has so far rejected the Marxist-Leninist approach of the Popular Front for the Liberation of Palestine on the grounds that it is part of the traditional revolutionary approach, and thus fails to overcome the impasse in which the Ba'ath and other Arab revolutionary movements have floundered. Fatah has so far relied on a nationalist and anti-imperialist (anti-Israel) approach. This approach has been more successful than that of the Popular Front, and its simplicity is made more attractive by the activities of Fatah inside Israeli-occupied territory. But at this stage, greater emphasis must be accorded to structures and organization. If Fatah and the Popular Front for the Liberation of Palestine fail to develop these structures, they will lose control over the non-Palestine Arabs, and the whole movement may fall prey to "warlordism." On the other hand, the Arab governments, conservatives and radicals alike, will view with alarm the development of an organized mass movement that can only threaten their continued existence, and will probably not countenance the development of these parallel organizations.

In its Palestinian context, Fatah represents the willingness of the Palestinian Arab to seize the initiative in securing what he believes to be his rights in Palestine. In its greater Arab context, it represents a reevaluation, if not an outright rejection, of Arab governments. It is in this context that increasing student and associational groups' unrest in the "revolutionary" Arab states must be viewed.

The approach of Fatah has been along the lines of two propositions suggested by Regis Debray; namely that guerrilla action leads to political action and political structures, and that the former is not dependent on the latter for success. Thus it is only now that Fatah is beginning to come to grips with the cultural inputs to what may become its ideological orientation and platform, and two trends appear. One trend calls for a reconciliation of Islamic tradition with the requirements of the day through the reform of Islam—reopening the doors to Ijtihad (religious interpretation and jurisprudence)—while the other trend suggests a completely secular left-of-center approach.

The prospect of a peaceful settlement may hasten these developments and bring about a major confrontation. There may be an attempt by the Palestinian liberation movements to take a short-cut approach: a direct bid to the masses without the benefit of parallel organizations. In such a situation they may find themselves stalemated, emotionally supported by the masses who, lacking organization, will not be a match for the organized, repressive force at the disposal of their governments.

This overall preoccupation with the Palestinian cause as the hard nut to crack, has potential as a vehicle for a Pan-Arab movement of liberation. The cause of Palestine, many involved Arabs feel, can only be served correctly through a Pan-Arab union. Liberation from without is pushing the agenda for liberation from internal rulers reluctant to gamble over sectional, particularistic interests. If and when a union of the Popular Front for the Liberation of Palestine and Fatah takes place, the desire for liberation from ruling elites will inevitably be intensified, and liberation from demoralizing and repressive regimes will become as much of a priority item on the agenda as is liberation from Zionism.

The Arabs may have a revolutionary experience coming, one that will rank among and parallel those of Italy in 1871 or Russia in 1917.

The New Left and Israel.

SHLOMO AVINERI

Since the Six Day War a critical attitude towards Israel has developed among student circles of the New Left. Frequently this criticism is not limited to opposing certain aspects of Israel's policy but even casts doubts on the legitimacy of the existence of the state. As Fatah propaganda increases in the West, helped by thousands of Arab students in European and American Universities, the stand of the Palestinian organizations derives ideological support from groups among the New Left.

The fact that some Jewish students (often among the most active members of the New Left) take part in this anti-Israel propaganda astounds the Israelis. They generally tend to deny the phenomenon or explain it away in psychological terms. In either event, this growing atmosphere of mutual misunderstanding has led to estrangement.

ISRAEL AND IMPERIALISM

Since World War II and the holocaust the socialist movements of Europe have generally been among the most ardent supporters of Israel and of her stand in the Israel-Arab conflict. However, even in the very early days of the Zionist movement, groups of *Poale Zion* (Zionist socialists) faced opposition from many factions within the Socialist International. Not only the *Bund*, but also non-Jewish socialists claimed that socialism would solve the problem of anti-Semitism and that Zionism, despairing of a socialist solution, based itself on narrow nationalist principals instead of a universal vision of socialist brotherhood.

Criticism of Zionism is not new in Socialist literature. Despite the efforts of the Socialist International in exposing anti-Semitism, especially in Russia, many of its leading spokesmen adopted an anti-Zionist position. Karl Kautsky for example, in his book *Race and Judaism* combined a stringent attack on anti-Semitism with a critical attitude towards Jewish settlement in Palestine. In the second edition of the book which appeared in 1921, he described Zionism as a tool of Western imperialism dominating the Arab world. He concluded his analysis with a dismal vision of the future: "Jewish settlement in Palestine will, of necessity, collapse with the disintegration of Anglo-French rule and the progress of Asia and Egypt. It is only a question of time and a very short time at that."

CURRENT VARIATIONS

Although the New Left does not constitute a cohesive unit, it holds certain ideas which can only bring about further estrangement from Israel. The Israeli-Arab conflict is viewed as analogous to the various struggles between white European and Afro-Asian communities. Since in these conflicts the New Left unreservedly supports the "Third World" (the blacks of South Africa and Rhodesia and, in the past, the Arabs of Algeria) Israel is conceived as a state of white, colonial settlers.

The fact that Israel is supported by America, and that part of this support derives from circles that regard Israel as a "bastion against the spread of communism," causes the Israel-Arab conflict to be viewed as one aspect of the cold war, with Israel supporting American interests against the local, national, socialist movements.

Israel's refusal to withdraw from the occupied territories unless her conditions for securing peace are met is produced as further evidence of her desire for conquest and settlement. The ideas of the "Movement for Greater Israel" are taken as a true indication of Israel's policies. In no other circles are statements by members of this movement so widely quoted or do they attract so much attention. Every extreme and "annexationist" statement is used to prove Israel's expansionist aims.

The fact that since the Six Day War the emphasis in the Israeli-Arab confrontation has shifted in the direction of the Palestinians has created the impression that the Arab war against Israel falls into the same category as the struggle of the FLN and the Vietcong. The myth of guerrilla warfare in underdeveloped countries, endorsed by the writings of Mao and Che Guevara, gives rise to the identification of Fatah with other movements. It is seen as a revolutionary and dynamic factor whose aims parallel those of the FLN and the Vietcong.

THE SLOGAN OF A SECULAR DEMOCRATIC PALESTINE

Perhaps the most important factor in arousing sympathy for Fatah and other Palestinian organizations is the changed content of their propaganda since the June War. Arab information personnel in general, and Fatah in particular, have perceived that among the factors producing the greatest hostility toward the Arab cause prior to the Six Day War were the almost universal Arab declarations of genocide. In their most extreme form they were voiced, for example, by Ahmed Shukairy: "Those Jews who remain in Palestine after the war will be allowed to return to their country of origin—but I suppose that the number of those remaining alive will be very small." This brought home to all the danger that Israel faced and could not but create sympathy for her.

Today Fatah claims that these extreme views were partly responsible for the Arab defeat. Fatah, it is said, does not intend to repeat these mistakes. Its aim is not to throw the Jews into the sea, nor even to destroy the state of Israel, but (and here there are slight differences in interpretation between the Fatah and the Popular Front) to ensure the rights of the Palestinians and create a state wherein Jews and Arabs can live together. To quote the *Fatah Manifesto* which was recently distributed in the West:

The Palestine Movement for National Liberation, Fatah, solemnly declares that the final aim of its struggle is to re-establish a free, democratic Palestinian State wherein all citizens, whatever their religion, shall hold equal rights.

The aim is the creation of a state in which "Moslems, Christians and Jews" will live with full and equal rights—as in Lebanon. This program, accepted in the West by people who have no access to nonpartisan information on events in the Middle East, evokes a vision of equality and democracy. Israel, on the other hand, is presented as a nationlistic, even a racialist state, intolerant and expansionist. The slogan of a "secular, democratic Palestine" or "a bi-national State" produces support for the Fatah in leftist circles that previously would not have tolerated such violently racist rhetoric as "the destruction of Israel" or "throwing the Jews into the sea."

CONFRONTING THIS SLOGAN

Traditional Israeli arguments are obviously not able to contend with this idea. The Israeli diplomatic stand is regarded by the New Left as irrelevant, just as the entire world of diplomacy is viewed as one aspect of the establishment against which they are rebelling. Customary Zionist arguments only confirm their conception of Israel's ethnocentric character and their belief in the danger facing the Arabs. Information regarding the basically liberal nature of the military administration in the occupied areas is also dismissed as irrelevant, since no liberal concepts hold any meaning for the New Left. Also, there are always the old stories of houses blown up, demonstrations dispersed, leaders imprisoned and banished to the East Bank and so forth, all of which proves that Israeli rule is, after all, an occupation.

Nor are the usual self-justifying apologetics—which invariably try to prove that Israel is always right and the Arabs always wrong—of any help in combatting this position. The only way to confront the arguments of the New Left is to set the reality of the Arab-Israeli struggle against their own theoretical position. It should be stressed that, unlike Vietnam or Cuba, the conflict in the Middle East is not one of Western imperialism versus a national liberation movement. It is a struggle between two movements for national liberation, the Jewish and the Arab, and that within the New Left criteria the pattern of Israeli society is far closer to their revolutionary image than is that of the Arabs. In other words, the revolutionary nature of Zionism from a social point of view has to be emphasized: the fact that in Zionism political aims and social reconstruction have gone hand in hand and that the combination of Zionism and socialism was fundamental to the political success of the Jewish national movement. Arab nationalism has not forged equally realistic tools to bring about social changes and the transformation of the traditional structure of Arab society.

Despite differences in theory Israel and the Israeli army bear a closer resemblance to North Vietnam. The parallel to South Vietnam in the Middle East is to be found not in Israel but in the military regimes of the Arab states which lack the capacity for political integration. The Israeli army—as a people's army—is far more akin to the armies of Communist China, Cuba or North Vietnam than to any Western army. Some Israelis may not like this comparison, but it is nonetheless valid.

Second, it is clear that the position taken by the great powers on the Israeli-Arab conflict has differed basically from that which they have adopted towards any other international conflict since World War II. There have been three wars in the Middle East and in each one their attitude has changed. We tend to forget that in 1948 it was Russia that not only supported the creation of the state of Israel but was the only power to facilitate the supply of arms to her.

Russia and America supported Israel while Britain and France took the Arabs side. In 1956 the situation changed completely with France and Britain supporting Israel, Russia supporting the Arabs and America, despite her general support for Israel, strongly opposing the Sinai Campaign and Israel's action. What happened in 1967 is well known—and here, of course, the interesting point is that France returned to her 1948 position. The picture that thus emerges is far different from the oversimplified concept of "imperialism versus progress."

Each twist and turn of the powers can be explained in terms of their interests at that particular time—but the overall picture which emerges makes it clear, without a shadow of doubt, that it is impossible to apply the simple formula of Western imperialism to the Israel-Arab conflict or to view it only as Israel versus the Arabs.

IGNORANCE OF HISTORY

The emphasis on the complex historical dimensions of the conflict is of special significance for the New Left whose members are accustomed to applying generalized formulae rather than making a detailed analysis of historical processes. To give one example: the Balfour Declaration is used as proof of the link between imperialism and Zionism but when set in proper historical context it acquires a different dimension. In the same year as the Balfour Declaration was proclaimed, the British encouraged and supported Arab nationalism in its rebellion against the Turks. Both national movements—the Arab and Jewish—were thus aided by British imperialism, and if this aid does not invalidate Arab nationalism it cannot therefore impugn the Jewish brand.

To give a further example: the emergence of the Fatah after the Six Day War is regarded as a new phenomenon. The point is being made that in conventional warfare a technologically strong state is more powerful, and thus Israel overcame the Arab armies; however, in guerrilla warfare the advantage lies with the less-developed society, and therefore what happened to the French in Algeria and what is happening to the Americans in Vietnam will finally happen to Israel.

The conventional reply is that the Israelis' bonds with their country are different from those felt by the French settlers or soldiers towards Algeria, and this, of course, is true. But there is another aspect to the debate: there is no historical validity to the claim that Fatah is a new phenomenon; the type of warfare being used by Fatah today is exactly the same as that used in the riots of 1936-39 and in the opening stages of the 1948 war. The Arabs have failed against Israel, not only in conventional warfare, but also in what they term guerrilla warfare.

To explain the roots of Arab defeat one would have to embark upon a comparative analysis of the structure of Arab and Israeli society, and this is impossible to undertake here. More pertinent, perhaps, is the geographical and topographical difference: the guerrilla wars of the FLN and the Vietcong succeeded because they were fought in jungle, swamp and mountain terrain. These conditions do not exist on the West Bank or in the Gaza Strip and so the Arab movement of opposition has no possibility of acquiring a territorial base and is doomed to failure.

Fatah is therefore impelled to resort to terrorism. Whilst in other guerrilla movements, terrorism is sometimes an adjunct to actual guerrilla warfare (and in these cases the New Left does not denounce its use), nevertheless the degeneration of the entire struggle into a war of terrorism testifies to its hopelessness. This is exactly what happened in 1936-39 and in 1948 and the current actions of Fatah and the other organizations follow the same pattern. Bombs in a supermarket or a university can kill people but cannot win a war. Far from being a new development, Fatah is repeating the mistakes of the movements which preceded it and which brought tragedy to the Palestinians. For the romantic generation of the New Left, Yasir Arafat may be a spellbinding personality, but placed alongside Fawzi Kaukji or Hassan Salame, despite the differences, we find a traditional phenomenon in the Arab world. The lack of innovation and the continuity in their mode of warfare against Israel are apparent.

THE NATIONAL ENTITIES

What sometimes appears at issue is the basic question of the legitimacy of the Zionist national movement. It is not sufficient to reply to Fatah propaganda slogans for a "democratic, secular Palestine" by saying that the only way in which this could be achieved would be by the destruction of the state of Israel, or by pointing out that this is not the line used by Fatah for its supporters in the Arab countries.

From the slogan of a "democratic, secular Palestine" it is possible to assume that the intention is to ensure individual civil rights and freedom of religious worship for the Jews. However, this is not the problem—these rights are assured to Jews in the West without difficulty. The two and a half million Jews in Israel want to ensure their rights, not only individual freedom and freedom of worship (and what about atheists and non-religious people?), but to live in a sovereign state of their own. They want what Fatah, even in its most liberally phrased declarations, is not prepared to grant them—the right of self-determination as a national entity within a sovereign territorial framework. The problem is not a personal one of a given number of individual Jews but of a framework for a specific human entity possessing its own culture, political structure and awareness of identity. In the same way the problem of the Palestinians is not that of individual rights to a certain house or plot of land but that of self-determination as a national body, and in this case it is recognized by the New Left.

The conclusion to be drawn from this comparison is that only by recognizing the rights of the Palestinians to self-determination can the answer be found to the claim for "a secular, democratic Palestine." Since the conflict is between two national entities, two movements for national liberation, the solution lies in the mutual recognition of the legitimacy of the two standpoints. Fatah is not prepared, in any form whatsoever, to recognize the legitimacy of Jewish nationalism—as far as they are concerned it does not exist. The Israeli case however must insist on recognizing the rights of the Palestinians to constitute—if they so wish—a national, political entity. The solution to the conflict must be sought in terms of a Palestinian state in Judaea and Samaria and Gaza (and in the long run also in Transjordan).

This solution—the establishment of a Palestinian state side by side with Israel—is sanctioned by historical experience. There are many examples to show that efforts to avoid a clash between two national movements by the creation of a "bi-national state" are doomed to tragic failure: Cyprus and Nigeria are two obvious examples and the fate of the non-Arab minorities in the Sudan and Iraq indicate the possible future nature of a "secular, democratic Palestine" however attractive it appears to the outsider.

DIASPORA ZIONISM AND THE NEW LEFT

A considerable section of the New Left, especially those who are Jews, judge Israel not by what she is but by those who support her in Western society. Since some of the foremost supporters of Israel in the Jewish community in the West are identified with the most prominent names among the Jewish plutocracy (the Rothschilds in France, Charles Clore and Isaac Wolfson in England and so forth) Israel is judged together with these millionaires. There is an even more widespread phenomenon—the type of Jewish person in the Diaspora whose identification with Israel results in his adopting a more extreme stand than the average Israeli. It has already been noted that the qualities which make the typical Diaspora Zionist a type not especially admired in Israel also alienate the young Jewish student in the Diaspora, who transforms his opposition to the Zionist establishment into opposition to Israel.

During a number of recent meetings in Western Europe between intellectuals, Israeli students and active members of the New Left, some of the ideas and arguments raised in this article were discussed. It became clear that it is possible to make members of the New Left question the facile parallels they draw between the Israel—Arab conflict and other situations in which they are politically and emotionally involved.

For instance, a group of Jewish Maoist students from Brussels left the Marxist-Leninist Organization of Students in Brussels after one of these meetings and set up a new group, called the "Organization of Marxist-Leninist-Zionist Students." They continue to hold their radical left opinions on all other matters but are now supporting, although not uncritically, the Israeli point of view.

This group has recently issued a booklet dealing with two issues: the right of self-determination for the Jews in Israel and a critical analysis of the Fatah. In the first part, the authors point out how the Left has historically negated Zionism although Lenin and his colleagues did not deny the right of the Jews to self-determination in an autonomous framework within the larger society. From this sprang the idea of Birobidjan. The authors show that the idea of Birobidjan was doomed to failure because it did not take into account the historical and cultural ties and the national consciousness that link a national group with a territory—a point strongly emphasized by one of the prophets of the New Left, Frantz Fanon. In contrast to Birobidjan, the two and a half million Jews in Israel have a deep and vital bond with the territory in which they live. Using the basic intellectual premises of the New Left and Leninist principles, backed by ideas from Frantz Fanon and Dov Ber Borochov (the theorist of the Labor Zionist Movement), the authors of this particular pamphlet affirm the legitimacy of the state of Israel.

The second part of the pamphlet deals with the social structure of Fatah: its middle-class conservative base is examined and the leading role played by intellectuals rather than the lower classes. Its ties with clerical, Moslem tradition and links with Kuwait and the oil tycoons are noted. Such facts are used to explain how the Fatah differs from the FLN and the Vietcong and why it will fail while they succeeded, and finally, why it is not worthy of the intellectual support of the New Left.

Closing Horizons:
Israelis and Nationalism

GIL CARL ALROY

I do not want to rove over the wide compass of problems that
have been touched upon here by these able speakers, but I would
like to say a few things about big power intervention in the
Middle East. My own perspective on this particular phenomenon
is derived not from diplomatic history, but rather from analysis
of the dynamics of the conflict in the Middle East. And if I am
led to any conclusion, it is that conventional interpretations of
big power intervention in the Middle East are seriously open to
question. The powers and the United Nations, usually portrayed
as rebuffed peacemakers, appear to me to aggravate and further
destabilize the area; almost inherently so. In fact the accumulated
record is so cogent in this respect that those who either propose
or support yet another version of big power intrusion simply
cannot get away with intimations and sometimes dubious logical
exercises. It seems to me that big power intervention can have
little to do with producing peace in the Middle East.

As I see it, the seemingly endless calamity to which Professor
Said addressed himself with compassion, that cost so many lives
of Jews and Arabs and that will probably go on costing so many
more, this calamity is in a profound sense sustained by a peculiar
incongruity between two sets of power relationships: one in the
area and the other in the international community. The fact of
international life that has been exposed here by Professor Hinsley

303

and Professor Perlmutter, is that within the area itself, the preponderance of Israeli power, because of its Western structure, is so great that one might in fact wonder whether, if it were not for the international community, even the most militant of Arabs would have very much hope about changing the situation.

In the international community, on the other hand, it seems to me the situation is precisely the opposite. Israel is a rather negligible quantity in the international community as opposed to the Arab nations, which with their associates and supporters are very heavily represented diplomatically in the United Nations and the Security Council. Indeed, this asymmetry in the international community between the positions of Israel and the Arab countries is even further exaggerated because so many large powers compete for Arab resources and good will. And so often, the real strengths of Israel are thus understated.

Because of the military superiority of Israel, the Arabs quite rationally retreat to the international community to seek redress and the reconstitution of the status quo ante. As Professor Perlmutter put it in his paper, in writing of the Arab point of view: "And above all what we can close by war and violence can be restored by diplomacy, political pressure and political exhortation and machinations between imperial and great powers who in the end opt in favor of 70 million Arabs, oil revenue, United Nations votes, status quo and strategic political considerations." This is a rather rational position narrowly defined. And for the life of me, I simply cannot understand how the present four power intrusion deviates from this prevailing pattern.

As the Rogers peace proposals clearly show—and they are not yet the end result of big power consultations—international intrusion can only tend toward restoration of the status quo under some new window dressing. International intrusion is premised upon two profoundly dubious assumptions. One, that Arab losses must always be restored after unsuccessful wars, which has the effect of convincing the Arabs that there is no penalty for trying to wipe Israel off the map. The other assumption is that Arab hostility, while bitter, is particularly flimsy, at one and the same time. It is assumed to be categorical, yet superficial and artificial—something to be turned on or off, like a faucet. Hence, side by side with the demand for the return of Arab losses after unsuccessful wars invariably appears the demand that the Arabs stop feeling about Israel the way they simply cannot help feeling.

Arab countries have repeatedly tried to give manifestation and reality to a strong sense of outrage that so many Arabs feel about the existence of a Jewish state of any size whatsoever in what they consider part of the Arab homeland. Parenthetically, we Americans have long had a rather superficial awareness of just how genuine and profound that sense of outrage was. In a way, I think that the older Zionist propaganda has misled us on this point. It has rather helped make us feel that there is a basically synthetic and artificial character to Arab opposition, a feeling so many Western liberals share. And hence we have tended to see this problem as an ordinary political one which it most decidedly is not. It is to this popular fallacy that the so-called big power search for the perfect formula appeals.

One must not confuse a mere conflict of interest among mutually tolerating contestants, where "balancing of claims" applies, with one in which survival is the issue. Nor can one transform the latter kind of conflict into the former by having one of the sides recite a few words. No amount of pursuit after the ultimately esoteric formula by diplomats can do this trick.

DISCUSSION AT THE THIRD PANEL
February 15, 1970

Horowitz: I would like to believe with Professor Hinsley that big power settlement of the Middle East struggle is possible. But I fail to detect in his paper the necessary critical examination of what political commonalities exist that would permit a mutual acceptance of outside regulation or outside control. Under the circumstances, why would big power settlement be superior to an attempt at settlement by the belligerents involved? Indeed, it seems to me that given the triadic nature of the struggle with the introduction of the Palestinian Arabs as a separate and distinctive factor, it might be difficult for even the major belligerents to arrive at a meaningful settlement. The assumption that the European and American powers can resolve world problems rests on a presumption that they have all the power—and it is precisely this presumption that the Third World contradicts.

With respect to the remarks made by Professor Perlmutter, I would center my criticism on why he assumes so categorically that it is the present role of the Soviet Union that has upset the existential balance of power. I find this kind of theorizing somewhat gratuitous, since it assumes an apriori balance which in fact has been profoundly irritating to major Arab interests, and which favors the Western capitalist powers to the detriment of central Arab concerns. When one employs a theory of political balance, this presumes that any new factor upsets that balance. In this sense, the penetration of the Soviet Union upsets that balance. There seems to be an assumption that without the existence of Soviet power the position of Israel would be stronger than at present. But by this kind of reasoning, one can construct a universe in which Arab apologists might properly declare that without the existence of United States power, their position would be stronger vis-a-vis the Israelis.

To Professor Said, I would address a similar kind of question. There is indeed a revolution of the Arab young and the Israeli young generation is indeed a fact—but those who still have power in the Arab world, while sharing with the young a certain rhetoric, do not necessarily share a common line of action. Is the Arab revolution defined in terms of Israel and the purging of the area of the Israeli state, or is it defined in terms of the problem of class formation and the liberation of the peoples from the yoke of colonialism; or if they are in fact problems that have to be attacked simultaneously, how in fact, does one handle the question of the Israeli regime? In what sense can Israel play a positive role in the formation of a Middle Eastern revolution and not simply be called a second item in the ordering of the priorities for the Middle Eastern revolution? It seems to me that the revolution that Professor Said talks about is first a revolution in social structure, and secondly a movement for the destruction of the Israeli nation. If the issue is one of timetables then the question is one of ordering priorities. However, do young Arab leaders really view their revolution this way? I would be very curious to know.

Professor Alroy raises the kind of issues Professor Perlmutter introduced, albeit somewhat differently. The question of the negligibility of Israel and the importance of Arabs and the lack of asymmetry therefore in foreign concern, perhaps overlooks the international Jewish community, which while not entirely a counterweight, is at least a factor in making Israel much more important than the state of Vermont. When one talks about balance of forces and balance of power, the existence of that international Jewish community becomes a serious factor as in point of fact all sides to the Middle East conflagration have always known. It might well be that considerable more symmetry in the balance of forces in the Middle East will be acknowledged once the international dimension is taken into account. In any event, it seems to me that Professor Alroy should show some appreciation of the role that the international Jewish community plays in any area-wide struggle.

Hinsley: You asked me a question which if I were to answer properly would require me to deliver another paper. The question is, how can I possibly expect the direct participants in this struggle, and in particular the Arabs, to accept an outwardly imposed settlement in view of the problems of national sovereignty and national feeling. Part of the answer is that Arab and Israeli nationalisms are, by European and American standards, at a very odd stage of development. Both of them are highly non-territorial in their concept of the nation. The Arabs for example are uncertain whether to regard themselves as Egyptian nationalists or as members of an Arab nation which is culturally conceived. All states in the Arab area are uncertain whether they are pan-Arabists, or whether they are competing secular states. This is because Arab nationalism continues to be at a peculiarly early stage of development. The one great step forward which it requires for stabilization, and for obtaining a platform from which it can undertake the really important work of internal revolution which Professor Said says is required, and to which many young Arabs are increasingly turning, is the presence of firm, fixed, territorial bounds of containment.

So long as that part of the world remains without boundaries that are accepted by both sides, and are guaranteed sufficiently long for them to take on the coat of custom, the Arab world will continue to dissipate its energies in what are on the whole peripheral activities. Now, in very much the same way, not a very great deal of attention has been paid so far by Israeli nationalism to territorial structure. The concept of the Israeli nation is highly religious and cultural rather than territorial. It is my firm belief from having studied a good deal of this despised history, both in terms of the problem of nationalism and in terms of the problem of the international system, that both Israeli and Arab nationalities and nationalisms require territorial settlements. This is really only the introduction to an answer to your question, which was: in the state of, as I would put it, primitive nationalism, to which both parties in the Middle East conflict still belong, how can they be expected to accept the bold intervention of the great powers in the form of a territorial settlement that I have suggested is now becoming possible.

I think I can better answer your question by sketching out what would happen as I see it, if the four powers were to agree on what were the territorial and other aspects of a firm settlement of the Middle East that they could recommend, and if they were then to dispatch instructions to Israel and the Arab states, to the effect that those states were to present themselves at Locarno at a certain date. They would all attend, and the great difficulty would not be that they would not accept the award, which of course would appear to be in the interests of everybody, Russia and America, France, Great Britain, the Arabs and Israelis. They would jump on it with alacrity. The difficulty would be that they would then be concerned with the problem of having to deal with their own societies and the problem of containing the revolutionary elements in those societies. We have long experienced the way these difficulties were controlled during the nineteenth century in Europe, and the powers were very influential in shaping that world.

Perlmutter: Concerning the theory of a balance of power, I hope that I have not claimed that the great powers are interested in a balance. I was referring to an orientation toward the balance, not as a description of the balance, but as a prescription of it. The orientation of the western powers toward a balance of power means the establishment and encouragement of status quo powers oriented toward the West. The Soviet orientation would be in favor of the establishment of power oriented to the status quo toward the Soviet Union. Therefore I consider the concept of balance of power as unrealistic precisely for the opposite reason that Professor Hinsley considers it realistic. In my views a concert of power is a concert of those powers who dominate while others participate less.

This assumes a high state of politics. Non-primitivism is the prerogative of highly cultured civilizations such as the United States, France and the Soviet Union. Low level civilizations—to use Professor Hinsley's term, primitive nationalisms—do not have the proper level of rationality, responsibility and capability and thus they have no right to concert the power. This is not the place to discuss whether the Balkans have really been concerted or not, but if I know my history of the Balkans, it's just the opposite.

Said: I see two dimensions of the question addressed to me by Professor Horowitz. One, was whether the rhetoric of the present-day young Arab intelligentsia is not identical with that of the more traditional Arab revolutionaries, such as the Ba'ath and others. And the second dimension referred to the agenda, so to speak: how do they view the state of Israel in this revolution. As to the first question, I think there is some difference in the rhetoric, perhaps not very apparent and perhaps not very significant. To a large extent the rhetoric of the traditional revolutionary movement centered mainly around the theme of the seizure of revolutionary power, around the theme of how one takes over power, where more recently one observes discussions centering around the theme of the revolutionary processes, goals and purposes. I'm not suggesting here that this latter point was not included in the former rhetoric; it was. There seems to be more attention paid to it now; however, because I observe greater attention centering around the theme of revolutionary processes and goals, this does not mean that they will achieve these goals and these purposes.

As to the second point, where does Israel figure in the present-day Arab revolutionary thrust, you use the phrase "destruction of Israel" and ask if the Arabs feel that is is inevitable. Again, I have the feeling that in respect to the non-Palestinian Arabs, we have to make a distinction. To the present-day Arab intelligentsia the liberation of Algeria, Syria and Iraq occupies a far more prominent place on their minds than liberation and destruction of Israel. Some of the young Arab revolutionaries or intelligentsia distinguish between the destruction of Israel as a state and the destruction of the Zionist organization. To these younger Arabs, if Israel becomes a multinational, multireligious society, then there is no problem. They will get along with it. They are trying to articulate this view at least in their own minds. They do not use the term "the destruction of Israel", they use a different term. They use either the term "national liberation" or "a society that will guarantee the rights of various citizens." In this matter the Palestinian Arab is in a slightly different situation from the non-Palestinian Arabs. But my feeling is this, the present-day thrust of revolution among these younger Arabs is really one very much directed to what they consider the inner contradictions of Arab society. They are trying to cope with what they consider to be political systems that are non-viable. And they observe that the non-viability of these political systems is a function of the inability of the present Arab governments to reconcile needs, demands, structures and environment. I am not saying these young revolutionaries are doing much about it, but this is what they are articulating at the present time.

Alroy: The war in 1967 had strong emotional consequences in the United States, and caused a state of shock and hysteria in the American-Jewish community including both religious and non-religious people, left and right, and even some members of the American Council for Judaism. In Israel the war has perhaps led to a closer identification with the situation of Jews in Europe in the 1940s before the holocaust, combined with determination that this shall bever be repeated. Incidentally, these are feelings that I think our policy-makers absolutely do not understand, just as they also do not understand the animosity of the Arabs. The greatest impact of the 1967 war was among the so-called Sabras, the native born Jews in Israel who prior to the war were described as almost totally ignorant of Jewry abroad and sometimes contemptuous of them, to boot.

I think that the feeling has developed very strongly in Israel and in the United States that if Israel has an ally in the world it can only be other Jews, especially those in the United States. This is true, but requires further analysis. That the Jewish communities in the West are influential is not to be denied. But the world Jewish communities do not possess what Mauritania possesses. That is sovereignty. They may possess large financial means and, particularly in periods of distress, are liberal with such assistance. But as a political force they are less obviously effective. It seems to me that in the United States, where the largest and most important Jewish community outside Israel exists, we could define its influence on American policy in terms of a negative parameter rather than as a positive force. I do not think that American Jewish power can positively influence American policy very much. Possibly they might, at certain times, put down the limit beyond which not even a Republican administration might go in attempts at pressuring Israel. But I have my doubts about that too. For instance, there is reason to believe that the present administration is confident of its capacity of manipulating Jewish opinion to a considerable degree. Consider also the very powerful and strongly Zionist community in France, of approximately one-half million Jews, and the extent of its influence on Pompidou's policies toward the Middle East. Of course they have some influence; for instance, French officials balance their hostile interventions against Israel with gracious statements that, after all, they concede that Israel has a right to exist—quite a concession to the one-half million Jews in France.

Mr. Merlin, who spoke here this morning, recently made a very interesting observation, something that I had noticed time and again myself. There is a curious pattern to the attitude of Western statesmen toward Israel. When they are out of power, they are friends; when they get into power, they invariably assume a different stance. I think this is indicative of the peculiar fluctuations and limitations of the effectiveness of Jewish power in western countries. For example, the supposedly notoriously Zionist newspaper, the *New York Times*, has consistently taken a position which according to the Prime Minister of Israel is inimical to the Israelis' vital interests. In consequence, somebody in Washington turns to somebody else and says, "What do you mean, the Jews are upset by my policies? Why the *New York Times* supports me." The problem of Jewish power has usually been oversimplified. Its effectiveness surely has been exaggerated for the most part.

Question: My question is directed to Professor Said and possibly to other members of the panel. It seems to me that one obstacle to peace at the present time is the inflamed anger of a significant number of Arab people. Not merely Arab masses, but possibly and especially Arab intelligentsia, intelligent young people who perhaps are joining Fatah. Professor Hinsley has also said that it may be very hard for the parties to enforce a settlement and to sell that settlement to their own people. It strikes me it might be especially hard to sell it to the Arab people. What might then be the basis for this kind of hatred or anger at the present time? Speakers yesterday and this morning suggested that it is the problem of the Arab refugees. If their problems were solved these animosities would be reduced significantly. I wonder if that really is an explanation for the anger at the present time, since we have no evidence that Arabs in the past have been so concerned for those related to them in other Arab countries. Perhaps the hatred at the present time is a traumatic result of the smashing defeat of the Six Day War. The kind of activity and hope and enthusiasm of many Arabs just prior to the war was afterwards dashed to disappointment by the blazing and rapid Israeli victory. The Arabs view Israel as having given them an unpardonable insult. This situation is similar to Arab attitude towards the Crusades, as an insult to the Arab culture of the past and an insult which perhaps has always been lingering there and caused inferiority feelings, vis a vis the West. If this is indeed the case, how can we somehow allow the Arabs to save face while preserving Israel's existence?

Said: I wouldn't call it hatred myself. Let me just give a very brief response to the question. I had occasion to travel in many Arab states several months after the Arab-Israeli war in 1967, in my capacity as an American specialist for the Department of State lecturing in universities. There are many factors involved. One, I had a feeling, a very strong feeling, that if Israel was located next to any state in Asia or Africa, with very few exceptions, Israel would make that state look very bad. This is an important point. The Arabs are neighbors to a state that is advanced, that is technological and that would have exposed almost any state in Africa or Asia. Another factor that is important here relates to the Arabs rather than to Israel. The Arabs are very frustrated. This frustration is not caused by the Israelis, but by their own social and economic problems. A third factor is a belief, a conviction on the part of the Arabs—and this applies to the majority of Arabs—that the United States is committed and dedicated to assist Israel against them; not to assist Israel to maintain a balance, but to assist Israel against them. And when you discuss it with Arabs they will cite chapter and verse. I do not believe that the great powers can successfully impose a peace. I think that so long as conflicts between states centered around the accumulation of victories in pursuit of national interests, the traditional balance of power might have applied. But we are dealing with a different situation. We are dealing with a situation of states pursuing what I call obscene national missions. And I equate here Zionism and Arab nationalism. Personally I am against such national missions. The role of the great powers in the Middle East at the present time is not the same as it was in the old days. In the old days we exercised the influence of power. Now we have to exercise the power of influence. How do you do it? Americans have little or no credibility with most of the Arabs. The Soviet Union has discovered that you cannot buy an Arab, you can only rent him and his maintenance is very high. Americans have discovered that you cannot influence Israel that much. Who is going to do it, who is going to carry it out?

Perlmutter: I'm trying to devise a typology of the Arab reaction to 1967. I think definitely that the aggravation after 1967 is important. And if I make a summary of the Arab reactions since 1967 based on the Arab literature written in various areas, one actually finds five schools; reformist, revolutionary, Islamic, establishment and Fatah. Two items are especially interesting. One is, what is the solution and prognosis and the other, what is the enemy and what comes first? To the reformist, the solution is change, educational and political, and the westernization and technological development of the regime. The enemy is Israel. To the revolutionaries, the revolution comes first, and it must be total. Economic, social, political and national liberation must occur at home. The enemy is imperialism in Israel. The priority of the two phenomena varies. Sometimes the revolution comes first; at other times the imperialism in Israel. The Islamic group's position is very simple. Its view is that we have suffered because we have betrayed Islam, and the enemy is Israel, world communism and the Arab socialist states. Obviously the return of Islam comes first and the latter are really long-run solutions. The establishment and Fatah views are the most interesting. The establishment's analysis is that what has occurred is that the regime really did not know what to do or how to reform itself but that it is now necessary to give confidence to the regime. First comes the destruction of Israel and imperialism and then there will be confidence in the regime. Fatah's position is very clear. It is symmetrical. Guerrilla warfare against Israel is war against Israel and the resolution of internal Arab conflict will be triggered by this. In other words, if we fight against Israel the capabilities that we establish will lead, after the liberation of Israel, to a social revolution.

Question: I have two questions. The first is to Professor Said. I followed with much attention your argument about changes in the Arab intelligentsia. Would you please say whether there would be an advantage to a solution in which the Palestinians who are now actually a majority on the East side of the Jordan, would take over the Jordanian government? And I have a second question to Professor Hinsley. I was a bit disturbed by your statement about nationalism in the Middle East. I would like to know your sources. Judaism is extraterritorial and where did you find that there is no connection between the Israelis in Israel and the territory?

Said: Perhaps the establishment of an Arab Palestinian state of Jordan and that part which at the present time is occupied by Israel might alleviate conflict, but I have not really thought about it very carefully. However, should the Arab commandoes take over Jordan, then in all probability they would not abandon their objective, their goal of what they consider to be the inevitable process of liberation, namely to go into Israel and to transform Israel into a multinational, multireligious society, in which the Arabs would then be dominant.

Hinsley: The answer to the second part of the question is very much contained in what Professor Said said when speaking about the pursuit on both of these sides of obscene national missions. The territorial concept in the Israel idea of the state, has been very much overwhelmed, especially with the growth of conflict, by the missionary, non-territorial side of nationalism. Until both sides have acquired territorial stabilization, this pursuit of obscene national missions will go on. One way of bringing about the territorial stabilization which is a precondition of movement toward more stable nationalism, is the one that I have suggested. Neither side thinks it is practicable, but nobody has suggested any other practicable way in which the conflict can be brought to an end.

Question: I would like to just make a few brief comments and address a question to Professor Hinsley. Hinsley really advanced a hypothetical situation and I think this hypothetical situation should be considered in opposition to the mechanistic typologies developed by modern political science. This hypothetical situation rests on the assumption that states can intermittently behave sensibly and rationally. Not permanently; the situation always remains precarious, and only a precarious balance and precarious arrangements can be established. Perhaps rationality and a sense of realism can break through and we can manage certain situations which seem to have got out of hand. I would like to ask Hinsley if his idea of a concert of the great powers imposing a solution involves at the same time a disengagement from the local conflict. It would have to involve at least their ceasing to supply arms to both sides, their supervising areas and their adopting policies that would bring about a compromise between the two sides. In this kind of realistic compromise, Israel's rights would be adequately, and more than adequately protected. Therefore, would Professor Hinsley agree that the concert can be accompanied by a process of disengagement and that if this does not happen and if the great powers continue to behave irrationally, then the Middle East will continue to be convulsed with conflict, violence, perhaps tragedy, and that this will continue for a long time, to the detriment of both Israel and the Arab people.

Hinsley: I do agree that the kind of settlement that would be possible, on the basis of agreement between the great powers would be one involving their own withdrawal from direct participation in the area, except as guarantors of a local settlement which they had imposed. Some of the speakers this afternoon have been assuming, no doubt because the distortions of the Cold War have not yet fully disappeared, that states, great states, can only concert together when they agree. The whole history of the diplomatic system proves that great states only concert when they don't agree. It is when they have got to compromise over something that they do not like to compromise, that they reach agreed and general settlements. The whole nature of the concert requires you to understand that apparent paradox. It will be because they, in their own interests, come to the view that they must retreat, that they will agree to the kind of settlement that I have suggested.

Question: I'd like to address my question to Professor Alroy. I felt very disturbed by the use of the word "hysteria" with respect to the Jewish community's reaction to the June war. Perhaps as a physician I'm more sensitive to the word hysteria, because we have very precise definitions in medicine as you do in the social sciences. The main thrust of hysteria is that it disables the human being from carrying on normal activities. Now the Jewish community reacted with surprise, with fright, with disturbance, but it was galvanized to action. And that I think endeared it to the Israeli community, and relationships have been much closer between Israel and the outside Jewish community since the war. For example, in Philadelphia, within four days from the war's beginning we had 100 physicians either on the way to Israel or ready to go the moment the government needed them to replace civilian doctors who had to go to the military installations. At the same time there were dozens of young men volunteering to fight in the Israeli army if they were requested. And it should be mentioned, beside all the fund raising activities that went on in the community generally, that the American Academic Association for Peace in the Middle East came into existence in that period. We're a non-sectarian group, but the professors in the universities were inquiring what they could do in this world crisis. And there was no hysteria, there was action.

Alroy: I know very little of the behavior of Jews throughout this area in late May and early June of 1967. My observations were of course scattered in other areas and I have relied on some studies, such as that by Marshall Sklane in what he calls Lakeville, which is a large suburban community near Chicago. It is interesting that what he found there falls into the kind of behavior that you as a physician would call hysteria. For instance, the inability to continue with ordinary daily activity; the inability to eat, sleep, concentrate on work. I will admit that in the social science fraternity we very often borrow terms from other disciplines and often misuse them. But "hysteria" was not entirely an inappropriate term in this case.

Horowitz: I would like to close this meeting with a quotation from a good Jew who is very highly regarded in the Arab world, Karl Marx: "We have moved from the weapon of criticism to a criticism of weapons." Maybe we should have begun that hours ago, but the hour is late. I think that the sobriety of the occasion was matched by the civility of the participants. I thank all of you and especially the panelists for a fine afternoon.

INDEX

Abduh, Muhammad, 281

Abdullah of Transjordan, Emir, 286; intervenes with Palestinians, 75-6; favors settlement, 175-7

Acheson, Dean, 97, 228, 241, 249

Afghani, Jamal al-Din al-, 281

Aflaq, Michel, 132, 138-41, 285

Aida 87

al-Ahd, 281

Al Ahram, 184

al-Aksa (mosque), 183

al'Ala'illi, Abd Allah, 282

al-Ami, Musa, 283

Al Azhar, 265

Ali, Rashid, 132

al-Ilhya', 139

al-Shari'ah, 281

al-tajriba al-murra, 133

al-Tali'a, 132

Aman, 11, 12

Amer, Abdul Hakim, 248

American Journal of Economics and Sociology, The, 29

American University, Beirut, 87, 227, 268

Amin, Mustafa, 230

Amit, General Meir, 238

Amman al Masa, 100

Antonius, George, 98, 169, 174

Arab Bureau, the, 171, 172

Arab Common Market, the, 113

Arab Congress (1919), the, 98

Arab Executive, the, 72

Arab Higher Committee, the, 74, 75, 77

Arab League, the, 175, 234

Arab League Council, the, 150

Arab National Bank, the, 80

Arab National Committee, the, 74

Arab National Fund, the, 80

Arab Refugees, the, (See also: UN, UNRWA, etc.), 13, 40, 58, 83, 95-6, 100, 106-7, 110, 168, 190, 207, 264; and Palestinian identity, 84-9; status in Jordan, 112-3, 192; claims to Israel, 114; numbers; 144, 147, 162, 191; and repatriation, 146, 148-9, 161; and UNRWA, 150-2, 156-7, 163, 165,; UN Resolutions on, 153-5, 158, 164, 2123; and Arab leaders, 159, 160; rehabilitation and development prospects, 166, 209-10

Arab Socialist Party, the, (Syria), (See also: Hourani, A.), 140-1, 249

Arab Socialist Union (U.A.R.), 287

Arab Summit Conference, the, (1969), 184

Arafat, Yasir, 178, 183, 280; image as leader, 90, 299; concept of Palestine, 191-2

Armistice Agreements, 1948, 198

Arsuzi, Zaki al, 132 9

Asad, Hafid, 141

Asali, Sabri al-, 134

Atasi, Nur Al-Din al-, 140, 142

Axis (See Nazi)

Azm, Abdul Rahman al-, 234

Ba'ath, 140, 230, 284-5, 287, 293, 309; constitution, 98-9; intellectual formation, 132-3, 136, 138-9; ideology, 219

Badeau, John, 167, 243, 248, 249

Baghdadi, Abd al-Latif, 240, 249

Baghdad Pact, the, 221, 224-26, 233, 237, 241

319

Baker, Dwight L., 30
Balfour Declaration, the, 93, 97, 99, 100, 101, 103, 175, 239; principles of, 102, 177, 203; beneficial effects, 104; defines Palestine, 105; Balfour's letter to Weizmann, 171; New Left's conception of, 298
Beeri, Eliezer, 247-8
Begin, Menachem, 166, 108
Ben Gurion, David, 153, 233, 249; on Arabs, 42, 240; on Orthodox, 120; early views, 195; on reform in Egypt, 239
Ben-Porath, Yoran, 92
Bentwich, Joseph, 30
Ben-Tzur, 142
Berger, Earl, 239, 249
Bernadotte, Count, 145
Berreby, Jean-Jacques, 178
Bevin, Ernest, 178
Bilby, Kenneth, 166, 208
Bitar, Salah al-Din al-, 132, 139, 141
Borochov, Dov Ber, 302
British Mandate, the, 70, 72-3, 99, 103, 105, 145, 185, 192, 203; Arab hostility to, 71, 74; creates Arab-Jewish conflict, 76
British Royal Commission on Palestine (1937), 73, 75, 76, 81, 85, 92
British White Paper, the (1939), 78, 80
Bunche, Ralph, 11, 177
Bustani, Butrus, 282
Byroade, Ambassador Henry, 230, 248

Caffery, Ambassador Jefferson, 230
Campbell, John, 247
Chamberlain, Houston Stewart, 136-7

Chamberlain, Neville, 240
Chamoun, Kamil, 232
Cheine, Anwar G., 248
Childers, Erskine B., 158, 248
Chomsky, Noam, 101
Christian Science Monitor, the 167
Clayton, General, 172-3
Cohen, Aaron, 92
Commentary 105

Condor, Colonel, 103
Copeland, Miles, 229-30, 247
Cremens, Charles, 247

Daim, Abd Allah Abd al-, 283
Dandashi, Abd al-Razzaq, al-, 134
Dayan, Moshe, 155, 196, 238
Debray, Regis, 294
Deir Yassin, 145, 168, 261
de Volney, Count, 103
Din, Ali Yusuf Nasir al-, 282
Din, Zakariyah Muhi al-, 230
Dodd, Peter and Barakat, Halim, 92
Dulles, Allen, 247
Dulles, John Foster, 228; and Suez, 222-3; and Baghdad Pact, 224-6; and State Dept., 231; and Nasser, 234; and Israel, 239, 241-2

Eban, Abba, 196
Eden, Sir Anthony, 178, 242, 247, 249; and U.S. policy, 222, 224; and Suez, 223; and Israel, 225, 241; and Baghdad Pact, 226, 23
Eichelberger, James, 230, 231
Eisenhower, Dwight D., 149
Eisenstadt, S.N., 66
El Ard, 86
ESCO Foundation for Palestine, Inc., 92
Eshkol, Levi, 42, 197, 274

Evening Bulletin, The, (Philadelphia), 167

Farah, Naj'ah Ka'war, 92
Farouk, King, 240
Fatah, 90, 178, 180, 214, 281,
295, 312-13, on Zionism, 96;
on Jews, 267; ideology, 268,
293-4, 302, 314; on Israel,
297, 300-1; terrorism, 154,
298-9
Fiesal, Emir, 100, 171, 172, 173,
176, 281
Feron, James and Speigel, Irving,
30
Fichte, 137
Forrestal, James, 241, 249
Frankfurter, Felix, 100
Frantz, Fanon, 95, 302
Free Officers Group, (Egyptian),
230
Friedmann, G., 67
Front of National Liberation, the,
(Algeria) (F.L.N.), 273, 287,
302
Fruki, R. I. Al-, 266

Gailani, Rashid 'Ali al-, 139, 240
galut, 13
Gandhi, Mahatma, 74
General Syrian Congress (1919),
98
gharib, 13
Ghazi, (King) of Iraq, 75, 135
ghurbah, 13
Giles, Frank, 92
Glubb, John Bagot, 166
Guevara, Che, 297
Gruen, George E., 30

hadith, 265
Haifa Congress (Arab), 72
Halpern, Manfred, 247
Hamaday, S. 261, 277
Hanoch, G., 67

Harb, 87
Hashemites (the), 83, 170, 173,
191, 140
Hebrew University, the, 66, 67,
86
Herman, S., 66
Herzl, Theodor, 101, 102, 259
Heykal, Muhammed Hassanein,
184, 185, 230, 258, 259
Hinnawi, Colonel Sami al-, 279
Hirsch, Baron, 193
Hirszowicz, 249
Hitler, Adolf (See also: Nazi), 81,
200, 209
Hogarth, Commander, 172, 173,
178
Hourani, A., (See also: Arab
Hurewitz, J.D., 166, 247, 249
Husain, (Sharif of Mecca), 170,
172, 173
Husaini(s), 72, 73, 74, 77, 78, 80
Husaini, Amin al- (Mufti of Jeru-
salem), 78, 98, 171, 173, 175,
240
Husaini, Ishak Musa, 248
Husri, Sati al-, 282
Hussein, Kamal Al-Din, 248
Hussein, King (of Jordan), 110,
112, 114, 178, 191-2
Hussein, Rashed, 92

Iberiam, Hasan, 240
Ibn Saud, King, 75, 175
Illiyat, Ari, 118
Institute for Mediterranean
Affairs, 168, 193
Institute of Higher Arabic Studies
(of the Arab League), 266
Israel Digest, the, 167
Istiqlal Party, the, 80
Itjihad, 294

Jahiliyyah, 135, 137
Jedid, General Salah, 140-2
Jerusalem Post Weekly, the, 118

Jerusalem Times, the 277
Jewish Agency, 22
Jewish National Fund, the, 104
jihad, 12, 87, 183, 268
Johnson, Dr. Joseph E., 149, 168
Johnston, Eric, 149
Joyce, Colonel Pierre C., 171
Juden und Araber, 133
Juma, Sa'as, 265
Jundi, Sami al-, 13, 136-42

Kai-shek, Chiang, 229
Kamal, Abd as Star, 248
Kamil, Mustafa, 281
Karameh, 91, 206
Karpat, Kemal, 193-4
Katzenelson, K., 66
Kaukji, Fawzi, 299
Kautsky, Karl, 296
Kawakibi, Abd al-Rahman al-, 281
Ka'war, Jamal, 92
Kazem, Mussa, 171, 173
Keith, A., 103
Kerr, Malcolm H., 142, 167, 228, 247, 249
Khadduri, Majid, 15, 249
Khartoum Conference, the, 246, 269, 272
Khouri, Fred J., 167
Khruschchev, 237, 245
kibbutz, 19, 28
Kimche, Jon, 166, 181, 208
King-Crane Commission, 101, 102
Kirk, George E., 166, 208
Klinov-Malul, R., 67
Knesset, 34-5, 42, 153, 199, 218
Knightley, Phillip, 170
Kolack, Shirley and Sol, 29
Kolko, Gabriel, 246
Koran (the), 265, 267
Kuwatli, al-, (President of Syria), 279

Lacouture, Jean and Simone, 247-8

Lausanne and Paris (Arab-Jewish meetings at) (See: Paris Peace Conference), 11, 71, 147
Lawrence (of Arabia), 170-1
League of Arab States, the, 80, 175, 283, 286
League of Arab Students, the, 78-9
League of Nations Mandate, 25
Lehrman, Hal, 166, 208
Little, Tom, 247
Look (magazine), 29
Louvish, M., 29
Lukasz-Hirszowicz, 248

Macmillan, Harold, 224, 226, 242, 247, 249
Makhos (Minister) (Syria), 133
Malik, Charles, 98
Mapai, 26
Mao, 297
Mapam, 26
Marshall, George C., 228
Matras, J., 67
McDonald, James G., 166
McMahon (letter), 101
Meglissin, 72
Meir, Golda, 153, 178; on Palestinian entity, 92, 115, 116, 117; on borders, 196; on Jewish identity 199, 200
Middle Eastern Studies, 143
Middle East Journal, the, 15, 142, 167
Misri, General Aziz ali al-, 240
Mitchell, Richard P., 248
Moskin, R., 30
Moslem Brotherhood, the, 235, 247-8
Muaridin, 73
Mufti of Jerusalem, the (See: Husaini, Amin al-)
Mu'nis, Hussein, 248
Muslim-Christian Societies (in Palestine), 71

Naguib, 249
Nashashibi(s), 72-4, 76, 80
Nasser, Gamal Abdel, 90, 106, 114, 178, 202, 221-2, 226, 233, 240-1, 248-9, 258, 280; and the Palestinians, 95, 269; on Egyptian nationalism, 184; pre June 1967, 154; on Arab refugees, 207; and the West, 228, 230, 242, 246; pan Arabism, 232, 234, 235-6; and military aid, 237-8
National Action League, the (Syria), 134
National Arab Party, the, (Syria), 134, 284
National Bloc, the, (Syria), 134
National Defense Party, the, 74, 77
National Charter, (of the U.A.R.), 271
Nazi(s) (ism), 136, 137, 174, 175, 240, 248
Neo-Destour Party, the, (Tunisian), 287
New Outlook, 168
New Republic, The, 29
Newsweek, 29, 30
New Yorker, The, 30
New York Times, The, 93, 124, 166-8, 247
Nietzche, 135, 137
Nixon Declaration, the, 93, 94
Nolte, Richard, 221, 243, 247, 249
Nolte, Richard, 248
Nutting, Anthony, 248

O'Ballance, Edgar, 166, 168, 208
Organization of Marxist-Leninist-Zionist Students, 301

Palestine Liberation Organization (PLO), 89, 90, 99, 192, 258, 267, 270

Palestinian Arab Conference, the, 71
Palestinian Arab Congress, the, 71
Palestinian Arab Party, the, 73, 80
Palestinian National Covenant, the, (also: Fatah Manifesto), 14, 267, 297
Pan-Arab Congress at Bludan, 77
Pan-Moslem Summit Conference, (1969), 183
Paris Peace Conference (1919) (See: Lausanne and Paris), 174, 175, 180
Peres, Y., 67
Peres, Yochanan, and Nira Yuval-Davis, 92
Peretz, Don, 166, 167
Perlmutter, Amos, 247, 249
Poale Zion, 295
Popular Front for the Liberation of Palestine, (PFLP), 293, 294, 297
Protocols of the Elders of Zion 264, 265

Qaddur, Abd al-Halim, 136
Qamhawi, Walid al-, 261

Ra'anan, Uri, 236-8, 248
Rawf, Abdul Muneim Abd al-, 248
Razzaz, Munif al-, 13, 140-2
Razzik, Aref Abdul, 77
Rida, Rashid, 281
Rhodes (Armistice Agreements), 10
Rogers, William P., 157, 158, 242, 304
Roosevelt, Kermit, 229-30
Rothschild, Baron, 193
Ruz al-Yusuf, 276

Sa'ab, Hasan, 286
Sa'adeh, Antun, 285

Sabri, Hasan, 240
Sacher, Harry, 166, 208
Sacks, Morris, 168
Sadat, Anwar al-, 248, 249
Safadi, Muta'al-, 142
Safran, Nadav, 15
Said, Nuri al-, 222, 223, 225, 226, 23, 240, 241, 242, 275, 286
Salame, Hassan, 299
Sayegh, F.A., 262, 277
Seale, Patrick, 247
Seltzer, M., 69
Seymour, Martin, 143
shaira, 75
Sharett, Moshe, 153, 196
Sharif, Kamil Isma'il al-, 248
Shawkat, Sami, 282
Shimoni, Yaakov, 92
Shishakli, Muhsin, 193
Shukairy, Ahmed, 99, 192, 258, 297
Shuval, Judith, 29, 67, 69
Simpson, Colin, 170
Smith, W.C., 261, 277
Spectator, The, 159
Spiro, M., 67
Storrs, Sir Ronald, 173
sulh(a), 11, 12, 113, 114, 115
Supreme Muslim Council, the, 72, 74, 75
Sykes-Picot Agreement, 101
Symes, Colonel G.S., 172
Syrian Congresses (1919), 71
Syrian Scientific Society (1857), 282
Syrian Social National Party (SSNP), 285

Tahtawi, Rif'at al-, 281
Tibawi, A.L., 13, 92
The Times (London), 167
Torrey, Gordon H., 142, 247
Toynbee, Arnold, 97
Treaty of Versailles, 256
Tripartite Agreement, the (1950), 23, 234, 238

Truman, Harry S., 147, 221, 222, 241
Tunisi, Khayr al-Din, 281
Tutsch, H.E., 269, 277

Ulam, Adam, 237, 248
Umran, Muhammad, 141
Uma al Arabia, 184, 202
UN Conciliation Commission, 11, 146, 147, 148, 149, 150, 152, 157, 213
UNESCO, 85, 92
UN Partition Resolution (1947), 25, 82, 93, 95, 98, 105, 144, 147, 162, 176, 187, 192, 195, 203, 225, 260
UN Security Council Resolution, Nov. 2, 1967, 155, 164, 198, 206, 212, 256, 270
UN Resolution 273 (1948), 148
UNRWA, 84, 95, 146, 148, 150, 151, 152, 155, 156, 159, 163, 164, 165
U.S. Foreign Policy Middle East Staff Study, 168

Vatad, M., 30
Von Horn, Maj. Gen. Carl, 167

Wadi Salib, 21
Wafd, the, 175, 284
Waters-Taylor, Colonel, 173
Weingrod, Alex, 29, 30
Weizmann, Chaim, 170, 172, 173;-Faisal Agreement, 100, 171, 176; on Arab nationalism, 102
Wheelock, Keith, 247
Williams, R.M., 69
Wilson, Woodrow, 102

Yaziji, Nasif, 282
Yost, Charles W., 167, 248

Zaghlul, Sa'd, 234

Zaim, Colonel Husni al-, 142, 279
zakat, 268
Zayat, Az-, 269
Zeezya, 87

Zenner, Walter, 29
Zionist Congress (1897), 96
Zulayyin, Yusuf, 140
Zurayk, Constantine, 283, 286

NOTES ON CONTRIBUTORS

Gil Carl Alroy   "Closing Horizons: Israelis and Nationalism"
Professor of political science, Hunter College, New York City.

Shlomo Avineri   "The New Left and Israel"
Chairman, department of political science, Hebrew University of Jerusalem, Israel.

Sylvia G. Haim   "The Ba'ath in Syria"
Authority on Arab history and author of *Arab Awakening*; resides in London, England.

Ben Halpern   "Israel and Palestine: The Political Use of Ethics"
Professor of Near Eastern and Judaic studies, Brandeis University, Waltham, Massachusetts.

Yehoshafat Harkabi   "Ending the Arab-Israeli Conflict"
Professor of international relations, Hebrew University of Jerusalem, and former Director of Military Intelligence in Israel.

F. H. Hinsley   "The Middle East and the Great Powers"
Teaches history at St. John's College, Cambridge University, England.

Irving L. Horowitz "Political Systems of the Middle East: Opening Remarks"
Chairman, department of sociology, Livingston College of Rutgers University and editor-in-chief of *trans*action magazine.

Eliyahu Kanovsky   "Economic Aspects of the Arab-Israeli Conflict"
Professor of economics, State University of New York at Stony Brook.

Fred Khouri   "Arab Refugees and the Arab-Israeli Dilemma"
Professor of political science, Villanova University, Villanova, Pennsylvania.

Jon Kimche   "The Second Arab Awakening"
Editor of *The New Middle East,* published in London, England.

Samuel Merlin   "Demography and Geography in Palestine"
Director of the Institute for Mediterranean Affairs, New York City.

Yochanan Peres   "Ethnic Relations in Israel"
Professor in the department of social relations, Harvard University, Cambridge, Massachusetts.

Don Peretz   "The Palestine Arabs: A National Entity"
Professor of political science and director of the Southeast Asia/North
Africa program at the State University of New York at Binghamton

Amos Perlmutter   "The Fiasco of Anglo-American Middle East Policy"
Visiting Ford professor, humanities department, Massachusetts Institute of
Technology; and research associate at the Center for International Affairs,
Harvard University, Cambridge, Massachusetts.

Abdul Aziz Said   "Clashing Horizons: Arabs and Revolution"
Professor of political science, American University, Washington, D.C.

Hugh H. Smythe   "Intergroup Relations in Israel"
Professor of sociology, Brooklyn College, of the City University of New
York.

Marie Syrkin   "Who are the Palestinians"
Emeritus professor of sociology, Brandeis University, Waltham, Massachusetts.

Sandra Weintraub   "Intergroup Relations in Israel"
Undergraduate assistant working for a degree in the department of
sociology at Brooklyn College of the City University of New York.